Mastering Django ORM

Performance Tuning and Advanced Query Optimization

Afsal MS

Apress®

Mastering Django ORM: Performance Tuning and Advanced Query Optimization

Afsal MS
Perumbavoor, Kerala, India

ISBN-13 (pbk): 979-8-8688-2588-0 ISBN-13 (electronic): 979-8-8688-2589-7
https://doi.org/10.1007/979-8-8688-2589-7

Managing Director, Apress Media LLC: Welmoed Spahr
Acquisitions Editor: Shaul Elson
Editorial Assistant: Gryffin Winkler

Cover designed by eStudioCalamar

Cover image designed by Freepik (www.freepik.com)

Distributed to the book trade worldwide by Springer Science+Business Media New York, 1 New York Plaza, New York, NY 10004. Phone 1-800-SPRINGER, fax (201) 348-4505, e-mail orders-ny@springer-sbm.com, or visit www.springeronline.com. Apress Media, LLC is a Delaware LLC and the sole member (owner) is Springer Science + Business Media Finance Inc (SSBM Finance Inc). SSBM Finance Inc is a **Delaware** corporation.

For information on translations, please e-mail booktranslations@springernature.com; for reprint, paperback, or audio rights, please e-mail bookpermissions@springernature.com.

Apress titles may be purchased in bulk for academic, corporate, or promotional use. eBook versions and licenses are also available for most titles. For more information, reference our Print and eBook Bulk Sales web page at http://www.apress.com/bulk-sales.

Any source code or other supplementary material referenced by the author in this book is available to readers on GitHub. For more detailed information, please visit https://www.apress.com/gp/services/source-code.

If disposing of this product, please recycle the paper

To Moothuma, who gave me a computer to play with;
to my family, whose love gave me strength;
to my teachers, who shaped my understanding;
to my mentors, who guided my steps;
and to my friends, who stood beside me through every high and low.
This book belongs to all of you.

Table of Contents

About the Author

Afsal MS is a Python and Django developer passionate about building scalable systems and teaching developers how to write clean, efficient code. With hands-on experience developing applications for ERP, logistics, the medical field, etc., he has spent years uncovering the practical strengths and pitfalls of Django ORM in production environments.

Afsal MS shares his knowledge regularly at parseltongue.co.in, a platform for Python and Django enthusiasts, where he breaks down complex concepts into actionable learning. His teaching style emphasizes clarity, real-world use cases, and lessons drawn from mistakes he made early in his career, making him uniquely positioned to guide readers through the hidden depths of Django ORM.

About the Technical Reviewer

Sheeban Wasi is a senior machine learning engineer with deep expertise in building production-grade agentic AI platforms for the finance and hedge fund industries. He holds an MS in Computer Science from Virginia Tech, where his thesis research focused on computer vision and 3D scene understanding, contributing to published work in the field.

He has architected and developed enterprise agentic AI platforms that integrate multi-agent orchestration, context engineering, and knowledge graph–powered reasoning over heterogeneous financial data sources spanning time-series and operational data stores. His engineering work spans the full model lifecycle from training and fine-tuning domain-adapted models to building evaluation pipelines and governance controls, to deploying reliable agentic systems in regulated production environments. He has particular depth in GraphRAG architectures, long-context memory systems, and the design of context runtimes that combine structured knowledge with large language model (LLM) reasoning.

Sheeban's research and engineering interests span computer vision, 3D scene understanding, multi-agent LLM systems, model training and post-training techniques, knowledge graph construction, context engineering, agent security and governance, and applied AI in regulated enterprise environments. He previously served as a technical reviewer for IEEE, BPB, etc., bringing a practitioner's lens focused on technical accuracy and conceptual clarity.

Acknowledgments

This book would not have been possible without the support and inspiration of many people.

I am deeply grateful to my teachers and mentors Fran K Baby, Arun Babu, Mithun Sreedharan, Vishnu Haridas, Kripa Sreedevi, Greeshma Radhakrishnan, Shinu Odol, Ajai Kumar, Arun Dasan, Lini, Geetha Mohan, Arun Prabha, Muhammed Sherin, Srijith Vijayamohan, Vineeth Nair, Amalesh, Nisar, Ajayan, and Jose Antony whose guidance shaped the way I approach learning and problem-solving. Their constant reminder to "look deeper" has been the foundation of this journey. I would also like to thank Jimmy Kappen for trusting me and encouraging my efforts.

My heartfelt thanks go to my friends who played a critical role during my college days: Nithin S, Arjun, Yacob, Rabah, Pranav, Pallavi, Maria, Nithin D, Akhil, Althaf, Bhavya, Pavitra, Anju, George Kurian, Reena, Teena, Vyas, Atmaram, and Stefan. I also cherish the friendships from my school days: Tom, Mrudhun, Thanveer, Thamees, Umarul Farooq, and Aslam Niyasi. Beyond these names, I extend my gratitude to all of my friends from Mecca School, National School, Asram HSS, and Model Engineering College, whose camaraderie, discussions, and encouragement left a lasting impact on me, both personally and academically.

I would also like to acknowledge my teachers: Beevi Teacher (my very first teacher), Prof. Vineetha Miss, Prof. Aparna Devi Miss, Prof. Rashid Sir, Prof. Sudheer Babu Sir, Geetha Miss, Sujith Sir, Resi Miss (Late), John Daniel (my C++ and SQL guru), Sajan Sir, Salini Miss, Sarama Miss, and Habeeba Miss as well as all of my teachers from Mecca School, National School, Asram HSS, and Model Engineering College. Their dedication to teaching and unwavering encouragement laid the foundation for my journey in learning and discovery.

A special word of appreciation goes to the **Django community** not only for creating a powerful framework but also for fostering a culture of openness, collaboration, and sharing that continues to inspire developers worldwide.

Finally, my deepest gratitude goes to my family and friends, whose patience, encouragement, and belief in me made it possible to devote countless hours to writing this book. Without their support, this work would never have reached completion.

Introduction

When I first started my journey with Django, I found the object-relational mapper (ORM) to be very simple and easy to use. Everything seemed straightforward, until I began working on real projects. That's when performance issues started appearing, and I often felt frustrated, even cursing the ORM at times.

One day, when I spoke with my mentor about these struggles, they encouraged me to dig deeper. That was when I realized that Django ORM is far more powerful than it appears at first glance. In fact, in most cases, it is fully capable of handling very large projects efficiently if used correctly.

I began exploring the ORM more seriously and soon discovered that it was a continuous journey. With every new Django release, new ORM features and improvements arrive, keeping the learning alive. Later, when I started leading projects and mentoring developers, I noticed that many of my mentees faced the same problems I once had; they were using the ORM but had very little understanding of what was happening under the hood.

That experience gave me the push to write this book. My goal is to explain how Django ORM works behind the scenes, how to optimize queries, and how to avoid the common mistakes I made (and have seen others make) while reviewing projects.

This book is my attempt to remove the mystery around Django ORM. It should no longer feel like a black box, but instead a powerful tool you can fully understand and control.

—Afsal

CHAPTER 1

Introduction to Django ORM

Django ORM is one of the key features that makes Django such a powerful and popular web framework. It allows developers to work with relational databases using Python objects instead of writing raw SQL, resulting in code that is cleaner, safer, and easier to maintain.

In this chapter, you'll explore what Django ORM is, why it is so widely used, and how it works behind the scenes when you interact with the database. By the end of the chapter, you'll understand the advantages Django ORM offers, its practical limitations, and when it is the right tool for the job. At that point, the ORM will no longer feel like a black box.

What Is Django ORM?

Django ORM is one of the core features that contributes to Django's popularity and productivity. It serves as a bridge between your application code and the underlying relational database, allowing developers to work with data without dealing directly with SQL syntax.

Instead of manually writing SQL statements for operations such as `INSERT`, `UPDATE`, and `SELECT`, developers define Python classes and interact with them using familiar methods. Django ORM translates these Python operations into the corresponding SQL queries behind the scenes, handling query generation and execution automatically.

More broadly, an object-relational mapper (ORM) is a technique that enables object-oriented interaction with relational databases. ORM tools create a clear mapping between database tables and in-memory objects. In Django, each model class corresponds to a database table, and each model field maps a column in that table. As a result, working with database records feels much like working with ordinary Python objects rather than rows and columns.

Afsal MS, *Mastering Django ORM*, https://doi.org/10.1007/979-8-8688-2589-7_1

This abstraction reduces boilerplate, improves readability, and forms the foundation for the practical examples you'll explore in the sections that follow.

Why Use Django ORM?

Django ORM is designed to simplify how applications interact with relational databases, allowing developers to focus more on business logic and less on database-specific details. The benefits go beyond convenience; they influence code quality, security, and long-term maintainability. Because schema changes are managed as part of the source code, everyone on the team stays synchronized with the same database state.

One of the most immediate advantages of Django ORM is that it eliminates the need to write raw SQL for most common operations. Instead, developers work with Python objects and methods, which reduces boilerplate and lowers the barrier to working with databases, especially for those more comfortable in Python than SQL.

Using Django ORM also leads to cleaner and more maintainable code. Database operations become part of the application object model, making the intent of the code easier to understand and reducing the likelihood of subtle bugs that can arise from handwritten SQL.

Another important benefit is database abstraction. Django ORM acts as a consistent interface across multiple database back ends, such as `PostgreSQL`, `MySQL`, and `SQLite`. This abstraction allows applications to switch database engines with minimal code changes, as Django handles differences in SQL syntax internally.

Security is also built into the ORM by default. Django ORM automatically escapes user input in queries, significantly reducing the risk of SQL injection attacks, one of the most common vulnerabilities in database-driven applications.

Finally, Django ORM contributes to faster development cycles. By automating query generation, schema management, and many repetitive database tasks, teams can move more quickly while reducing errors. A real-world example often cited is the Kerala flood relief platform developed in 2018 using Django, which demonstrated how quickly scalable applications can be built during emergency situations.

Together, these advantages explain why Django ORM is a core part of the Django ecosystem and a key reason many teams choose the framework for real-world applications.

With these benefits in mind, let's dive into how Django ORM works in practice by first looking at how models - the foundation of ORM - are defined.

Defining a Model

Models are the building blocks of Django ORM. They are used to define the structure of the tables using Python objects. If you know the table structure, then it's an intuitive task to make a model.

To make this clear, let's define a simple Book model to see how Django ORM works in practice.

Listing 1-1. Defining a simple Django model

```
from django.db import models

class Book(models.Model):
    title = models.CharField(max_length=255)
    author = models.CharField(max_length=100)
    published_date = models.DateField()
```

The Book class inherits from `models.Model`, which tells Django that this class represents a database table. Each attribute is the column of the table. Don't worry about the fields as of now; we will learn more about them in the upcoming chapters.

`title` and `author` are `CharField` which is equivalent to VARCHAR in SQL, and `published_date` is `DateField` which is equivalent to DATE in SQL. Together, this class corresponds to a table that stores details about books.

Once the model is defined, Django ORM converts this class to a SQL on running command. Detailed steps will be explained in upcoming sections.

To understand this mapping more clearly, let's look at the SQL that Django might generate for the Book model.

Listing 1-2. SQL table generated for the Book model

```
CREATE TABLE myapp_book (
    id BIGSERIAL PRIMARY KEY,
    title VARCHAR(255) NOT NULL,
    author VARCHAR(100) NOT NULL,
    published_date DATE NOT NULL
);
```

The SQL in Listing 1-2 shows how the model in Listing 1-1 is translated into the SQL. If you look closely into the SQL, we can see that the table name is **myapp_book** which is due to Django automatically appending the app name before the model's name. Django also provides a way to change it if needed. Another thing we noticed is that there are `id` fields which are not in models in the SQL. This is because Django automatically adds a primary key if we do not explicitly define models. The rest of the fields are intuitive, i.e., `VARCHAR` for title and author and `DATE` for the published date.

In simple terms, a class is equivalent to a database table, and its attributes correspond to the columns in that table.

This clear and predictable mapping is what makes the Django ORM very simple and intuitive to use.

With this model as the reference, we can now explore how Django ORM uses it to generate queries for creating, retrieving, updating, and deleting data without requiring you to write SQL by hand.

How Django ORM Generates SQL

Now that we have seen how we can create a table using Django models, let's move toward a simple example that shows how Django ORM generates SQL for insert operations.

To illustrate this, we'll look at a simple example that creates a new record using the Book model defined earlier. As shown in Listing 1-3, inserting data with Django ORM involves creating a model instance and saving it.

Listing 1-3. Creating and saving a model instance

```
book = Book(title="Harry Potter", author="J.K. Rowling", published_
date="1997-06-26")
book.save()
```

We can see that we are creating a Python object and the `save` method is called. For a developer, this is an intuitive task, as it aligns naturally with how Python code is written. However, in the background the Django ORM automatically generates insert queries.

The generated query will look like what is shown in Listing 1-4.

Listing 1-4. SQL generated for inserting a record

```
INSERT INTO myapp_book (title, author, published_date)
VALUES ('Harry Potter', 'J.K. Rowling', '1997-06-26');
```

This query inserts a new row into the `myapp_book` table using the values provided in the Python object. Django ORM automatically handles details such as quoting values, escaping input, and matching Python field types to database column types.

The key takeaway here is that Django ORM does not replace the SQL, but instead it generates SQL for you. But understanding this makes you write better and more efficient code. Also debugging will be more efficient and easier.

In the next section, you will see how we can print the generated SQL in the shell. This is very useful when debugging and optimizing the query.

Inspecting SQL Queries Generated by Django ORM

Being able to see the generated SQL is a valuable thing because this helps us to optimize and debug the code faster. Also, this helps the developer to know what is happening under the hood.

Django provides us with a `query` attribute for inspecting the query. Let us check this with our book example. Let us fetch all the book records from the database and inspect the generated SQL query.

As shown in Listing 1-5, this can be done using Django's interactive shell.

Listing 1-5. Inspecting SQL generated by a QuerySet

```
# Import the Book model
from myapp.models import Book

# Retrieve all books
books = Book.objects.all()

# Print the generated SQL query
print(books.query)
```

When this code is executed, Django outputs the SQL statement that would be sent to the database to retrieve all `Book` records. The output will look similar to the query shown in Listing 1-6.

Listing 1-6. SQL generated for retrieving all books

```
SELECT "myapp_book"."id", "myapp_book"."title", "myapp_book"."author",
"myapp_book"."published_date"
FROM "myapp_book";
```

Being able to view the generated SQL is especially useful when optimizing queries or diagnosing performance issues such as unnecessary joins or missing filters. It also reinforces an important idea: Django ORM is not hiding SQL from you; it is generating it transparently and predictably.

With this visibility into ORM-generated queries, now we can learn more about the Django ORM flow.

The Django ORM Workflow

Until this point, we learned about the ORM, how it works, how we can inspect the SQL, etc. Now we will start from the database settings to basic operations using Django ORM.

Database Settings

The workflow begins with database configurations. This tells Django where to connect. This configuration is defined in the DATABASES setting in the project's **settings.py** file. Django gives us a fixed place for this to make settings centralized and easy to configure.

When we start a new project in Django, it comes with default settings which connect to the SQLite database as shown in Listing 1-7.

Listing 1-7. Default database settings in Django

```
# settings.py

DATABASES = {
    'default': {
        'ENGINE': 'django.db.backends.sqlite3',
        'NAME': BASE_DIR / 'db.sqlite3'
    }
}
```

The example in Listing 1-7 shows the connection settings for SQLite. SQLite is a file-based database which is great for learning and prototyping. For production systems, teams often prefer more powerful database back ends such as PostgreSQL or MySQL, especially when scalability and concurrency are required. Django can connect with various databases using the same settings.

Now we can learn how to connect to other database back ends.

Listing 1-8. Example PostgreSQL settings in Django

```
DATABASES = {
    'default': {
        'ENGINE': 'django.db.backends.postgresql',
        'NAME': 'mydatabase',
        'USER': 'myuser',
        'PASSWORD': 'mypassword',
        'HOST': 'localhost',
        'PORT': '5432'
    }
}
```

This is a sample PostgreSQL setting for Django (Refer Listing 1-8). Now let's dive into each of the keys in those settings in more detail.

ENGINE

`ENGINE` specifies which database back end we should use. Here in this case, we are using `django.db.backends.postgresql` which tells Django that the generated SQL must be compatible with the PostgreSQL. When the back end changes, we can easily change the configuration here. Some of the common ENGINE settings are

- 'django.db.backends.sqlite3' (default)
- 'django.db.backends.postgresql'
- 'django.db.backends.mysql'
- 'django.db.backends.oracle'

NAME

`NAME` refers to the name of the database to which Django connects. In SQLite is the path of the database file for the other database if it names the database. This must match the name of the database server.

USER

USER tells Django which user is using to authenticate when we connect to the database. This user is doing all the database operations such as creating tables, fetching data, inserting records, etc.

PASSWORD

PASSWORD is the password associated with the user specified earlier. Django uses this password to connect with the database. It is a better approach to read this value from environment variables rather than specifying directly in the code. This helps us to prevent exposing sensitive information.

HOST

HOST specifies where the database back end is running. This can be on the same machine, a different machine, or a managed database service. In production, this will be on different servers or on a managed database service. The value will either be the hostname or IP address.

PORT

The port settings are the network port which is used to connect with the database back end. Its value varies according to the database and its settings. In the case of PostgreSQL, it is 5432.

Now learn how to set up the database settings. The next step involved is defining the models for our application. We have already seen how to define the model in Listing 1-1. In Django, each application has a file called **models.py** where models for that application are written. Like settings, Django gives us a proper place to write the code. We will define a model and its relationship according to the requirements. We will learn about these details in the next chapter. As of now we are good to go to the next step which is **migrations**.

Migrations

Once models are defined and connections are established, Django ORM needs a way to keep the database schema in sync with the Python code. This is where migrations come in. Migrations track and manage how the application's database schema evolves over time.

At a high level migrations contain all actions like renaming, adding new fields, updating the fields, etc. Migration file is automatically created by Django when we run the command for it. A migration file contains all the necessary details related to the schema. Since the migration files are part of the source code, this ensures that all the environments and developers are in sync.

Creating a migration file is very easy; once the model is defined, run the command `python manage.py makemigrations` in your terminal which creates a new file in the **migrations** folder of your app. This command checks what things changed after the last migration. If nothing changes, then it shows no change detected.

Let us look at how the book migration file looks like in Listing 1-9.

Listing 1-9. Sample Migration File

```
from django.db import migrations, models

class Migration(migrations.Migration):

    initial = True

    dependencies = [
    ]

    operations = [
        migrations.CreateModel(
            name='Book',
            fields=[
                ('id', models.BigAutoField(auto_created=True, primary_
                key=True, serialize=False, verbose_name='ID')),
                ('title', models.CharField(max_length=255)),
                ('author', models.CharField(max_length=100)),
                ('published_date', models.DateField()),
            ],
        ),
    ]
```

This is the autogenerated file created inside the migration folder. If we read this file, we will get an idea that ORM is asking to create a table for book using the same fields as we specified in **models.py.** We have to create the migration files on every schema change. This migration file must be part of the source code to maintain consistency across the environment.

Now we have created a history for the changes in the schema. But this change is not synced with the database. For that we have another command called `python manage.py migrate`. When we run this command, all the unapplied migrations are applied, and all the changes are synchronized with the database. To keep track of the migrations, Django creates a table in our database. It saves the last applied migrations of each application, when they apply, etc. When we run this command, Django checks if there are any pending migrations; if so, it applies them automatically. If there are none, it shows that message in the terminal to the user.

Let us recap the flow: first we have to configure the `DATABASES` setting in the **settings.py** file. We will define the models in **models.py** of the applications. It is a Python class inherited from `models.Model` once the model is defined. We will generate a migration file by running the `python manage.py makemigrations` command in the terminal. When we run these migrations, a file is created inside the migration folder of the app. To reflect the change in the database, we must run another command - `python manage.py migrate`. This will sync the unapplied changes to the database. If you want to unapply the migration, we can run `python manage.py migrate <previous migration name>`. When this is executed it rolls back to the previous stage. If Django cannot roll back, it will throw an error. This process is repeated according to the requirements. Now we can move to the next section on the benefits of using Django ORM.

Practical Benefits of Django ORM

While the earlier section introduced why Django ORM is widely used, this section focuses on how those benefits appear in real-world development scenarios.

One of the most immediate advantages of Django ORM is its ease of use. Compared to writing raw SQL, the ORM allows developers to create tables, modify schemas, and perform database transactions using just a few lines of Python code. This lowers the learning curve and makes database interactions more approachable, especially for developers who are already comfortable with Python. Consider the examples in Listing 1-10.

Listing 1-10. Ease of usage

```
from myapp.models import Book
# Create and save a record
Book.objects.create(
    title="Atomic Habits",
    author="James Clear",
    published_date="2018-10-16"
)
```

```
# Fetch all books
books = Book.objects.all()
```

Because Django ORM simplifies database operations, it also saves a significant amount of development time. Tasks such as query generation, schema changes, and environment consistency are handled automatically. This allows developers to focus on business logic rather than worrying about SQL syntax or database-specific quirks.

Security is another major benefit. Django ORM automatically escapes user input when constructing queries, which helps protect applications from SQL injection attacks, a common and dangerous vulnerability when working with raw SQL. While secure design is still the developer's responsibility, the ORM provides a strong default safety layer. Let's consider the example in Listing 1-11.

Listing 1-11. Security

```
#Unsafe raw SQL
cursor.execute(f"SELECT * FROM users WHERE username = '{username}'")
#Safe ORM query
User.objects.filter(username=username)
```

The ORM automatically escapes user input, reducing the risk of SQL injection.

Django ORM also offers excellent database portability. It supports multiple database back ends, including PostgreSQL, MySQL, and SQLite, through a unified interface. This abstraction makes it possible to switch database engines in the future with minimal changes to application code, as Django handles back-end-specific SQL internally. Consider the example in Listing 1-12.

Listing 1-12. Portability example

```
# Same query works across PostgreSQL, MySQL, SQLite
books = Book.objects.filter(author="James Clear")
```

This code does not change even if the underlying database changes.

The object-oriented nature of Django ORM further improves code readability and maintainability. Database tables are represented as Python classes, and rows are represented as objects, making the codebase easier to understand and reason about. This structure benefits experienced developers while also helping beginners write clearer, more organized code. Consider the example in Listing 1-13.

Listing 1-13. OOP concept

```
book = Book.objects.get(id=1)
print(book.title)
```

Database rows are treated as Python objects, making the code more intuitive.

Finally, migrations are treated as first-class source code. Every schema change is versioned, tracked, and shared across the team, ensuring consistency between development, testing, and production environments. This approach eliminates the uncertainty of manual database changes and makes schema evolution predictable.

Let us summarize these sections. Django is popular because of

- Core Strength
- Ease of Use
- Faster Development
- Built-In Security
- Database Portability
- Object-Oriented Design
- Migration System

At the same time, no abstraction is without trade-offs. To use Django ORM effectively, it is just as important to understand where its strengths end and its limitations begin. In the next section, we'll take a closer look at the situations where Django ORM may fall short and when it makes sense to step outside the ORM and work closer to SQL.

Limitations of Django ORM

While Django ORM provides many advantages, it is not a perfect fit for every situation. Understanding its limitations is just as important as understanding its strengths. Knowing where the ORM falls short helps you make informed decisions about when to rely on it and when not to.

One trade-off of using an ORM is performance overhead. Because Django ORM adds an abstraction layer on top of SQL, certain operations may be less efficient than carefully optimized raw queries. In most applications, this overhead is negligible, but in performance-critical paths it can become noticeable.

Django ORM can also struggle with very complex queries. Advanced SQL features such as recursive common table expressions (CTEs), window functions, or highly specialized reporting queries are not always easy or practical to express using the ORM alone. In such cases, using raw SQL or database views often results in clearer and more performant solutions.

Another common pitfall is the N+1 query problem. When relationships are not handled correctly using functions like `select_related` or `prefetch_related`, a seemingly simple query can result in many unnecessary database hits. This issue is not unique to Django ORM, but it can surprise developers who are new to how QuerySets work. Consider the example in Listing 1-14.

Listing 1-14. N+1 query

```
books = Book.objects.all()

for book in books:
    print(book.author.name)
```

In Listing 1-14 we are accessing the book's author using `book.author.name.` This triggers one query for fetching the books and an N additional query for fetching the author. This is why it is called the N+1 query issue. If the data is large, this will cause big performance issues. Let's consider the example in Listing 1-15.

Listing 1-15. N+1 Query Fix using select_related

```
books = Book.objects.select_related('author')

for book in books:
    print(book.publisher.name)
```

Here we are optimizing the query using `select_related`. Here we fetch the author's details in a single query. We will learn this in detail in the upcoming chapters.

Django ORM also abstracts many database-specific features. While this abstraction enables portability, it can limit access to powerful back-end-specific capabilities such as PostgreSQL's JSONB optimizations, materialized views, or advanced indexing strategies. Although Django provides some extensions, full access to these features often requires custom SQL.

Bulk operations introduce additional constraints. Methods like `bulk_create` and `bulk_update` improve performance, but they bypass model methods and signals. This can lead to unexpected behavior if your application relies on validation of logic, hooks, or side effects defined at the model level. Debugging can also be challenging at times. Because QuerySets are lazy and SQL is generated only when a query is executed, it may not always be obvious when or how many database queries are being made. Without careful inspection, this can result in hidden performance issues.

Finally, relying heavily on the ORM without understanding basic SQL concepts can lead to inefficient designs. Django ORM is a powerful tool, but it works best when developers have a solid grasp of how relational databases behave underneath the abstraction.

Let us summarize this section. The limitations of Django ORM are

- Not Always the Perfect Fit
- Performance Overhead
- Handling Complex Queries
- N+1 Query Problem
- Limited Access to Database-Specific Features
- Bulk Operations Bypass Model Logic
- Lazy Evaluation and Debugging Challenges
- Requires SQL Understanding

These limitations do not diminish the value of Django ORM; instead, they define its boundaries. In the next section, we'll look at how Django ORM is used in real-world systems and why it continues to be trusted by companies operating at scale.

Notable Companies Using Django ORM

Understanding how a tool performs in real-world systems helps build confidence beyond examples and tutorials. Django ORM is not just a convenience for small projects; it has been used successfully in large, high-traffic applications where reliability, scalability, and developer productivity matter.

Many well-known technology companies adopted Django ORM during critical growth phases of their products. These organizations relied on Django ORM to move quickly while managing increasingly complex data models.

Instagram used Django ORM extensively in its early years to support rapid feature development and massive user growth. **Pinterest** similarly leveraged Django ORM to iterate quickly as user activity scaled. **Dropbox** used Django as part of its web stack to manage metadata and back-end services during its rapid expansion.

Django ORM has also been adopted in content-heavy and data-intensive environments. Organizations such as ***The Washington Post*** and ***National Geographic*** rely on Django for large-scale content management and fast delivery. **Mozilla** uses Django across several internal and public-facing systems, benefiting from its stability and security model.

Even scientific and public sector organizations have turned to Django ORM. **NASA** uses Django for public-facing applications where data integrity and security are critical, while **Eventbrite** has used Django ORM to manage large volumes of events and ticketing data.

These examples highlight an important point: Django ORM is not chosen because it hides SQL, but because it enables teams to balance speed, safety, and long-term maintainability. When used with an understanding of its strengths and limitations, the ORM scales well beyond simple use cases.

With this real-world context in mind, we can now step back and summarize what this chapter has covered before moving on to the next stage of working with Django ORM.

Summary

In this chapter, you explored the foundations of Django ORM and why it is such a central part of the Django framework. You learned what an ORM is and how Django ORM allows developers to interact with relational databases using Python objects rather than raw SQL, making database-driven development cleaner and more approachable.

We examined why Django ORM is widely used, highlighting its benefits in terms of ease of use, security, database portability, and development speed. You also saw how models define database structure, how migrations track and apply schema changes, and how Django translates ORM operations into SQL behind the scenes.

Just as importantly, we discussed the practical limitations of Django ORM. Understanding performance trade-offs, complex query constraints, and common pitfalls such as the N+1 query problem helps ensure the ORM is used effectively rather than blindly. Real-world examples from companies using Django ORM at scale reinforced its credibility as a production-ready tool.

With this conceptual foundation in place, the next chapter moves into hands-on design. You'll dive into Django model fields and their attributes, learning how to choose the right field types and configure them correctly to build reliable, maintainable data models.

CHAPTER 2

Deep Dive into Model Fields

Django ORM offers a rich set of model field types that allow you to define your database structure effectively. Understanding these fields, their attributes, and their practical applications is key to creating well-organized data models. This chapter explores some of the most used fields in Django, complete with examples, attributes, SQL representations, and guidance on when to use each field type.

Field Options

Before diving into the field types, we can first check what fields options are available and what they mean. Let us learn them one by one. The first one is `null`.

null

The `null` attribute controls whether a database column can store a `NULL` value. It directly affects the database schema. When `null` attributes are set to **True**, then at the SQL level, it allows `NULL`. By default, `null` is False. `NULL` in the database world is equivalent to **None** in the Python world. Let's see this with an example (Refer Listings 2-1 and 2-3).

Listing 2-1. Example model with null

```
class Example(models.Model):
    name = models.CharField(max_length=100, null=True)
```


Afsal MS, *Mastering Django ORM*, https://doi.org/10.1007/979-8-8688-2589-7_2

Listing 2-2. Equivalent SQL representation

```
CREATE TABLE example (
    id BIGSERIAL PRIMARY KEY,
    name VARCHAR(100) NULL
);
```

Listing 2-3. Example model without null

```
class Example(models.Model):
    name = models.CharField(max_length=100)
```

Listing 2-4. Equivalent SQL representation

```
CREATE TABLE example (
    id BIGSERIAL PRIMARY KEY,

    name VARCHAR(100) NOT NULL
);
```

If you refer to Listing 2-2, we can see that the field name accepts null value at the database level. But if we check Listing 2-4, we can see that the field does not accept a null value.

Now we move to the other option which is blank.

blank

The `blank` attribute is almost identical to the `null` attribute. But here there is no database-level change. This determines whether empty values are accepted in the forms.

Misunderstanding the difference between blank and null is a common confusion among developers. A good rule of thumb is to think of blank as an application-level constraint and null as a database-level constraint. Choosing the correct combination ensures clean data modeling and predictable application behavior.

Tip For `CharField` and `TextField`, prefer using `blank`=True rather than `null`=True.

Django represents empty text values as an empty string ('') in the database, not as NULL.

Avoiding `null`=True for text fields keeps your data model simpler and more consistent. Now we will move to choices.

choices

The `choices` attribute in Django model fields is used to limit the possible values that a field can take. It provides a fixed set of options, and in forms or the admin interface, this field will appear as a dropdown menu with these predefined choices. This helps enforce data at the application level only. At the database level, there are no constraints.

The choices attribute expects an iterable of 2-tuples. The first element of each tuple is the actual value stored in the database, and the second element is the human-readable name shown in forms or admin.

Let's see how we can use this with an example.

Listing 2-5. Choice example

```
class Product(models.Model):
    STATUS_CHOICES = [
        ('A', 'Available'),
        ('O', 'Out of Stock'),
        ('D', 'Discontinued'),
    ]
    status = models.CharField(max_length=1, choices=STATUS_CHOICES)
```

In this model (Refer Listing 2-5), the status field is a CharField that can only take one of three values: "A" (Available), "O" (Out of Stock), or "D" (Discontinued). This restriction is enforced by the choices option, which provides these specific options for forms and serializers, showing the human-readable names to users.

Important The `choices` constraint is enforced only at the Django application level (in forms, serializers, and model validation) and does not create any restriction at the database level.

Using tuples was an older way of setting choices in the field. Now we have a class-based way of doing this, which is enumeration type. Enumeration types provide better readability and code completion and help avoid duplication of values.

Let's see the same example using enumeration type.

Listing 2-6. Enumeration type example

```
from django.db import models

class Status(models.TextChoices):
    AVAILABLE = 'A', 'Available'
    OUT_OF_STOCK = 'O', 'Out of Stock'
    DISCONTINUED = 'D', 'Discontinued'

class Product(models.Model):
    status = models.CharField(max_length=1, choices=Status.choices)
```

Here in this example (Refer Listing 2-6), we define a class instead of tuples. This makes it easy to manage and reuse.

Now we will move to `db_column`.

db_column

The `db_column` attribute in Django is used to customize the column name of the table. By default, column names are the same as those of the fields. We have seen these in previous examples. In case you want to customize the column, you can use this attribute.

Let's check this with an example.

Listing 2-7. Customized column_name example

```
class Employee(models.Model):
    full_name = models.CharField(max_length=100, db_column="emp_name")
```

Listing 2-8. Customized column_name SQL equivalent

```
CREATE TABLE my_app_employee (
    id BIGSERIAL PRIMARY KEY,
    "emp_name" varchar(100) NOT NULL
);
```

In Listing 2-7, the **full_name** field is defined with the `db_column` attribute set to **emp_name**. If the `db_column` attribute were not specified, Django would use **full_name** as the column name in the corresponding SQL table. However, as shown in Listing 2-8, the generated SQL uses **emp_name** as the column name instead of **full_name** because of this explicit configuration.

Let's move to the next option which is `db_comment`.

db_comment

The `db_comment` attribute in Django is used to add comments to a column. This is mainly for users who do database administration and are not working with the application code.

Let's check this with an example.

Listing 2-9. Example of column with db_comment

```
class Product(models.Model):
    price = models.DecimalField(max_digits=10, decimal_places=2, db_
    comment="Price in USD")
```

Listing 2-10. SQL equivalent of db_comment

```
CREATE TABLE product (
    id BIGSERIAL PRIMARY KEY,
    price DECIMAL(10, 2) NOT NULL
);
COMMENT ON COLUMN product.price IS 'Price in USD';
```

In Listing 2-9, the **price** field is defined with the `db_comment` attribute set to "**Price in USD**." This will create a comment in the table for that field. Let's investigate Listing 2-10. We can see that there is a comment in the equivalent SQL query; this is very useful for those who only want to manage the database.

Let's move to the next option which is `default`.

default

The `default` attribute in Django is used to set the default value for a column. Default attributes are working at the application level, not at the database level. Default attributes can be static value or callable. Let's check both of them with examples.

Listing 2-11. Example of static default

```
class Task(models.Model):
    status = models.CharField(max_length=20, default="pending")
```

Here is an example (Refer Listing 2-11) of the column **status** that has a default of **pending.** If we don't specify a status during creation, Django ORM automatically adds this in the insert query.

Listing 2-12. Example of dynamic default

```
import datetime

class Event(models.Model):
    created_at = models.DateTimeField(default=datetime.datetime.now)
```

Here is an example (Refer Listing 2-12) of the column **created_at** that has a dynamic default. Here instead of a value we will give a **callable.** During the creation process Django ORM calls the function and its value is added to the insert query.

Let's move to the next option which is `db_default.`

db_default

The `db_default` attribute in Django is like `default.` The difference is that `db_default` is working at the database level. This is introduced in Django 5.0, so use it only if you are using Django 5.0 and above. `db_default` is more efficient than `default` as Django does not extra overload for adding the default values.

Let's check this with an example.

Listing 2-13. Example of db_default

```
class Order(models.Model):
    status = models.CharField(max_length=10, db_default="pending")
```

Listing 2-14. SQL equivalent of db_default

```
CREATE TABLE order (
    id BIGSERIAL PRIMARY KEY,
    status varchar(10) DEFAULT 'pending' NOT NULL
);
```

In the Listing 2-13 **status** column, it has `db_default` and its value is pending. If we check its equivalent SQL in Listing 2-14, we can see that the database level has `DEFAULT` and its value is **pending**.

Let's move to the next option which is `db_index.`

db_index

The `db_index` attribute tells Django ORM that this field needs to be indexed for faster lookup. By default, `db_index` is False. Some exceptions are primary key fields, fields with foreign key and one-to-one relationships, and unique constraints; we must specify which needs to be indexed.

Let's check this with an example.

Listing 2-15. Example of db_index

```
class Customer(models.Model):
    email = models.CharField(max_length=255, db_index=True)
```

Listing 2-16. SQL equivalent of db_index

```
CREATE TABLE customer (
    id BIGSERIAL PRIMARY KEY,
    email VARCHAR(255) NOT NULL
);

CREATE INDEX customer_email_idx ON customer (email);
```

In the Listing 2-15 **customer** column, `db_index` is set to True. If we check its equivalent SQL in Listing 2-16, we can see that an index is created for that specific column. This makes the query faster. It is advised to add `db_index` for frequently queried fields.

Let's move to the next option which is `db_tablespace`.

db_tablespace

The db_tablespace attribute tells the Django ORM **where the database should physically store a table or an index**, provided the database back end supports tablespaces. A tablespace is a logical storage unit inside the database that maps to a specific disk location.

By default, Django uses the database's default tablespace. We only need to specify db_tablespace when we want finer control over storage, for example, storing indexes on faster disks or separating large tables.

Let us check with an example.

Listing 2-17. db_tablespace example

```
class Order(models.Model):
    order_number = models.CharField(max_length=20,
    db_tablespace="orderspace")
```

In the above example (Refer Listing 2-17), **order_number** is saved to a different db_tablespace tablespace. This can result in improved speed; Django doesn't create a tablespace for you. Also, your database must support this.

Let's move to the next option which is editable.

editable

The editable attribute tells the Django ORM whether this needs to be shown in Django admin and forms. If this is set to False, this will not show in Django admin. By default, the value is True.

Let's check this with an example.

Listing 2-18. editable example

```
class SecretKey(models.Model):
    key = models.CharField(max_length=255, editable=False)
```

The key field in the model SecretKey will not be visible in Django admin and model forms (Refer Listing 2-18). This restriction is only at the application level, not at the database level.

Let's move to the next option which is error_messages.

error_messages

error_messages is used to customize the error message shown in Django admin. If we need to show custom errors instead of the default one, this is useful.

Let's check this with an example.

Listing 2-19. error_messages example

```
class Product(models.Model):
    name = models.CharField(
        max_length=100,
        error_messages={"max_length": "Name cannot exceed 100 characters!"}
    )
```

If the number of characters for the field name exceeds 100, it will show this error message instead of the default message (Refer Listing 2-19).

Let's move to the next option which is help_text.

help_text

help_text is used to create a custom tool tip for fields in Django admin. Let's check this with an example (Refer Listing 2-20).

Listing 2-20. help_text example

```
class UserProfile(models.Model):
    bio = models.TextField(help_text="Write a short biography about
    yourself.")
```

When we check Django admin, this will show a tool tip.

Let's move to the next option which is primary_key.

primary_key

The primary_key attribute tells Django ORM this field is the primary key for the table. We have already seen that Django automatically adds **id** fields in the SQL (check previous examples). But if we specify a field as the primary key, then that **id** field will not be there in the SQL.

Let's check this with an example.

Listing 2-21. Example of primary_key

```
class Country(models.Model):
    name = models.CharField(max_length=13, primary_key=True)
```

Listing 2-22. Equivalent SQL

```
CREATE TABLE country (
    name varchar(13) NOT NULL PRIMARY KEY
);
```

In Listing 2-21, the **name** column is set as the primary_key for that field. Now, look at the equivalent SQL in Listing 2-22. We can see that the id field is not there; instead the name is set as the primary key.

Let's move to the next option, which is `unique`.

unique

The `unique` attribute tells the Django ORM that the value in that field is unique. This is set at the database level. If we are duplicate values, it will raise integrity errors.

Listing 2-23. Example of unique

```
class UserInfo(models.Model):
    username = models.CharField(max_length=150, unique=True)
```

Listing 2-24. Equivalent SQL

```
CREATE TABLE userinfo (
    id BIGSERIAL PRIMARY KEY,
    username varchar(150) NOT NULL UNIQUE
);
```

In Listing 2-23, the **username** column is set as unique for that field. This adds a unique constraint at the database level. So, no two users with the same username can exist. If we check the equivalent SQL in Listing 2-24, we can see that username is set as `UNIQUE`.

Let's check three options together because they work the same way. They are `unique_for_date`, `unique_for_month`, and `unique_for_year`.

unique_for_date, unique_for_month, unique_for_year

These three options ensure that the value is unique for the date, month, and year. This is not enforced at the database level; instead, it works at the application level.

Let us check this with an example.

Listing 2-25. Example of unique_for_date

```
class BlogPost(models.Model):
    title = models.CharField(max_length=200, unique_for_
    date="published_date")
    published_date = models.DateField()
```

In Listing 2-25, the **title** column has `unique_for_date` set and its value is `published_date`. This ensures that the title is unique for the date which means we cannot use the same title for the same date. Likewise `unique_for_month` ensures it is unique for the month, and `unique_for_year` ensures that it is unique for the year.

Let's check another option which is `verbose_name`.

verbose_name

The `verbose_name` attribute is used to set the user field name in Django admin screens. It has no effect at the database level.

Let's check this with an example.

Listing 2-26. verbose_name example

```
class Product(models.Model):
    price = models.DecimalField(max_digits=10, decimal_places=2,
    verbose_name="Product Price")
```

When we check Django admin (Refer Listing 2-26), we can see that it shows as **Product Price** instead of **price**.

Let's move to the next option which is `validators`.

validators

The `validators` attribute is used to set custom validations for the field. This works at the application level, not at the database level.

Let's check this with an example.

Listing 2-27. validator example

```
from django.core.validators import MinValueValidator

class Product(models.Model):
    price = models.DecimalField(
        max_digits=10, decimal_places=2,
        validators=[MinValueValidator(0)]
    )
```

In Listing 2-27 we added `MinValueValidator` which is a built-in validator. What it does is ensure that the min value of the price is zero. If anything below zero is given, it will raise a validation error. Django provides lots of built-in validators; they are

- **MinValueValidator**: Minimum numeric value
- **MaxValueValidator**: Maximum numeric value
- **MinLengthValidator**: Minimum string length
- **MaxLengthValidator**: Maximum string length
- **RegexValidator**: Pattern matching
- **EmailValidator**: Email format validation
- **URLValidator**: URL format validation
- **validate_slug**: ASCII slug validation
- **validate_unicode_slug**: Unicode slug validation
- **FileExtensionValidator**: File type restriction
- **DecimalValidator**: Decimal precision validation

We can make custom validations that we will learn later.

We have covered the options for Django fields. Now we will move to the main building blocks of models, which are the fields.

Fields can be classified into two: **data fields** and **relationship fields**. Let us learn about them one by one. First we will learn about data fields.

Data Fields

The data fields are used to store actual values in database tables. The fields are mapped to columns in the table. According to the field type, it is mapped to datatypes like text, number, Boolean, date, etc.

Let us check all data fields in Django one by one. The first one is `CharField`.

CharField

`CharField` is one of the most used fields in Django. This is used to store a short piece of text where the maximum length is known in advance. This is used to store data like name, title, username, etc. `CharField` has a required field option, which is `max_length`, for specifying the maximum length of the text. Along with `max_length` we can also use options like `blank`, `null`, etc., which we have learned earlier. The maximum length of the text is validated both at the application and database levels.

Let us check this with an example.

Listing 2-28. Example model with CharField

```
class Example(models.Model):
    name = models.CharField(max_length=100, null=True)
```

Listing 2-29. SQL equivalent of CharField

```
CREATE TABLE example (
    id BIGSERIAL PRIMARY KEY,
    name VARCHAR(100) NULL
);
```

In Listing 2-28, we have defined a model named **Example**, and it has a field **name** which is of the type `CharField`. Its maximum length is defined as 100. The fields also allow NULL value. Let us check its equivalent SQL in Listing 2-29. We can see that it defines a table named example and has a field named **name**, and its type is VARCHAR **(100).** The Django ORM maps `CharField` to VARCHAR. We have also mentioned it is nullable, so name has `NULL`.

Now we are clear with how to store text with a known max length. What if the length of the text is unknown? There comes `TextField`.

TextField

`TextField` is used to store text which has no predefined length. This is used to store data like blog content, product description, comments, etc. We can use options like `blank`, `null`, etc., which we have learned earlier. We can use `max_length` for `TextField` also, but it is enforced at the application level, not at the database level.

Let us check this with an example.

Listing 2-30. Example model with TextField

```
class Example(models.Model):
    description = models.TextField(null=True)
```

Listing 2-31. SQL equivalent of TextField

```
CREATE TABLE example (
    id BIGSERIAL PRIMARY KEY,
    description TEXT NULL
);
```

In Listing 2-30, we have defined a model named **Example**, and it has a field **description** which is of the type `TextField`. The fields also allow NULL value. Let us check its equivalent SQL in Listing 2-31**;** we can see that it defines a table named **example** and has a field named **description** and its type is TEXT**.** The Django ORM maps `TextField` to TEXT.

Now we will learn about storing whole numbers using `IntegerField`.

IntegerField

`IntegerField` is used to store a whole number. This is used to store data like age, quantity, count, etc. The range of values for this field is from -2,147,483,648 to 2,147,483,647.

Let us check this with an example.

Listing 2-32. Example model with IntegerField

```
class Example(models.Model):
    quantity = models.IntegerField()
```

Listing 2-33. SQL equivalent of IntegerField

```
CREATE TABLE example (
    id BIGSERIAL PRIMARY KEY,
    quantity INTEGER NOT NULL
);
```

In Listing 2-32, we have defined a model named **Example**, and it has a field **quantity** which is of the type `IntegerField`. Let us check its equivalent SQL in Listing 2-33**;** we can see that it defines a table named **example** and has a field named **quantity** and its type is `INTEGER`**.** The Django ORM maps `IntegerField` to `INTEGER`.

Django provides a variety of integer fields based on the range of values you expect to store:

> **`PositiveBigIntegerField:`** Stores only positive integers from **0** to **9,223,372,036,854,775,807**. Use this when you expect extremely large numbers that will never be negative, for example, storing counter, external ids, etc.
>
> **`PositiveIntegerField:`** Stores positive integers from **0** to **2,147,483,647**. Ideal values like age, quantities, or counts that stay well within this range are always positive.
>
> **`PositiveSmallIntegerField:`** Stores small positive integers from **0** to **32,767**. Perfect for fields like rating (0–5), quantity of items (if known to be small), or status codes.

SmallIntegerField: Stores integers from **–32,768** to **32,767**. Use this when your values can be both negative and positive but still small in range such as temperature differences, small balances, or offset values.

Now we have learned about IntegerField; we will move to BooleanField.

BooleanField

BooleanField is used to store Boolean data. Mainly we are using this field to store flags, status, etc.

Let us check this with an example.

Listing 2-34. Example model with BooleanField

```
class Example(models.Model):
    is_active = models.BooleanField(default=True)
```

Listing 2-35. SQL equivalent of BooleanField

```
CREATE TABLE example (
    id BIGSERIAL PRIMARY KEY,
    is_active BOOLEAN NOT NULL
);
```

In Listing 2-34, we have defined a model named **Example**, and it has a field **is_active** which is of the type BooleanField. Let us check its equivalent SQL in Listing 2-35**.** We can see that it defines a table named **example** and has a field named **is_active** and its type is BOOLEAN. The Django ORM maps BooleanField to BOOLEAN.

Now let's move to the next field which is DateTimeField.

DateTimeField

DateTimeField is used to store date and time data. This is mainly used for timestamp of an event, created time of an object, etc. DateTimeField has two extra options; they are auto_now and auto_now_add**.** If auto_now is True, Django ORM automatically sets the field to the current date and time each time the object is updated/created. If `auto_now_add` is True, Django ORM automatically sets the field to the current date and time only when the object is created. They are very useful in tracking changes in an object.

Let us check this with an example.

Listing 2-36. Example model with DateTimeField

```
class Example(models.Model):
    created_at = models.DateTimeField()
```

Listing 2-37. SQL equivalent of DateTimeField

```
CREATE TABLE example (
    id BIGSERIAL PRIMARY KEY,
    created_at datetime NOT NULL
);
```

In Listing 2-36, we have defined a model named **Example**, and it has a field **created_at** which is of the type `DateTimeField`. Let us check its equivalent SQL in Listing 2-37. We can see that it defines a table named **example** and has a field named **created_at** and its type is `datetime`. The Django ORM maps `DateTimeField` to `datetime`.

Now let's move to the next field which is `DateField`.

DateField

`DateField` is used to store date. This is mainly used for storing date of an event, date of birth, etc. `DateField` has also two extra options which are the same as those of `DateTimeField`.

Let us check this with an example.

Listing 2-38. Example model with DateField

```
class Example(models.Model):
    dob = models.DateField()
```

Listing 2-39. SQL equivalent of DateField

```
CREATE TABLE example (
    id BIGSERIAL PRIMARY KEY,
    dob date NOT NULL
);
```

In Listing 2-38, we have defined a model named **Example**, and it has a field **dob** which is of the type `DateField`. Let us check its equivalent SQL in Listing 2-39**.** We can see that it defines a table named **example** and has a field named **dob** and its type is `date`**.** The Django ORM maps `DateField` to `date`.

Now let's move to the next field which is `EmailField`.

EmailField

`EmailField` is used to store email addresses. `EmailField` is a modified `CharField` regex validation on the value saved in this field. This is enforced at the application level and not the database level. Like `CharField` it has a `max_length` option; by default it's set as 254. But we can change this if we need it.

Let us check this with an example.

Listing 2-40. Example model with EmailField

```
class Example(models.Model):
    email = models.EmailField(unique=True, max_length=254)
```

Listing 2-41. SQL equivalent of EmailField

```
CREATE TABLE example (
    id BIGSERIAL PRIMARY KEY,
    email VARCHAR(254) NOT NULL UNIQUE
);
```

In Listing 2-40, we have defined a model named **Example**, and it has a field **email** which is of the type `EmailField`. Let us check its equivalent SQL in Listing 2-41**.** We can see that it defines a table named **example** and has a field named **email** and its type is VARCHAR, which means there is no difference between `EmailField` and `CharField` at the SQL level.

Now let's move to the next field which is `FloatField`.

FloatField

FloatField is used to store floating numbers. These fields are mainly used for storing percentage, sensor reading whose precision is not critical, etc. Values saved here are equivalent to Python float type.

Let us check this with an example.

Listing 2-42. Example model with FloatField

```
class Example(models.Model):
    temperature = models.FloatField()
```

Listing 2-43. SQL equivalent of FloatField

```
CREATE TABLE example (
    id BIGSERIAL PRIMARY KEY,
    temperature REAL NOT NULL
);
```

In Listing 2-42, we have defined a model named **Example**, and it has a field **temperature** which is of the type FloatField. Let us check its equivalent SQL in Listing 2-43. We can see that it defines a table named **example** and has a field named **temperature**, and its type is REAL. The Django ORM maps FloatField to REAL.

Now let's move to the next field which is DecimalField.

DecimalField

DecimalField is also used to store floating numbers. But here we have more control over the decimal points. These fields are mainly used for places where we need precision like scientific records, measurements, price, etc. Values saved in these fields are equivalent to the decimal type in Python. DecimalField has two more options; they are max_digits and decimal_places. max_digits is used to specify the total number of digits allowed in the number. decimal_places is used to specify the number of digits after the decimal point.

Let us check this with an example.

Listing 2-44. Example model with DecimalField

```
class Example(models.Model):
    amount = models.DecimalField(max_digits=10, decimal_places=2)
```

Listing 2-45. SQL equivalent of DecimalField

```
CREATE TABLE example (
    id BIGSERIAL PRIMARY KEY,
    amount NUMERIC(10, 2) NOT NULL
);
```

In Listing 2-44, we have defined a model named **Example**, and it has a field **amount** which is of the type `DecimalField`. Let us check its equivalent SQL in Listing 2-45. We can see that it defines a table named **example** and has a field named **amount**, and its type is `NUMERIC`. The Django ORM maps `DecimalField` to `NUMERIC`. The amount fields store a number with a maximum digit of 10 and it has two decimal places.

Now let's move to the next field which is `AutoField`.

AutoField

`AutoField` is an `IntegerField` that automatically increases its value. In most cases, values are not manually assigned to this field. It is primarily used for primary key columns. In Django, if a primary key is not explicitly defined in a model, Django automatically creates an `AutoField` to serve as the primary key.

Let us check this with an example.

Listing 2-46. Example model with AutoField

```
class Example(models.Model):
    pass
```

Listing 2-47. SQL equivalent of AutoField

```
CREATE TABLE example (
    id BIGSERIAL PRIMARY KEY
);
```

In Listing 2-46, we have defined a model named **Example**, with no fields. Let us check its equivalent SQL in Listing 2-47. We can see that it defines a table named **example** and has a field named **id**, and its type is `integer`. We can see that it is set as the primary key, and it is autoincremented. We have a variation of AutoField `BigAutoField`. The only change is the range. It stores numbers ranging from 1 to 9,223,372,036,854,775,807.

Now let's move to the next field which is `DurationField`.

DurationField

`DurationField` stores periods of time. It is equivalent to the timedelta in Python. This can be used for time differences, durations, or time intervals, such as tracking how long an event lasts.

Let us check this with an example.

Listing 2-48. Example model with DurationField

```
class Example(models.Model):
    duration = models.DurationField()
```

Listing 2-49. SQL equivalent of DurationField

```
CREATE TABLE example (
    id BIGSERIAL PRIMARY KEY,
    duration INTERVAL NOT NULL
);
```

In Listing 2-48, we have defined a model named **Example**, with a field named **duration**. Let us check its equivalent SQL in Listing 2-49. We can see that it defines a table named **example** and has a field named **duration**, and its type is `INTERVAL`.

Note If we use `DurationField` on PostgreSQL, the datatype used is an `INTERVAL`, and on Oracle the datatype is INTERVAL DAY(9) TO SECOND(6). Otherwise, a bigint of microseconds is used.

Now let's move to the next field which is `FileField`.

FileField

FileField is a specialized variation of CharField used to upload and store files through Django models and forms. Internally, it stores the file path as a string in the database, while the actual file is saved to the configured storage back end. It automatically handles file uploads and requires the MEDIA_ROOT and MEDIA_URL settings to be properly configured. The upload_to option specifies the directory or callable that determines where uploaded files are stored, enabling organized file management. The max_length option defines the maximum length of the file path that can be stored in the database (default is 100). FileField supports both local and custom storage back ends and is commonly used for managing user-uploaded content such as images, documents, and other media files.

Let us check this with an example.

Listing 2-50. Example model with FileField

```
class Example(models.Model):
    document = models.FileField(upload_to='uploads/')
```

Listing 2-51. SQL equivalent of FileField

```
CREATE TABLE example (
    id BIGSERIAL PRIMARY KEY,
    document VARCHAR(100) NOT NULL
);
```

In Listing 2-50, we have defined a model named **Example**, with a field named **document**. Let us check its equivalent SQL in Listing 2-51**.** We can see that it defines a table named **example** and has a field named **document**, and its type is VARCHAR. This means internally there is no difference between FileField and CharField. Here we have specified upload_to as **uploads**, so the file is stored inside MEDIA_ROOT/uploads/<file_name>. Its URL will be MEDIA_URL/uploads/<filename>.

Now let's move to the next field which is FilePathField.

FilePathField

`FilePathField` is a specialized variation of `CharField` that stores the path of an existing file located on the server's filesystem. It does not handle file uploads or manage file content. Instead, it allows selection from files within a predefined directory specified by the path option. The `match` option can be used to filter the available file choices based on a regular expression pattern, allowing only matching file names to be selected. The `recursive` option determines whether subdirectories under the specified path should be included when searching for files. The file path is stored as a string in the database, and the `max_length` option controls the maximum length of this stored path (default is 100). The FilePathField is primarily used for referencing static, configuration, or server-side files and is not suitable for user-uploaded data.

Let us check this with an example.

Listing 2-52. Example model with FilePathField

```
class Example(models.Model):
    path = models.FilePathField(
        path='/var/www/media',
        match=".*\.txt$", recursive=True)
```

Listing 2-53. SQL equivalent of FilePathField

```
CREATE TABLE example (
    id BIGSERIAL PRIMARY KEY,
    path VARCHAR(100) NOT NULL
);
```

In Listing 2-52, we have defined a model named **Example**, with a field named **path**. Let us check its equivalent SQL in Listing 2-53**.** We can see that it defines a table named **example** and has a field named **path**, and its type is `VARCHAR`. This means internally there is no difference between `FilePathField` and `CharField`. This field allows selection of any **.txt** file located anywhere under **/var/www/media** and its **subdirectories**, without uploading or modifying the file itself.

Now let's move to the next field which is `GenericIPAddressField`.

GenericIPAddressField

`GenericIPAddressField` is a specialized variation of `CharField`, and it is stored in the database as a character-based column rather than a numeric IP type. Because GenericIPAddressField is implemented as a variation of CharField, Django relies on application-level validation to ensure that only valid IP addresses are stored, while the database simply stores the value as text. It has an option called `protocol`; its possible values are `'both'`, `'IPv4'`, or `'IPv6'`.

Let us check this with an example.

Listing 2-54. Example model with GenericIPAddressField

```
class Example(models.Model):
    ip_address = models.GenericIPAddressField(protocol='both')
```

Listing 2-55. SQL equivalent of GenericIPAddressField

```
CREATE TABLE example (
    id BIGSERIAL PRIMARY KEY,
    ip_address VARCHAR(39) NOT NULL
);
```

In Listing 2-54, we have defined a model named **Example**, with a field named **ip_address**. Let us check its equivalent SQL in Listing 2-55. We can see that it defines a table named **example** and has a field named **ip_address**, and its type is `VARCHAR`. This means internally there is no difference between `GenericIPAddressField` and `CharField`. All the IP validation is done at the application level.

Now let's move to the next field which is `ImageField`.

ImageField

`ImageField` is a specialized variation of `FileField` which accepts image files only; it has all the options of `FileField`. There are two more options for `ImageField`. They are `width_field` and `height_field`. The `height_field` and `width_field` options allow Django to save the image dimensions into separate model fields. When an image is uploaded or updated, Django reads the image metadata and automatically populates these fields with the image height and width values. These fields must be defined explicitly in the model, and they are typically implemented using `PositiveIntegerField`.

Let us check this with an example.

Listing 2-56. Example model with ImageField

```
class Example(models.Model):
    image = models.ImageField(upload_to='images/')
```

Listing 2-57. SQL equivalent of ImageField

```
CREATE TABLE example (
    id BIGSERIAL PRIMARY KEY,
    image VARCHAR(100) NOT NULL
);
```

In Listing 2-56, we have defined a model named **Example**, with a field named **image**. Let us check its equivalent SQL in Listing 2-57. We can see that it defines a table named **example** and has a field named **image**, and its type is `VARCHAR`. This means internally there is no difference between `ImageField` and `CharField`.

Now let's move to the next field which is `JSONField`.

JSONField

`JSONField` is used to store JSON data. This is used to store configuration, metadata, etc.

Let us check this with an example.

Listing 2-58. Example model with JSONField

```
class Example(models.Model):
    metadata = models.JSONField()
```

Listing 2-59. SQL equivalent of JSONField

```
CREATE TABLE example (
    id BIGSERIAL PRIMARY KEY,
    metadata JSONB NOT NULL
);
```

In Listing 2-58, we have defined a model named **Example**, with a field named **metadata**. Let us check its equivalent SQL in Listing 2-59. We can see that it defines a table named **example** and has a field named **metadata**, and its type is `JSONB`. Django ORM maps `JSONField` to `JSONB (Postgres)/JSON (MySQL)/ TEXT (SQLite)`.

Now let's move to the next field which is `SlugField`.

SlugField

`SlugField` is a specialized `CharField` used to store user-readable tags, usually URLs. It is mainly used to store URLs for blogs. It has `max_length` and `allow_unicode` options. If `allow_unicode` is set as True, then the fields allow Unicode characters. The default `max_length` length of `SlugField` is 50.

Let us check this with an example.

Listing 2-60. Example model with SlugField

```
class Example(models.Model):
    slug = models.SlugField()
```

Listing 2-61. SQL equivalent of SlugField

```
CREATE TABLE example (
    id BIGSERIAL PRIMARY KEY,
    slug VARCHAR(50) NOT NULL
);
```

In Listing 2-60, we have defined a model named **Example**, with a field named **slug**. Let us check its equivalent SQL in Listing 2-61**.** We can see that it defines a table named **example** and has a field named **slug**, and its type is `VARCHAR`. We can see that `SlugField` is internally equivalent to `CharField`.

Now let's move to the next field which is `TimeField`.

TimeField

`TimeField` is used to store time. This is mainly used for storing data of an event, appointment time, etc. `TimeField` has also two extra options which are the same as those of `DateTimeField`.

Let us check this with an example.

Listing 2-62. Example model with TimeField

```
class Example(models.Model):
    appointment_time = models.TimeField()
```

Listing 2-63. SQL equivalent of TimeField

```
CREATE TABLE example (
    id BIGSERIAL PRIMARY KEY,
    appointment_time TIME NOT NULL
);
```

In Listing 2-62, we have defined a model named **Example**, with a field named **appointment_time**. Let us check its equivalent SQL in Listing 2-63**.** We can see that it defines a table named **example** and has a field named **appointment_time**, and its type is `TIME`. Django ORM maps `TimeField` to `TIME`.

Now let's move to the next field which is `URLField`.

URLField

`URLField` is a specialized variation of `CharField` which accepts URLs. It is mainly used to save websites, links, etc. The default `max_length` length of `URLField` is 200.

Let us check this with an example.

Listing 2-64. Example model with URLField

```
class Example(models.Model):
    website = models.URLField(max_length=200)
```

Listing 2-65. SQL equivalent of URLField

```
CREATE TABLE example (
    id BIGSERIAL PRIMARY KEY,
    website VARCHAR(200) NOT NULL
);
```

In Listing 2-64, we have defined a model named **Example**, with a field named **website**. Let us check its equivalent SQL in Listing 2-65. We can see that it defines a table named **example** and has a field named **website**, and its type is VARCHAR. This means internally URLField is equivalent to CharField.

Now let's move to the next field which is UUIDField.

UUIDField

UUIDField is used to store UUIDs. It can be used as primary key fields instead of autogenerated primary key, Storing API keys, can we use in publicly exposing ids. etc.

Let us check this with an example.

Listing 2-66. Example model with UUIDField

```
class Example(models.Model):
    identifier = models.UUIDField(default=uuid.uuid4)
```

Listing 2-67. SQL equivalent of UUIDField

```
CREATE TABLE example (
    id BIGSERIAL PRIMARY KEY,
    identifier UUID NOT NULL
);
```

In Listing 2-66, we have defined a model named **Example**, with a field named **identifier**. Let us check its equivalent SQL in Listing 2-67. We can see that it defines a table named **example** and has a field named **identifier**, and its type is UUID. In some databases instead of UUID, it saves as VARCHAR.

Now let's move to the next field which is BinaryField.

BinaryField

BinaryField is used for storing raw binary data. This field is suitable for data such as encrypted values, image data, or any other binary content. Use this field when you need to store binary data like encoded files, hashed passwords, or other raw data formats that are not directly human-readable.

Let us check this with an example.

Listing 2-68. Example model with BinaryField

```
class Example(models.Model):
    binary_data = models.BinaryField()
```

Listing 2-69. SQL equivalent of BinaryField

```
CREATE TABLE example (
    id BIGSERIAL PRIMARY KEY,
    binary_data BYTEA  NOT NULL
);
```

In Listing 2-68, we have defined a model named **Example**, with a field named **binary_data**. Let us check its equivalent SQL in Listing 2-69. We can see that it defines a table named **example** and has a field named **binary_data**, and its type is `BYTEA`.

We have completed the data fields and now we are moving to another type which is relationship fields. Let us dive into it.

Relationship Fields

We know relationships are the core idea behind the RDMS. Django ORM provides fields for relationships, and it makes accessing related objects very easy.

ForeignKey

`ForeignKey` is one of the most important relational fields in Django. It is used to create a **many-to-one** relationship between two models. In simple terms, `ForeignKey` allows one model to reference another model, thereby establishing a relationship at the database level.

`ForeignKey` is commonly used when multiple records in one table are related to a single record in another table. Typical examples include a book belonging to an author, an employee belonging to a department, or an order linked to a customer.

Unlike data fields such as CharField or IntegerField, ForeignKey does not store raw data. Instead, it stores a reference (usually the primary key) of another model.

Listing 2-70. Model with ForeignKey

```
class Author(models.Model):
    name = models.CharField(max_length=100)

class Book(models.Model):
    title = models.CharField(max_length=200)
    author = models.ForeignKey(Author, on_delete=models.CASCADE,
        related_name='books')
```

Listing 2-71. SQL equivalent of ForeignKey

```
CREATE TABLE author (
    id BIGSERIAL PRIMARY KEY,
    name VARCHAR(100) NOT NULL
);
CREATE TABLE book (
    id BIGSERIAL PRIMARY KEY,
    title VARCHAR(200) NOT NULL,
    author_id INTEGER NOT NULL,
    FOREIGN KEY (author_id) REFERENCES author (id) ON DELETE CASCADE
);
```

In Listing 2-70, we have defined two models: **Author** and **Book**. The **Book** model contains a field named **author**, which is a `ForeignKey` pointing to the **Department** model. This means that each **book** is associated with exactly one **author**, while an **author** can have multiple **books**.

If we look at the SQL equivalent in Listing 2-71, Django creates a column named **author_id** in the employee table. Internally, Django stores the primary key value of the related **Author** record in this column. This is how Django maintains relationships at the database level. We will learn more about accessing these in the upcoming chapter.

Now we will learn more about the options for `ForeignKey`.

The `ForeignKey` field provides several parameters to control its behavior.

The first one is `to`.

to

This is the first and required parameter. It specifies the model which the `ForeignKey` refers to.

Listing 2-72. to parameter example

```
author = models.ForeignKey(
    Author, on_delete=models.CASCADE,related_name='books')
```

Here we are passing the **to** option as a positional argument; its value is the name of the class we need to refer to. Here we are referring to the Author model (Refer Listing 2-72).

We can see another argument if that code is on_delete. Let's check what its use is.

on_delete

This is a required parameter that defines what happens when the referenced object is deleted. Django enforces this behavior at the application level.

Let us look at all available on_delete options in detail.

Let us see what models.CASCADE does.

models.CASCADE

When the referenced object is deleted, all related objects are also deleted.

Listing 2-73. models.CASCADE example

```
author = models.ForeignKey(Author, on_delete=models.CASCADE)
```

In Listing 2-73 we have used the **models.CASCADE** option which means when an author is deleted from the database, then all the related books will be deleted automatically. This is like a cascade delete in SQL. Now we will move to the next option which is models.PROTECT.

models.PROTECT

Prevents deletion of the referenced object if related objects exist.

Listing 2-74. models.PROTECT example

```
author = models.ForeignKey(Author, on_delete=models.PROTECT)
```

In Listing 2-74 we have used the **models.PROTECT** option which means if an **author** has **books**, Django will raise a **ProtectedError** and will not allow the **author** to be deleted.

Now we will move to the next option which is models.RESTRICT.

models.RESTRICT

This is similar to models.PROTECT, but it is more context aware. We can learn this with an example.

Listing 2-75. models.RESTRICT example

```
class Author(models.Model):
    name = models.CharField(max_length=100)
class Book(models.Model):
    title = models.CharField(max_length=200)
    author = models.ForeignKey(Author, on_delete=models.CASCADE)
class Review(models.Model):
    text = models.CharField(max_length=200)
    book = models.ForeignKey(Book, on_delete=models.RESTRICT)
```

In Listing 2-75 we have three models – Author, Book, and Review. Book has reference to Author, and its delete behavior is `models.CASCADE`. Review has reference to Book, and its delete behavior is `models.RESTRICT`. If we are trying to delete a book with a review, then it will raise a **RestrictedError.** So, we can protect all books with reviews. But if we delete the author, it will delete the book cascaded, and the reviews will be deleted cascaded.

Now we are moving to the next option which is models.SET_NULL.

models.SET_NULL

Sets the ForeignKey value to NULL when the reference object is deleted. For this option, null=True must be specified.

Listing 2-76. models.SET_NULL example

```
author = models.ForeignKey(Author, on_delete=models.SET_NULL, null=True)
```

In Listing 2-76 the author field's delete behavior is set as `models.SET_NULL`. If an author is deleted from the database, the field author in the book table is set as null. `null=True` is a must for these settings. Now we will move to the next option which is `models.SET_DEFAULT`.

models.SET_DEFAULT

Sets the ForeignKey value to a default value when the reference object is deleted. A default value must be provided.

Listing 2-77. models.SET_DEFAULT example

```
author = models.ForeignKey(Author, on_delete=models.SET_DEFAULT, default=1)
```

In Listing 2-77 the author field's delete behavior is set as `models.SET_DEFAULT`. If an author is deleted from the database, the field author in the book table is set as 1. The `default` is a must for these settings, and related objects with a default value must exist on the database also. Let's move to `models.SET`.

models.SET()

Allows setting the `ForeignKey` to a specific value or callable. Here, the values can be dynamically changed.

Listing 2-78. models.SET example

```
def get_anonymous_author():
    return Author.objects.get(name="Anonymous")
author = models.ForeignKey(Author, on_delete=models.SET(get_anonymous_
author))
```

In Listing 2-78 the author field's delete behavior is set as `models.SET`. And a function named `get_anonymous_author` is passed as the argument for this. When we delete the author, then this function is called and an author object with the name "Anonymous" is set as the new value. This method gives more control over deletion than the default and setting null.

Let us move to the last behavior which is `models.DO_NOTHING`.

models.DO_NOTHING

No action is taken when the reference object is deleted.

Listing 2-79. models.DO_NOTHING example

```
author = models.ForeignKey(Author, on_delete=models.DO_NOTHING)
```

In Listing 2-79 the author field's delete behavior is set as `models.DO_NOTHING`. If we delete the author, nothing happens. This may result in database integrity errors if the database enforces foreign key constraints.

Now we have learned the two required options for `ForeignKey` and its deletion behavior; let's learn about `related_name`.

related_name

Defines the name used for reverse relationships. We will learn more about this in the upcoming chapter in detail. For now, we will move to another option which is `db_constraint`.

db_constraint

Controls whether a database-level foreign key constraint is created. It is a Boolean, and the default value is True. In most cases, it is better to not use this option. This is useful for legacy data where we are not sure about data integrity. Let's move to another option which is `to_field`.

to_field

Specifies a field other than the primary key to reference. But make sure that the field is unique.

Listing 2-80. to_field example

```
author = models.ForeignKey(Author, on_delete=models.DO_NOTHING,
to_field='name')
```

In Listing 2-80 the author field's `to_field` is set as **name**, so instead of storing the id of the author, this will store the name of the author. But the catch is that the author's name must be unique for this to work properly.

Now we have learned about `ForeignKey` in detail; let's move to another relationship field which is `OneToOneField`.

OneToOneField

`OneToOneField` in Django defines a **one-to-one relationship** between two models. Each record in one model is **linked to exactly one record** in another model. This is often used for **profile extensions**, where additional information is stored in a separate model or we extend a model without modifying the original model, etc. It has the same required options as the `ForeignKey`. And the internal working is the same, except there is only one connection between the objects.

Listing 2-81. Example for OneToOneField

```
from django.db import models
from django.contrib.auth.models import User

class Profile(models.Model):
    user = models.OneToOneField(User, on_delete=models.CASCADE)
    bio = models.TextField(blank=True)
```

```
    phone_number = models.TextField()
    address = models.TextField(null=True)
```

Listing 2-82. SQL equivalent for OneToOneField

```
CREATE TABLE profile (
    id BIGSERIAL PRIMARY KEY,
    user_id INTEGER UNIQUE NOT NULL,
    bio TEXT NOT NULL,
    phone_number TEXT NOT NULL,
    address TEXT NULL,
    FOREIGN KEY (user_id) REFERENCES auth_user (id) ON DELETE CASCADE
);
```

In Listing 2-81, we have defined two models: **Profile** and **User** (predefined in Django). The **Profile** model contains a field named **user**, which is a `OneToOneField` pointing to the **User** model (predefined in Django). This means that each **profile** is associated with exactly one **user**; this is like extending the user and new fields are added.

If we look at the SQL equivalent in Listing 2-82, Django creates a column named **user_id** in the profile table. Internally, Django stores the primary key value of the related **user** record in this column. This is how Django maintains relationships at the database level. We can see that internally `OneToOneField` and `ForeignKey` are the same, but for the `OneToOneField` there is a `UNIQUE` constraint at the database level. In another way, we can say that `OneToOneField` is `ForeignKey` with `unique=True`.

Let's move to the last relationship field which is `ManyToManyField`.

ManyToManyField

The `ManyToManyField` in Django is used to represent a **many-to-many relationship** between two models. In this type of relationship, a single record in one model can be associated with multiple records in another model, and at the same time, each record in the second model can also be associated with multiple records in the first model. Django manages this relationship by automatically creating an intermediate table that stores references to both models.

A ManyToManyField should be used when neither side of the relationship can be represented using a simple ForeignKey. Common real-world examples include students enrolling in multiple courses while each course can have multiple students, authors writing multiple books while each book can have multiple authors, and users belonging to multiple groups while each group can contain multiple users.

Let us check this with an example.

Listing 2-83. Example for ManyToManyField

```
class Student(models.Model):
    name = models.CharField(max_length=100)

class Course(models.Model):
    title = models.CharField(max_length=200)
    students = models.ManyToManyField(Student, related_name="courses")
```

In Listing 2-83 we can see two models named **Student** and **Course.** In the **Course** model there is a field named **students** which is a ManyToManyField referencing the **student** model. So, a student can enroll in multiple courses, and each course has multiple students. But how does Django ORM handle this situation? Let us check the internal of the same.

Listing 2-84. SQL equivalent of ManyToManyField

```
CREATE TABLE student (
    id BIGSERIAL PRIMARY KEY,
    name VARCHAR(100) NOT NULL
);

CREATE TABLE course (
    id BIGSERIAL PRIMARY KEY,
    title VARCHAR(200) NOT NULL
);

CREATE TABLE course_students (
    id BIGSERIAL PRIMARY KEY,
    student_id INTEGER NOT NULL,
    course_id INTEGER NOT NULL,
    FOREIGN KEY (student_id) REFERENCES student(id) ON DELETE CASCADE,
```

```
    FOREIGN KEY (course_id) REFERENCES course(id) ON DELETE CASCADE,
    UNIQUE(student_id, course_id)
);
```

Django automatically creates the course_students table as the intermediate table (Refer Listing 2-84). This table stores the relationship between students and courses by keeping foreign key references to both tables. The unique constraint ensures that the same student cannot be associated with the same course more than once. Django ORM handles insertion and deletion to this intermediate table.

ManyToManyField has also to, related_name, etc. One special option for ManyToManyField is through.

Let us learn the working of through.

In some cases, the relationship itself needs to store additional data. For example, when tracking the date on which a student enrolled in a course, the automatically generated intermediate table is not sufficient. In such scenarios, a custom intermediate model can be defined using the **through** parameter.

Listing 2-85. Example for ManyToManyField with through

```
class Student(models.Model):
    name = models.CharField(max_length=100)

class Course(models.Model):
    title = models.CharField(max_length=200)
    students = models.ManyToManyField(Student, through="Enrollment")

class Enrollment(models.Model):
    student = models.ForeignKey(Student, on_delete=models.CASCADE)
    course = models.ForeignKey(Course, on_delete=models.CASCADE)
    enrollment_date = models.DateField(auto_now_add=True)
```

In Listing 2-85, the Enrollment model functions as the intermediate table and stores additional information about the relationship, such as the enrollment date. Since a custom through model is defined, Django does not create an automatic many-to-many table.

That is the end of the relationship fields. Let us summarize what we learned in this chapter.

Summary

In this chapter, we explored Django's wide variety of model fields, from basic datatypes like CharField and IntegerField to specialized fields like JSONField, UUIDField, and BinaryField. Each field type maps to an underlying database column type and offers attributes for customization, such as null, blank, default, and choices. We also looked at relationship fields ForeignKey, OneToOneField, and ManyToManyField that define links between models. Additionally, we covered common field options to control behavior, validation, indexing, and display in the Django admin. Understanding these field types and options ensures that your models are both accurate and efficient, forming a strong foundation for your Django applications. We have added a cheat sheet for data fields (see Table 2-1), field options (see Table 2-2), and different deletion behaviors (see Table 2-3).

In the next chapter we will dive deeper into database operations using Django ORM. We will learn about QuerySet, how to do CRUD (Create, Retrieve, Update, and Delete) operations, and some advanced lookups.

Appendix A

Table 2-1. *Django data field summary*

Field Type	Description	Typical Use Cases
CharField	Fixed-length text field	Names, titles, usernames, short textual data
TextField	Large unrestricted text	Long descriptions, comments, blog content
IntegerField	Signed whole numbers	Quantities, counts, IDs
PositiveIntegerField	Positive integers only	Positive counts, stock quantities
PositiveSmallIntegerField	Small positive integers	Ratings (e.g., 0–5), statuses
SmallIntegerField	Small signed integers	Temperature differences, small offset values
BigIntegerField	Large signed integers	Large counters, IDs exceeding standard int size

(continued)

Table 2-1. (*continued*)

Field Type	Description	Typical Use Cases
PositiveBigIntegerField	Large positive integers	Large wallet balances, huge counters
BooleanField	True/False binary value	Active flags, toggles
DateTimeField	Date and time	Timestamps for creation/modification
DateField	Date only	Birth dates, event dates
TimeField	Time only	Opening hours, appointment times
EmailField	Email address with validation	User emails, contact forms
URLField	URL string with validation	Websites, social links
FloatField	Floating point numbers	Sensor Datas, ratings with decimals
DecimalField	Fixed precision decimal numbers	Currency, financial data
AutoField	Auto-incrementing integer (primary key)	Primary key by default
BigAutoField	Large auto-incrementing integer	Large primary keys
DurationField	Time interval (`timedelta`)	Duration of events
FileField	File upload path (string)	Uploaded documents, files
ImageField	Image upload path (file + validation)	User avatars, product images
FilePathField	Filesystem path of a file (string)	Referencing files on server filesystem
GenericIPAddressField	IP address (IPv4/IPv6)	Storing IP addresses
JSONField	JSON encoded data	Metadata, flexible structured data
SlugField	URL-friendly short labels	SEO-friendly URLs, slugs
UUIDField	Universally unique identifiers	API keys, unique tokens
BinaryField	Binary data storage	Cryptographic hashes, binary blobs

***Table 2-2.** Django field options summary*

Option Name	Description	Usage/Example	Effect/Notes
null	Allows storing NULL in database	`null=True`	Field can store NULL; for string fields, prefer blank=True
blank	Allows form input to be empty	`blank=True`	Field is not required in forms; independent of `null`
choices	Restricts field values to a predefined set	`choices=[('A', 'Available'), ('O', 'Out')]`	Provides dropdown in forms; not enforced at DB level
db_column	Sets custom column name in database	`db_column='emp_name'`	Changes actual DB column name
db_comment	Adds comment/ description to DB column	`db_comment='Price in USD'`	Adds DB-level comment (supported in some DBs)
db_default	Sets database-level default value	`db_default='pending'`	More efficient than Python `default`; done at DB side
db_index	Adds database index on this field	`db_index=True`	Speeds up queries filtering on this field
db_tablespace	Specifies tablespace for field's column (DB-specific)	`db_tablespace= 'orderspace'`	Used in advanced DB setups (Oracle, PostgreSQL)
default	Sets Python-side default value	`default='Unnamed'`	Used by Django when creating new instances
editable	Mark field as editable/ non-editable in forms/ admin	`editable=False`	Field excluded from admin and ModelForms

(continued)

Table 2-2. (*continued*)

Option Name	Description	Usage/Example	Effect/Notes
error_ messages	Customizes validation error messages	`error_messages={'max_ length': 'Too long!'}`	Overrides default validation messages
help_text	Adds descriptive help text for field in admin	`help_text='Enter product description'`	Displays tool tip in Admin
primary_key	Marks the field as primary key	`primary_key=True`	Field becomes PK; no automatic `id` field created
unique	Enforces uniqueness constraint	`unique=True`	Creates uniqueness constraint at DB level
unique_for_ date	Ensures uniqueness for field per date in another date field	`unique_for_ date='published'`	Not enforced DB-side; enforced in Django validation
unique_for_ month	Ensures uniqueness for field per month in another date field	`unique_for_ month='published'`	As above
unique_for_ year	Ensures uniqueness for field per year in another date field	`unique_for_ year='published'`	As above
validators	List of validators to apply on field	`validators=[MinVa lueValidator(0), MaxValueValidator(10)]`	Runs validation using provided callables
verbose_name	Human-friendly name for field	`verbose_name='Product Title'`	Used in admin and forms

Table 2-3. *on_delete behavior cheat sheet*

Option	Behavior
CASCADE	Deletes the related objects when the referenced object is deleted
PROTECT	Prevents deletion of the referenced object if related objects exist
RESTRICT	Prevents deletion of the referenced object if related objects exist but is context aware
SET_NULL	Sets the foreign key field to NULL when the referenced object is deleted (requires null=True)
SET_DEFAULT	Sets the foreign key field to its default value when the referenced object is deleted
SET()	Calls a function or assigns a specific value when the referenced object is deleted
DO_NOTHING	Does nothing; leaves the foreign key value as is (may cause integrity errors)

Appendix B

Concept check

1. What is the difference between CharField and TextField?
2. Why is it better to use DecimalField instead of FloatField for storing currency values?
3. What is the role of auto_now and auto_now_add in DateTimeField and DateField?
4. What's the difference between null=True and blank=True in a Django field?
5. Which field would you use for storing
   - A blog post body
   - An image
   - A website URL
   - A unique API key

6. How does Django handle primary keys if you don't specify one in your model?
7. What is the purpose of the `choices` attribute in a field?
8. Which relationship field would you use for
    - Linking a profile to a user (one to one)
    - Linking books to authors (many to many)
    - Linking an order to a customer (many to one)

Exercise 1: Library System

Create a model for a library system with the following fields:

- `Book`: title, author_name, published_date, price
- `Member`: name, email, join_date, is_active

Which field types will you choose for each field, and why?

Exercise 2: Blog Application

Create a `BlogPost` model with

- `title` (short text, required)
- `slug` (URL friendly identifier, unique)
- `content` (long text, optional)
- `published_date` (date only, set when created)
- `is_published` (Boolean, default: False)

Write the model in Django ORM.

Exercise 3: Relationships

Model the following scenario:

- An `Author` can write multiple `Books`.
- A `Book` can belong to multiple `Categories`.

Exercise 4: Custom Constraints

Define a `Product` model with

- `name` (max length 100, required)
- `price` (must be positive, use validators)
- `status` (choices: Available, Out of Stock, Discontinued, default "Available")

Write the Django model and explain why you chose each field type.

Exercise 5: Thinking in Django

For each of the following scenarios, decide the **best field type**:

1. Storing a student's roll number (unique, short text)
2. Saving a JSON configuration (structured but flexible data)
3. Keeping track of login timestamps
4. Storing a user's profile picture
5. Keeping track of a movie's duration

CHAPTER 3

Working with QuerySets, CRUD Operations, and Advanced Lookups

In the last chapter, we explored Django model fields and their options, laying the groundwork for defining your data structure. Building on that foundation, this chapter dives into Django's QuerySets, a powerful and flexible way to interact with your database. We'll begin by introducing the models you'll work with, then examine QuerySets' key features such as lazy evaluation, chainability, iterable behavior, and caching. You'll learn how to perform CRUD (Create, Retrieve, Update, and Delete) operations efficiently, followed by a detailed look at advanced lookups with explanations, ORM examples, SQL translations, and sample outputs. Additionally, we cover aggregations, annotations, and working with relationships both forward and reverse. The chapter concludes by revisiting CRUD operations alongside their SQL equivalents, with sample outputs throughout to help solidify your understanding.

Note The SQL shown in this chapter is conceptual and may vary depending on the database back end.

Before diving, we can define a model that explains all the concepts in this chapter.

Afsal MS, *Mastering Django ORM*, https://doi.org/10.1007/979-8-8688-2589-7_3

Listing 3-1. Model for explaining all the concepts in this chapter

```
from django.db import models

class Author(models.Model):
    name = models.CharField(max_length=100)

    def __str__(self):
        return self.name

class Genre(models.Model):
    name = models.CharField(max_length=50)

    def __str__(self):
        return self.name

class Book(models.Model):
    title = models.CharField(max_length=200)
    author = models.ForeignKey(Author, on_delete=models.CASCADE)
    genres = models.ManyToManyField(Genre, blank=True)
    price = models.DecimalField(max_digits=6, decimal_places=2, null=True,
    blank=True)
    number_of_pages = models.IntegerField(null=True, blank=True)
    published_date = models.DateField(null=True, blank=True)
    created_at = models.DateTimeField(auto_now_add=True)

    def __str__(self):
        return self.title
```

In Listing 3-1 we have three models; they are **Author**, **Genre**, and **Book**. Both Author and Genre have only name fields. Book has title, author which is `ForeignKey` to Author, genres which is `ManyToManyField` to Genre, price, number of pages, published_date, and created_at.

We have used the proper datatype accordingly.

Now we are clear with the model. Let's learn about `QuerySet`.

QuerySet Overview

In Django, a QuerySet is a collection of database records that you obtain by querying a model. It represents the result of a database query and allows you to retrieve, filter, and manipulate data using Python code instead of writing raw SQL. It behaves similarly to a Python list in terms of iteration but represents a database query.

Now we will learn about the properties of QuerySet. The first one is QuerySets are lazy.

QuerySets Are Lazy

Django constructs the SQL query but does not execute it until the QuerySet is **evaluated** (e.g., iteration, casting to list, slicing that needs rows, len(), etc.). Let us explain this with an example.

Listing 3-2. QuerySets are lazy

```
books = Book.objects.all() #No Query executed here
print(list(books))
```

In Listing 3-2 we can see that books = Book.objects.all(). This will not trigger a database query. Database query is executed only when print(list(books)). This is why we call QuerySets lazy. Let us move to the next property which is QuerySets can be chained.

QuerySets Can Be Chained

Each operation on a QuerySet returns a new QuerySet, allowing multiple operations to be chained together. So we can apply as many queries as possible back-to-back. Even if we do lots of back-to-back queries, Django ORM combines them to a query.

Listing 3-3. QuerySet can be chained example

```
books = Book.objects.filter(author__name="J.K. Rowling").
    filter(price__gte=300)
print(books)
```

Listing 3-4. QuerySet can be chained equivalent SQL

```
SELECT b.*
FROM book AS b
JOIN author AS a ON b.author_id = a.id
WHERE a.name = 'J.K. Rowling' AND b.price >= 300;
```

In Listing 3-3 we can see that we have applied multiple filters back-to-back. But in Listing 3-4 there is only one query. Let us move to the next property which is QuerySets are **iterable**.

QuerySets Are Iterable

We know that in Python any object which can be looped over one at a time is called **iterable**. The QuerySet in Django is an iterable. We can loop over the QuerySet using loops in Python like a list.

Listing 3-5. QuerySets are iterable

```
for b in Book.objects.all():
    print(b.title)
```

Output

```
Harry Potter and the Philosopher's Stone
Harry Potter and the Chamber of Secrets
The Hobbit
The Lion, the Witch and the Wardrobe
```

In Listing 3-5 we can see that we are iterating the QuerySet using a loop. Each iteration of the QuerySet gives the object of the model which can be accessed like a class. This is similar to a list in Python. Let us move to the next property which is QuerySets cache results.

QuerySets Cache Results

This is a very important property of QuerySet which makes Django ORM powerful. Django ORM will not trigger multiple queries for the same QuerySet. **Once** a query is triggered, the result will be cached, so no database hit will be there. Let us check this with an example.

Listing 3-6. QuerySets cache results

```
qs = Book.objects.all()
print(list(qs))  # Executes SQL
print(list(qs))  # Uses cached results (no new SQL)
```

In Listing 3-6 we can see that we are printing the same `QuerySet` two times. But the database query will be triggered only once. The second time it will not fire any query; instead it uses the data in the cache which makes the Django ORM very efficient.

Now we have a good idea about `QuerySet`. Now we can move to **CRUD** operations of Django models.

CRUD Operations

CRUD operations form the foundation of working with data in any database-driven application. In Django, CRUD (`Create`, `Read/Retrieve`, `Update`, and `Delete`) is performed through the ORM using `QuerySet` and model instances, allowing you to interact with the database using clean, expressive Python code rather than raw SQL. This section introduces how Django handles each of these operations, explains the underlying behavior of the ORM, and shows how common data manipulation tasks map to their SQL equivalents. Through practical examples and sample outputs, you'll learn how to safely and efficiently manage data throughout the lifecycle.

Let's see how we can do the `Create` operations.

Create (Insert)

As the name suggests, it is the process of creating a new row in the table. In Django ORM, we are creating instances of models and calling their methods. We have different ways of creating the object.

Let us check them one by one. First is using the `create` method.

Using create

Using `create` is the simplest way to create a record in Django. We are passing all the parameters to the create method. The syntax is **<model_name>.objects.create(arguments). objects** is called a manager; we will learn more about this in the upcoming chapter. It is the default manager for all the models. Let us check this with an example.

Listing 3-7. Create using create method

```
author = Author.objects.get(name="J.K. Rowling")
book = Book.objects.create(title="Harry Potter", author=author)
print(book)
```

Output

```
<Book: Harry Potter>
```

Equivalent SQL

```
INSERT INTO book (title, author_id) VALUES ('Harry Potter', 1);
```

In Listing 3-7 we are using the `create` method for creating the record. We are passing all the required fields. If we do not pass the field if it has a default value, it will be passed; otherwise a **null** value is taken. Here we are passing the title and the author. If we check the equivalent SQL, we can see that it is an insert query with **title** as **Harry Potter** and **author_id** as **1**. Do you wonder where this 1 comes from? This is because the author is a `ForeignKey`, so we are passing the author object in the above example. Django ORM automatically takes the primary key value of the related object and generates the SQL. Now let's move to using the `save` method.

Using save

Using the `save` method is also equivalent to the create method but here we are not using the manager. Instead, we are creating an instance of the model class and calling the `save` method.

The actual object is created only after the save method is called. This method is useful for cases where we have conditional values before saving, like if number_of_pages > 500, then the price is 500. Let us check with an example.

Listing 3-8. Create using save method

```
author = Author.objects.get(name="J.R.R. Tolkien")
book = Book(title="The Hobbit", author=author)
book.save()
print(book)
```

Output

```
<Book: The Hobbit>
```

Equivalent SQL

```
INSERT INTO book (title, author_id) VALUES ('The Hobbit', 2);
```

In Listing 3-8 we are using the save method for creating the record. Here we are passing all the required parameters, and we call the save method. If we do not pass the field if it has a default value, it will be passed; otherwise a **null** value is taken. Here we are passing the title and the author. If we check the equivalent SQL, it is the same as the create method. Let us move to create using bulk_create.

Using bulk_create

Both methods create a single record at a time. But bulk_create, as the name suggests, creates multiple records at a time. This is very useful for creating multiple records efficiently. The syntax is similar to the create method, but we are passing a list of book objects. Let us check with an example.

Listing 3-9. Create using bulk_create

```
author = Author.objects.get(name="J.K. Rowling")
Book.objects.bulk_create([
    Book(
        title="Harry Potter and the Philosopher's Stone",
        author=author
    ),
    Book(
        title="Harry Potter and the Chamber of Secrets",
        author=author
    ),
])
print(list(Book.objects.filter(author=author)))
```

Output

```
[<Book: Harry Potter and the Philosopher's Stone>,
 <Book: Harry Potter and the Chamber of Secrets>]
```

Equivalent SQL

```
INSERT INTO book (title, author_id)
VALUES
    (' Harry Potter and the Philosopher's Stone ', 1),
    (' Harry Potter and the Chamber of Secrets ', 1);
```

In Listing 3-9, we are using the `bulk_create` method for creating the record. Here, multiple records are created in a single query. This is a very efficient way to create multiple records. We are passing a list of book objects to the `bulk_create` method. If we see the equivalent SQL, we can see that the only difference is that values have multiple entries.

Now we can move to `Read/Retrieve`.

Retrieve (Read)

`Read/Retrieve` is the process of fetching the records from the database. In this section, we will learn how to fetch records from the database with different methods. How to order the records according to our needs.

Let us learn the first one using `get`.

Using get

The `get` method is used to fetch a single matching record. If there is no record, then it will raise a `DoesNotExist` exception. Also, if there is more than one record, it will raise a `MultipleObjectsReturned` exception. The get method expects the fields we are checking. If more than one field is given, then a condition is applied between the fields. It is best to filter using the primary key or unique fields as they return only one record. Let us check with an example.

Listing 3-10. Fetch using get

```
author = Author.objects.get(name="J.K. Rowling")
print(author)
```

Output

```
<Author: J.K. Rowling>
```

Equivalent SQL

```
SELECT * FROM author WHERE name = 'J.K. Rowling' LIMIT 21;
```

In Listing 3-10, we are using the `get` method for fetching the records. Here we are fetching the **author** with the **name “J.K. Rowling”**. Did you wonder why the limit is 21 in the SQL? This is a constant fixed in Django ORM. It is used for a safety buffer.

What if I need to get multiple records? There comes the next method which is `filter`.

Using filter

Using `filter` we can fetch multiple matching records at a time. Here also we are passing the fields that need to be filtered. If multiple fields are passed, then an AND condition is applied in the query. Here, the output of the filter will be a `QuerySet`. Let us check this with an example.

Listing 3-11. Fetch using filter

```
books = Book.objects.filter(author__name="J.K. Rowling", price=300)
print(list(books))
```

Output

```
[<Book: Harry Potter and the Philosopher's Stone>,
 <Book: Harry Potter and the Chamber of Secrets>]
```

Equivalent SQL

```
SELECT b.*
FROM book AS b
JOIN author AS a ON b.author_id = a.id
WHERE a.name = 'J.K. Rowling' AND b.price = 300;
```

In Listing 3-11, we are using the `filter` method for fetching the records. Here we are fetching a book that is written by **J.K. Rowling,** and the price of the book is 300. Do you wonder why **author__name** is used in the query? This is because the author is a `ForeignKey`, but we can access the fields using a double underscore (__). Let’s check the equivalent SQL. We can see that there is a SQL join between the book and author as we reference the author’s name in the query. Django ORM has done this for us. Now we learn another way to fetch the record which is `exclude`.

Using exclude

`exclude` works exactly the opposite of `filter`. Here we will get all the records which are not matching the argument passed. Let us check this with an example.

Listing 3-12. Fetch using exclude

```
books = Book.objects.exclude(author__name="J.K. Rowling")
print(list(books))
```

Output

```
[<Book: The Hobbit>, <Book: The Lion, the Witch and the Wardrobe>]
```

Equivalent SQL

```
SELECT b.*
FROM book AS b
JOIN author AS a ON b.author_id = a.id
WHERE NOT (a.name = 'J.K. Rowling');
```

In Listing 3-12, we are using the exclude method for fetching the records. Here we are fetching a book that is not written by **J.K. Rowling**. Let's check the equivalent SQL. We can see that there is a SQL join between the book and author as we reference the author's name in the query. We can see that it is like the filter method except there is a not in the where clause.

Now we have learned how to retrieve the records from databases. Sometimes we need to retrieve the records in a specific order. Django ORM gives us an intuitive way to order the records. Let us check this method which is order_by.

Ordering the QuerySet

You can control the order of results using order_by. By default, Django does not guarantee any ordering unless specified in the model Meta class. The syntax of the ordering is very simple; just give the name of the fields to order. If we need to reverse order, then place a - (minus) sign before the field name. We can place more than one field in order_by. Ordering is applied from left to right, and each subsequent field acts as a tiebreaker when the previous fields have equal values. Let us check with an example.

Listing 3-13. order_by examples

```
books = Book.objects.order_by("title")
print(list(books))

# Order by price (descending)
books = Book.objects.order_by("-price")
print(list(books))
```

Output

```
[<Book: Harry Potter and the Chamber of Secrets>,
 <Book: Harry Potter and the Philosopher's Stone>,
 <Book: The Hobbit>,
 <Book: The Lion, the Witch and the Wardrobe>]
```

```
[<Book: The Order of the Phoenix>,
 <Book: The Hobbit>,
 <Book: Harry Potter and the Chamber of Secrets>,
 <Book: Pocket Classics: Fairy Tales>]
```

Equivalent SQL

```
SELECT * FROM book ORDER BY title ASC;
SELECT * FROM book ORDER BY price DESC;
```

In Listing 3-13, in the first example we are ordering the book using title, and in the second example we are ordering the book using descending order of the price. If we check the equivalent SQL, we can see that the query contains an `ORDER BY` clause. Now we have learned how to retrieve and order the QuerySets. We can move to the `Update` operation.

Update

We use multiple ways to update records using Django ORM. The first one is using the `save` method.

Using the save method

We have already seen the `save` method during creation. The same method can be used for updating also. The `save` method works differently for new objects and existing objects. For new objects it is a create operation, and for existing objects it will be an update operation. Let us check with an example.

Listing 3-14. Update using save method

```
book = Book.objects.get(
    title="Harry Potter and the Chamber of Secrets"
)
book.price = 400
book.save()
```

Equivalent SQL

```
UPDATE book set price=400 where id=1;
```

In Listing 3-14, first we fetch a book with the title name "Harry Potter and the Chamber of Secrets." Then we have updated the price to 400. But here the value of the object is changed but not reflected in the database. When we call the save method, Django ORM fires a query for updating the price. We can see that the equivalent SQL is an update query. Let us move to the next method, which is `bulk_update`.

Using bulk_update

`bulk_update` is similar to the `bulk_create` method. We are updating multiple records using a single query. Here we are passing the list of objects and fields we are going to update. It is a more efficient method to update multiple records as it fires only a single query. Let us check with an example.

Listing 3-15. Update using bulk_update method

```
books = Book.objects.filter(author__name="J.K. Rowling")
for b in books:
    b.price = (b.price or 0) + 50
Book.objects.bulk_update(books, ['price'])
```

Equivalent SQL

```
UPDATE book
SET price = CASE
    WHEN id = 1 THEN 550
    WHEN id = 2 THEN 650
END
WHERE id IN (1, 2);
```

In Listing 3-15, what we are doing is fetching all the books written by **J.K. Rowling.** Then we update the price increment by 50 at the instance level. Then we call the `bulk_update` method with books and specify that the price needs to be updated. If we check the SQL, we can see multiple when and then statements. Now we can move to another method, which is the `update` method.

Using update

update is also a bulk update method. But the difference from bulk_update is that it works on the QuerySets but bulk_update works on the list of instances. Update is mainly used for updating multiple records to single values. Let us check with an example.

Listing 3-16. Update using update method

```
Book.objects.filter(author__name="J.K. Rowling").update(price=400)
```

Equivalent SQL

```
UPDATE book
SET price = 400.00
WHERE author_id IN (SELECT id FROM author WHERE name = 'J.K. Rowling');
```

In Listing 3-16, what we are doing is fetching all the books written by **J.K. Rowling**. Then we update the price of all the books to 400. Here it is not updating at the instance level; instead, it updates all the matching records to given values. If we check the equivalent SQL, we can see the difference from the bulk_update method. Now we can move to the last operation which is Delete.

Delete

Delete, as the name says, deletes the record from the database. This method works both at the instance level and the QuerySet level. Let us check this with an example.

Listing 3-17. Delete an instance

```
book = Book.objects.get(title="The Hobbit")
book.delete()
```

Equivalent SQL

```
DELETE FROM book WHERE id IN (40);
```

Listing 3-18. Delete a QuerySet

```
Book.objects.filter(price=100).delete()
```

Equivalent SQL

```
DELETE FROM book WHERE id IN (41, 42);
```

In Listing 3-17 we are doing a delete operation on a single instance, and in Listing 3-18 we are doing a delete operation on `QuerySet`. But if we check the SQL, both look the same.

That is the end of CRUD operations; now we can learn the set operation on `QuerySet`.

Set Operations on QuerySet

Django `QuerySet` supports set operations, allowing multiple `QuerySets` of the same model to be combined using familiar Python operators. These operations treat `QuerySets` as mathematical sets and enable developers to express complex query logic in a clear and readable way. By using operators such as union, intersection, and symmetric difference, QuerySets can be merged or compared without writing raw SQL.

Set operations work only between `QuerySets` that return the same model and apply their logic at the database level whenever possible. Django translates these operations into efficient SQL expressions, such as OR and AND conditions, depending on the structure of the `QuerySet` involved. The result is always a new `QuerySet`, preserving Django's lazy evaluation behavior.

By leveraging set operations, developers can construct expressive queries that closely mirror real-world conditions while keeping the code concise and maintainable.

Let us check the `union` operations of the `QuerySet`.

union

The `union` operator is used to combine the `QuerySet` into one. In mathematical union, it takes the unique value of a combined `QuerySet`. This is useful when we need different types of queries on a model, but we need to combine them. At the database level union is equivalent to `UNION`. Let us check this with an example.

Listing 3-19. QuerySet union

```
qs1 = Book.objects.filter(author__name="J.K. Rowling")
qs2 = Book.objects.filter(author__name="J.R.R. Tolkien")
qs = qs1.union(qs2)
print(list(qs))
```

Output

```
[<Book: Harry Potter and the Philosopher's Stone>,
 <Book: Harry Potter and the Chamber of Secrets>,
 <Book: The Hobbit>]
```

Equivalent SQL

```
SELECT * FROM book AS b
JOIN author AS a ON b.author_id = a.id
WHERE a.name = 'J.K. Rowling'
UNION
SELECT * FROM book AS b
JOIN author AS a ON b.author_id = a.id
WHERE a.name = 'J.R.R. Tolkien';
```

In Listing 3-19 we are combining the two `QuerySets` which are qs1 and qs2 using the `union` operator. So the result will be the combined items in both `QuerySets`. If we check the equivalent SQL, we can see that it has two select queries and combines them using the `UNION` operator.

Now we can move to the next one `intersection`

intersection

The `intersection` operator filters the common item in both QuerySets. This is useful to combine two QuerySets and find the common item between them. At the database level, it uses an `INTERSECT` operator. Let us check this with an example.

Listing 3-20. QuerySet intersection

```
qs1 = Book.objects.filter(price=300)
qs2 = Book.objects.filter(author__name="J.K. Rowling")
qs = qs1.intersection(qs2)
print(list(qs))
```

Output

```
[<Book: Harry Potter and the Chamber of Secrets>]
```

Equivalent SQL

```
SELECT * FROM book AS b
JOIN author AS a ON b.author_id = a.id
WHERE b.price = 300
INTERSECT
SELECT * FROM book AS b
JOIN author AS a ON b.author_id = a.id
WHERE a.name = 'J.K. Rowling';
```

In Listing 3-20 we are checking the `intersection` of two queries. The first one is a list of all books with a price of 300 and the second is a list of all books written by J.K. Rowling. Then our result will be a list of all books written by J.K. Rowling with a price of 300. If we check the SQL, we can see that it is using the `INTERSECT` operator.

Now we can move to the next operator which is `difference`.

Difference

The `difference` operator filters out items in the first list which are not in the second list. It is like subtracting the item from the first list which is present in the second list. At the database level, the `EXCEPT` operator is used. Let us check this with an example.

Listing 3-21. QuerySet difference

```
qs1 = Book.objects.filter(author__name="J.K. Rowling")
qs2 = Book.objects.filter(price=300)
qs = qs1.difference (qs2)
print(list(qs))
```

Output

```
[<Book: Harry Potter and the Philosopher's Stone>,
 <Book: Pocket Classics: Fairy Tales>]
```

Equivalent SQL

```
(
  SELECT * FROM book AS b
  JOIN author AS a ON b.author_id = a.id
```

```
  WHERE a.name = 'J.K. Rowling'
)
EXCEPT
(
  SELECT * FROM book AS b
  JOIN author AS a ON b.author_id = a.id
  WHERE b.price = 300
);
```

In Listing 3-21 we are checking the `difference` between two queries. The first one is a list of all books with a price of 300, and the second is a list of all books written by J.K. Rowling. Then our result will be a list of all books written by J.K. Rowling at the price of not 300. If we check the SQL, we can see that it is using the `EXCEPT` operator.

Now we can move to the advanced lookups in Django ORM.

Advanced Lookups

Django ORM provides a powerful and expressive way to query the database, and at the heart of this power are lookups. In earlier sections, we used basic field comparisons to retrieve data, such as matching exact values or filtering simple conditions. While these lookups are sufficient for straightforward queries, real-world applications often require more complex and flexible querying capabilities. This is where advanced lookups become essential.

Advanced lookups allow you to express complex database conditions directly in Python code without writing raw SQL. They enable operations such as partial matching, range of comparisons, case-insensitive searches, date and time filtering, relationship traversal, and set-based conditions. By combining these lookups, you can precisely describe what data you need while keeping your queries readable, maintainable, and efficient.

Django implements advanced lookups using a consistent double-underscore (__) syntax, which makes it possible to chain conditions, traverse relationships, and apply transformations within a single QuerySet. These lookups are lazily evaluated, meaning Django constructs the SQL query only when the data is needed, allowing you to build complex queries incrementally and efficiently.

Let us check the advanced lookups one by one. The first one is `contains`.

contains

This lookup is used to match a substring within a text field. It is a case-sensitive matching. At the database level, it is a LIKE query. Let us check this with an example.

Listing 3-22. contains example

```
qs = Book.objects.filter(title__contains="Magic")
print(list(qs))
```

Output

```
[<Book: The Magic Treehouse>]
```

Equivalent SQL

```
SELECT * FROM book WHERE title LIKE '%Magic%';
```

In Listing 3-22 we are filtering the books with the title containing the word "**Magic**". Here, filtering is case-sensitive. So only the exact matching items are filtered. If we see the SQL, it is LIKE query.

Let us move to the next which is icontains.

icontains

This works the same as that of contains. The only difference is that it is case-insensitive. At the database level it is using the LIKE query.

Listing 3-23. icontains example

```
qs = Book.objects.filter(title__icontains="magic")
print(list(qs))
```

Output

```
[<Book: The Magic Treehouse>, <Book: MAGIC Spells>]
```

Equivalent SQL

```
SELECT * FROM book WHERE UPPER(title) LIKE UPPER('%magic%');
```

In Listing 3-23 we are filtering the books with the title containing the word "**magic**". Here, filtering is case-insensitive. So if the title contains **magic,** then it is filtered. If we check the SQL, it is a `LIKE` query. But the comparison is done on the text which is converted to uppercase.

Let us move to the next one which is `date`.

date

The `date` lookup is used to compare the date portion of a `DateTimeField`. This is very useful when we need all the records on a given day.

Let us check this with an example.

Listing 3-24. date example

```
from datetime import date
qs = Book.objects.filter(created_at__date=date(2025, 6, 19))
print(list(qs))
```

Output

```
[<Book: The Hobbit>]
```

Equivalent SQL

```
SELECT * FROM book WHERE DATE(created_at) = '2025-06-19';
```

In Listing 3-24, we are using the date lookup. We know that the created_at is `DateTimeField` which means it contains data and time. But if we need a book object created on a particular date here 19-06-2025. In the equivalent SQL, we can see that we are casting the `DateTimeField` to date using `DATE` and then compare that date with the given date.

Now we can move to the next one which is `day`.

day

The day lookup is used to match the day value from a `DateField/DateTimeField`. This is useful to fetch records of what is created on a particular day of the month.

Let us check with an example.

Listing 3-25. day example

```
qs = Book.objects.filter(published_date__day=19)
print(list(qs))
```

Output

```
[<Book: The Lion, the Witch and the Wardrobe>]
```

Equivalent SQL

```
SELECT * FROM book WHERE EXTRACT(DAY FROM published_date) = 19;
```

In Listing 3-25, we are using the day lookup. We know that the published_date is `DateField`. Here what we do is filter all the books that are published on the 19th. If we check the SQL, what it does is use `EXTRACT`. It takes `DAY` from the published_date and compares the value given.

Let us move to the next lookup which is `endswith`.

endswith

The endswith lookup is used to filter fields with matching suffix. This is a case-sensitive filtering. At the database level, it is a `LIKE` query.

Let us check with an example.

Listing 3-26. endswith example

```
qs = Book.objects.filter(title__endswith="Azkaban")
print(list(qs))
```

Output

```
[<Book: Harry Potter and the Prisoner of Azkaban>]
```

Equivalent SQL

```
SELECT * FROM book WHERE title LIKE '%Azkaban';
```

In Listing 3-26 we are using the `endswith` lookup for filtering books that end with Azkaban. Here we get all the records that exactly match considering the case. If we check the SQL, we can see that it is a `LIKE` query.

Let us move to the next one which is `iendswith`.

iendswith

iendswith works exactly like endswith; the only difference is here it's case-insensitive.

Let us check with an example.

Listing 3-27. iendswith example

```
qs = Book.objects.filter(title__iendswith="azkaban")
print(list(qs))
```

Output

```
[<Book: Harry Potter and the Prisoner of Azkaban>]
```

Equivalent SQL

```
SELECT * FROM book WHERE UPPER(title) LIKE UPPER('%azkaban');
```

In Listing 3-27 we are filtering using iendswith. Here the case doesn't matter if any title that ends with Azkaban is being filtered. If we check the SQL, it is a LIKE query, but the comparison is performed after changing them to uppercase.

Let us move to the next lookup which is exact.

exact

The exact lookup is used to filter the exact records matching the exact string. Here it is case-sensitive. The interesting part is without lookup, if we pass the field name, it works in the same way. The exact lookup makes the code more explicit.

Let us check with an example.

Listing 3-28. exact example

```
qs = Book.objects.filter(title__exact="The Hobbit")
print(qs)

qs2 = Book.objects.filter(title="The Hobbit")
print(qs2)
```

Output

```
[<Book: The Hobbit>]
```

SQL

```
SELECT * FROM book WHERE title = 'The Hobbit';
```

In Listing 3-28 we are using the `exact` lookup for filtering the book, and also we are using a direct field to filter the book. Both of them work the same way. Both filter books that match the given text, and they are case-sensitive. The use of `exact` makes the code more explicit. At the SQL level, it is checking the fields with a matching value.

Let us move to the next lookup which is `iexact`.

iexact

`iexact` works the same way as `exact`. But here it is case-insensitive.

Let us check this with an example.

Listing 3-29. iexact example

```
qs = Book.objects.filter(title__iexact="the hobbit")
print(list(qs))
```

Output

```
[<Book: The Hobbit>]
```

Equivalent SQL

```
SELECT * FROM book WHERE UPPER(title) = UPPER('the hobbit');
```

In Listing 3-29 we are using `iexact` for filtering the book. Here a book with the title "the hobbit" is filtered. It does not care about the case. If we check the equivalent SQL, we can see that the comparison is done in the uppercase.

Let us move to the next lookup which is `in`.

in

The `in` lookup is used to filter records matching from list items. This is equivalent to IN in SQL. This lookup is useful when we need to match records from a list of items.

Let us check with an example.

Listing 3-30. in example

```
qs = Book.objects.filter(
    author__name__in=["J.R.R. Tolkien", "C.S. Lewis"]
)
print(list(qs))
```

Output

```
[<Book: The Hobbit>, <Book: The Lion, the Witch and the Wardrobe>]
```

Equivalent SQL

```
SELECT * FROM book
INNER JOIN author
    ON book.author_id = author.id
WHERE author.name IN ('J.R.R. Tolkien', 'C.S. Lewis');
```

In Listing 3-30 we are fetching all the books that are written by J.R.R. Tolkien or C.S. Lewis. For that we are using the `in` lookup. If we check the SQL, we can see that we are using an `IN` operator.

Let us move to the next one which is `isnull`.

isnull

The `isnull` lookup is used to check if a field is `NULL` or not. If we pass True as the value, then it filters all records with value `NULL`. And if False, it filters all records which are not `NULL.`

Let us check with an example.

Listing 3-31. isnull example

```
qs = Book.objects.filter(published_date__isnull=True)
print(list(qs))
```

Output

```
[<Book: Untitled Manuscript>]
```

Equivalent SQL

```
SELECT * FROM book WHERE published_date IS NULL;
```

In Listing 3-31 we are fetching all the books with published_date as null. If we check the equivalent SQL, we can see that `IS NULL` is used. If we are passing False, then the query will become `IS NOT NULL`.

Let us move to the next lookup which is `gt`.

gt

The `gt` lookup is used to filter the records which are greater than the given value. This is mainly used in numerical fields like integer, float, etc. At the database level, the greater than operator is used.

Let us check with an example.

Listing 3-32. gt example

```
qs = Book.objects.filter(number_of_pages__gt=500)
print(list(qs))
```

Output

```
[<Book: The Order of the Phoenix>]
```

Equivalent SQL

```
SELECT * FROM book WHERE number_of_pages > 500;
```

In Listing 3-32 we are fetching all the books with number_of_pages greater than 500. If we check the SQL, we can see that the > operator is used for comparison which is very intuitive.

Let us move to the next one which is `gte`.

gte

gte works exactly like gt. Here the matching value contains the equal values also.

Let us check with an example.

Listing 3-33. gte example

```
qs = Book.objects.filter(number_of_pages__gte=1000)
print(list(qs))
```

Output

```
[]
```

Equivalent SQL

```
SELECT * FROM book WHERE number_of_pages >= 1000;
```

In Listing 3-33 we are fetching all the books with number_of_pages greater than or equal to 1000. If we check the SQL, we can see that the >= operator is used for comparison.

Let us move to the next one which is hour.

hour

The hour lookup is used to fetch the match hour of a DateTimeField/TimeField. This is very useful in situations where we get activities that happen during an hour. The possible range of values is 0–23.

Let us check with an example.

Listing 3-34. hour example

```
qs = Book.objects.filter(created_at__hour=14)
print(list(qs))
```

Output

```
[<Book: The Hobbit>]
```

SQL

```
SELECT * FROM book WHERE EXTRACT(HOUR FROM created_at) = 14;
```

In Listing 3-34 we are fetching all the books created at the 14th hour. Upon checking the SQL, we can see that using `EXTRACT`, we extract hour components from created_at and match the given value.

Let us move to the next lookup which is `lt`.

lt

`lt` is used for filtering a value less than the given value. This is also useful for numeric fields. At the database level it is using the < operator.

Let us check with an example.

Listing 3-35. lt example

```
qs = Book.objects.filter(price__lt=100)
print(list(qs))
```

Output

```
[<Book: Pocket Classics: Fairy Tales>]
```

Equivalent SQL

```
SELECT * FROM book WHERE price < 100;
```

In Listing 3-35 we are fetching all the books with a price less than 100. If we check the SQL, we can see that we are using the < operator.

Let's move to the next one which is `lte`.

lte

`lte` works exactly the same, except it includes the value equal to the given value.

Let us check with an example.

Listing 3-36. lte example

```
qs = Book.objects.filter(price__lte=300)
print(list(qs))
```

Output

```
[<Book: Pocket Classics: Fairy Tales>]
```

Equivalent SQL

```
SELECT * FROM book WHERE price <= 300;
```

In Listing 3-36 we are fetching all the books with a price less than or equal to 300. If we check the SQL, we can see that we are using the <= operator.

Let us move to the next lookup which is `minute`.

minute

The `minute` lookup is used to fetch the match minute of a `DateTimeField/TimeField`. This is very useful in situations where we get activities that happened during a minute. The possible range of values is 0–59.

Let us check with an example.

Listing 3-37. minute example

```
qs = Book.objects.filter(created_at__minute=30)
print(list(qs))
```

Output

```
[<Book: The Hobbit>]
```

Equivalent SQL

```
SELECT * FROM book WHERE EXTRACT(MINUTE FROM created_at) = 30;
```

In Listing 3-37 we are fetching all the books created at the 30th minute. Upon checking the SQL, we can see that using `EXTRACT`, we extract minute components from created_at and match the given value.

Let us move to the next one which is `month`.

month

The `month` lookup is used to fetch the match month of a `DateTimeField/DateField`. This is very useful in situations where we get activities that happen during a month. The possible range of values is 1–12.

Let us check with an example.

Listing 3-38. month example

```
qs = Book.objects.filter(created_at__month=6)
print(list(qs))
```

Output

```
[<Book: The Hobbit>]
```

Equivalent SQL

```
SELECT * FROM book WHERE EXTRACT(MONTH FROM created_at) = 6;
```

In Listing 3-38 we are fetching all the books created at the 6th month. Upon checking the SQL, we can see that using `EXTRACT`, we extract month components from created_at and match the given value.

Let us move to the next one which is `quarter`.

quarter

The `quarter` lookup is used to fetch the match quarter of a `DateTimeField/DateField`. This is very useful in situations where we get activities that happen during a quarter. The possible range of values is 1–4.

Let us check with an example.

Listing 3-39. quarter example

```
qs = Book.objects.filter(created_at__quarter=2)
print(list(qs))
```

Output

```
[<Book: The Hobbit>]
```

Equivelent SQL

```
SELECT * FROM book WHERE EXTRACT(QUARTER FROM created_at) = 2;
```

In Listing 3-39 we are fetching all the books created in the 2nd quarter. Upon checking the SQL, we can see that using `EXTRACT`, we extract quarter components from created_at and match the given value.

Let us move to the next one which is `range`.

range

The range lookup is used to filter records matching values in the given range. This is useful for fetching records matching a range, records created between two dates, etc. At the database level it is implemented using a `BETWEEN-AND` combination.

Let us check with an example.

Listing 3-40. range example

```
qs = Book.objects.filter(number_of_pages__range=(100, 500))
print(list(qs))
```

Output

```
[<Book: The Hobbit>, <Book: The Lion, the Witch and the Wardrobe>]
```

Equivalent SQL

```
SELECT * FROM book WHERE number_of_pages BETWEEN 100 AND 500;
```

In Listing 3-40 we are fetching all the books with a number of pages between 100 and 500. If we check the SQL, we can see that it is using the `BETWEEN-AND` combination.

Let us move to the next one which is `regex`.

Regex

The `regex` lookup is used to fetch fields with regex expressions. This useful finding text in a large text. This is case-sensitive in matching. The generated SQL query varies according to the database back end.

Let us check with an example.

Listing 3-41. regex example

```
qs = Book.objects.filter(title__regex=r'^The')
print(list(qs))
```

Output

```
[<Book: The Hobbit>, <Book: The Lion, the Witch and the Wardrobe>]
```

PostgreSQL

```
SELECT * FROM book WHERE title ~ '^The';
```

MySQL/MariaDB

```
SELECT * FROM book WHERE title REGEXP '^The';
```

In Listing 3-41 we are fetching all the books starting with The. Here if we check the SQL, it is different in Postgres and MySQL. In Postgres it uses the ~ operator with regex expression. For MySQL, it uses the REGEXP operator.

Let us move to the next one which is `iregex`.

iregex

`iregex` works the same way as regex. But here it is case-insensitive. At the database level, there is only the regex change.

Let us check with an example.

Listing 3-42. iregex example

```
qs = Book.objects.filter(title__iregex=r'^the')
print(list(qs))
```

Output

```
[<Book: The Hobbit>, <Book: The Lion, the Witch and the Wardrobe>]
```

PostgreSQL

```
SELECT * FROM book WHERE title ~* '^the';
```

MySQL/MariaDB

```
SELECT * FROM book WHERE title REGEXP '^(?i)the';
```

In Listing 3-42 we are fetching all the books starting with The. Here it is case-insensitive. Here if we see the SQL, it is different in Postgres and MySQL. In Postgres it uses the ~ operator with regex expression. For MySQL, it uses the REGEXP operator.

Let us move to the next one which is `second`.

second

The second lookup is used to fetch the match second of a DateTimeField/TimeField. This is very useful in situations where we get activities that happen during a second. The possible range of values is 0–59.

Let us check with an example.

Listing 3-43. second example

```
qs = Book.objects.filter(created_at__second=0)
print(list(qs))
```

SQL

```
SELECT * FROM book WHERE EXTRACT(SECOND FROM created_at) = 0;
```

Output

```
[<Book: The Hobbit>]
```

In Listing 3-43 we are fetching all the books created at the 0th second. Upon checking the SQL, we can see that using EXTRACT, we extract second components from created_at and match the given value.

Let us move to the next one which is startswith.

startswith

startswith is used to fetch the field with a matching prefix. This is case-sensitive. At the database level, it's a LIKE query.

Let us check with an example.

Listing 3-44. startswith example

```
qs = Book.objects.filter(title__startswith="Harry")
print(list(qs))
```

Output

```
[<Book: Harry Potter and the Philosopher's Stone>,
 <Book: Harry Potter and the Chamber of Secrets>]
```

Equivalent SQL

```
SELECT * FROM book WHERE title LIKE 'Harry%';
```

In Listing 3-44 we are filtering all the books starting with **Harry.** The search is case-sensitive.

If we check the SQL, it is a `LIKE` query.

Let us move to the next one which is `istartswith`.

istartswith

`istartswith` works exactly like `startswith`; the only difference is here it's case-insensitive.

Let us check with an example.

Listing 3-45. istartswith example

```
qs = Book.objects.filter(title__istartswith="harry")
print(list(qs))
```

Output

```
[<Book: Harry Potter and the Philosopher's Stone>,
 <Book: Harry Potter and the Chamber of Secrets>]
```

Equivalent SQL

```
SELECT * FROM book WHERE UPPER(title) LIKE UPPER('harry%');
```

In Listing 3-45 we are filtering all the books starting with **Harry**. The search is case-insensitive.

If we check the SQL, it is a `LIKE` query, but checking is done in the uppercase.

Now let's move on to `time`.

time

The time lookup is used to filter the record using the time port of a `DateTimeField`. This is useful where we need to find activity within a time frame. At the database level, it takes the time component and compares with the input.

Let us check with an example.

Listing 3-46. time example

```
from datetime import time
qs = Book.objects.filter(created_at__time=time(14, 30))
print(list(qs))
```

Output

```
[<Book: The Hobbit>]
```

Equivalent SQL

```
SELECT * FROM book WHERE CAST(created_at AS time) = '14:30:00';
```

In Listing 3-46, we are filtering all the books created at 14:30. If we check the equivalent SQL, we can see that it first CAST the created_at to time and compares this with the input given.

Let us move to the next one which is `week`.

week

The `week` lookup is used to fetch the match week of a `DateTimeField/DateField`. This is very useful in situations where we get activities that happen during a week. The possible range of values is 1–52 or 53. Working may change according to the database back end.

Let us check with an example.

Listing 3-47. week example

```
qs = Book.objects.filter(created_at__week=25)
print(list(qs))
```

Output

```
[<Book: The Hobbit>]
```

Equivalent SQL

```
SELECT * FROM book WHERE EXTRACT(WEEK FROM created_at) = 25;
```

In Listing 3-47 we are fetching all the books created at the 25th week. Upon checking the SQL, we can see that using EXTRACT, we extract week components from created_at and match the given value.

Let us move to the next one which is week_day.

week_day

The week_day lookup is used with DateTimeField and DateField to filter records based on a specific weekday. This is useful in scenarios such as retrieving activities that occur on a particular day of the week. The lookup accepts integer values in the range 1–7. However, the weekday-to-number mapping is database-dependent, as different databases follow different conventions for the start of the week.

Let us check with an example.

Listing 3-48. week_day example

```
qs = Book.objects.filter(created_at__week_day=1)  # Sunday in Django
print(list(qs))
```

Output

```
[<Book: The Hobbit>]
```

Equivalent SQL

```
SELECT * FROM book WHERE EXTRACT(DOW FROM created_at) + 1 = 1;
```

In Listing 3-48, we are fetching all the books created on Sunday. Although the Django query uses value 1, the underlying database uses a different numbering system for weekdays. This mismatch is handled internally by Django and is database specific. In PostgreSQL, EXTRACT (DOW) returns values from 0 (Sunday) to 6 (Saturday). Django adjusts this by adding 1 so that the values fall in the range 1–7.

Because of these inconsistencies, Django provides the iso_week_day lookup, which follows the ISO 8601 standard and offers consistent behavior across databases.

iso_week_day

The iso_week_day lookup is used with DateTimeField and DateField to filter records based on a specific weekday following the ISO 8601 standard. According to this standard, the week starts on Monday, and the values range from 1 (Monday) to 7 (Sunday).Unlike week_day, the behavior of iso_week_day is consistent across all database back ends, making it the preferred choice for reporting and business logic.

Let us check with an example.

Listing 3-49. iso_week_day example

```
qs = Book.objects.filter(created_at__iso_week_day=1)  # Monday
print(list(qs))
```

Output

```
[<Book: The Hobbit>]
```

Equivalent SQL

```
SELECT * FROM book WHERE EXTRACT(ISODOW FROM created_at) = 1;
```

In Listing 3-49, we are fetching all books created on Monday using ISO 8601 weekday numbering. Since both Django and PostgreSQL follow the same ISO convention for iso_week_day, the value used in the ORM query and the value checked in the SQL expression are identical. This standardized behavior eliminates database-specific differences and makes iso_week_day more reliable than week_day when working across multiple database systems.

Let us move to the next one which is year.

year

The year lookup is used with DateTimeField and DateField to filter records based on the calendar year extracted from the date value. This lookup follows the Gregorian calendar year and is commonly used for yearly reports and date-based filtering.

Let us check with an example.

Listing 3-50. year example

```
qs = Book.objects.filter(created_at__year=2025)
print(list(qs))
```

Output

```
[<Book: The Hobbit>]
```

Equivalent SQL

```
SELECT * FROM book WHERE EXTRACT(YEAR FROM created_at) = 2025;
```

In Listing 3-50, we are fetching all books created in the calendar year 2025.

The year lookup simply extracts the year component from the date and matches it against the given value.

Let us move to the last lookup which `iso_year`.

iso_year

The `iso_year` lookup is used with `DateTimeField` and `DateField` to filter records based on the ISO 8601 week-based year. The ISO year may differ from the calendar year for dates that fall near the start or end of a year, as ISO weeks are defined relative to Thursdays.

Let us check with an example.

Listing 3-51. iso_year example

```
qs = Book.objects.filter(created_at__iso_year=2025)
print(list(qs))
```

Output

```
[<Book: The Hobbit>]
```

Equivalent SQL

```
SELECT * FROM book WHERE EXTRACT(ISOYEAR FROM created_at) = 2025;
```

In Listing 3-51, it is filtering all the books created in ISO calendar year 2025. Using extract, we take the ISO year component and match the record.

Now we have learned all the advanced lookups. Now we are moving to aggregation in Django.

Aggregations

In many applications, it is necessary to compute summary information from a collection of database records. Examples include counting the total number of rows, calculating averages, or finding minimum and maximum values. Django supports these operations through its aggregation framework, which allows such calculations to be performed efficiently at the database level.

The `aggregate` () method applies one or more aggregate functions such as `Count`, `Sum`, `Avg`, `Min`, and `Max` to an entire `QuerySet` and returns the result as a single dictionary. Unlike normal `QuerySet` operations, aggregations do not return model instances; instead, they return computed values that summarize the data.

By delegating these calculations to the database, aggregations reduce the amount of data transferred to application code and take advantage of the database's optimized query execution. This makes them well suited for reporting, analytics, and high-level summaries.

Let us check out different aggregation functions with examples. The first one is `Count`.

Count

`Count` is used to get the number of records. This is often required for analysis.

Let us check with an example.

Listing 3-52. Count example

```
from django.db.models import Count

print(Book.objects.aggregate(Count('id')))
```

Output

```
{'id__count':<count of books>}
```

Equivalent SQL

```
SELECT COUNT(book.id) AS id__count FROM book;
```

In Listing 3-52 what we are doing is taking the number of books in the database. Django provides a Count function for this. Combining the aggregate and Count, we can get the number of records. In the SQL, we can see that it uses the COUNT function.

Let us move to the next one which Sum.

Sum

Sum is used to get the sum of values in a particular field. This is often required for analysis.

Let us check with an example.

Listing 3-53. Sum example

```
from django.db.models import Sum

print(Book.objects.aggregate(Sum('price')))
```

Output

```
{'price__sum':<sum of all the books in the database>}
```

Equivalent SQL

```
SELECT SUM(book.price) AS price__sum FROM book;
```

In Listing 3-53 what we are doing is taking the sum of prices of all the books. Django provides a Sum function for this. Combining the aggregate and Sum, we can get the sum of prices. In the SQL, we can see that it uses the SUM function.

Let us move to the next one which is Avg.

Avg

Avg is used to get average values in a particular field. This is often required for analysis.

Let us check with an example.

Listing 3-54. Avg example

```
from django.db.models import Avg

print(Book.objects.aggregate(Avg('price')))
```

Output

```
{'price__avg':<average price of the books>}
```

Equivalent SQL

```
SELECT AVG(book.price) AS price__avg FROM book;
```

In Listing 3-54, what we are doing is taking the average price of all the books. Django provides an Avg function for this. Combining the `aggregate` and `Avg`, we can get the average price. In the SQL, we can see that it uses the `AVG` function.

Let us move to the next one which is `Max`.

Max

`Max` is used to get the maximum value of a given field. This is often required for analysis.

Let us check with an example.

Listing 3-55. Max example

```
from django.db.models import Max

print(Book.objects.aggregate(Max('price')))
```

Output

```
{'price__max':<max value of the book>}
```

Equivalent SQL

```
SELECT MAX(book.price) AS price__max FROM book;
```

In Listing 3-55, we are fetching the maximum price of the book. Django provides a `Max` function for this. Combining the `aggregate` and `Max`, we can get the Max price. In the SQL, we can see that it uses the `MAX` function.

Let us move to the next one which is `Min`.

Min

Min is used to get the minimum value of a given field. This is often required for analysis.

Let us check with an example.

Listing 3-56. Min example

```
from django.db.models import Min

print(Book.objects.aggregate(Min('price')))
```

Output

```
{'price__min':<min price of the books>}
```

Equivalent SQL

```
SELECT MIN(book.price) AS price__min FROM book;
```

In Listing 3-56, we are fetching the minimum price of the book. Django provides a Min function for this. Combining the aggregate and Min, we can get the lower price. In the SQL, we can see that it uses the MIN function.

Now we have learned about aggregation, which is useful for overall analysis of records. Sometimes in our application we need computed values per instance level. For this, Django provides annotation. Let dive into it.

Annotating QuerySets with Computed Values

In many applications, the data stored in the database is not always sufficient on its own. Often, applications need computed values, such as counts, totals, averages, or calculated values, based on existing records. Django's annotation provides a powerful way to compute such values directly at the database level and include them in QuerySet results.

The annotate () method allows developers to add computed, per-row values to a QuerySet without modifying the underlying database schema. These values are calculated as part of the SQL query and are exposed as temporary attributes on each returned model instance.

Let us check with an example.

Listing 3-57. Annotate example

```
from django.db.models import Count
authors = Author.objects.annotate(total_books=Count('book'))
print([f"{a.name} ({a.total_books})" for a in authors])
```

Output

```
['J.K. Rowling (2)', 'J.R.R. Tolkien (1)', 'C.S. Lewis (1)']
```

Equivalent SQL

```
SELECT a.*, COUNT(b.id) AS total_books
FROM author AS a
LEFT JOIN book AS b ON a.id = b.author_id
GROUP BY a.id;
```

In Listing 3-57, the `annotate` method is used together with the `Count` aggregation function to compute the number of books written by each author. The query operates on the **Author** model and adds a derived field named **total_books** to each returned object.

The expression `Count('book')` instructs Django to count the number of related book records for every author. Since this is an annotation, the calculation is performed per author, and the resulting count is attached to each Author instance as a temporary attribute. This attribute does not exist in the database schema and is available only for the lifetime of the `QuerySet`.

When the `QuerySet` is evaluated, Django translates the annotation into a SQL query that performs a LEFT JOIN between the author and book tables and groups the results by author. The LEFT JOIN ensures that authors without any related books are still included in the result set, with their count evaluated as zero.

The GROUP BY clause causes the database to compute the count of related books separately for each author. Django then maps the computed value (total_books) back onto the corresponding author objects.

As a result, each author in the `QuerySet` can be accessed like a normal model instance, with the additional **total_books** attribute representing the number of books associated with that author.

In the next section we are digging deeper into querying of relationship fields.

Dig Deeper into Relationship Fields

In this section, we will dig deeper into the working of relationships. Our main goal is to learn different ways of querying `OneToOneField`, `ForeignKey`, and `ManyToManyField`. Also, we will cover how to add and clear `ManyToManyField`.

First, let's look at `ForeignKey`.

Querying ForeignKey

In Django, querying a `ForeignKey` works in two directions. They are **forward querying** and **reverse querying**. Forward querying is filtering from the model which has the `ForeignKey` fields. In our case, the book has the `ForeignKey` field, so filtering book is called forward querying. Reverse querying is filtering from the referenced model. In our case from the Author model.

Let us consider the case we need to filter all the books by J.K. Rowling using forward querying.

Listing 3-58. Forward querying of ForeignKey

```
rowling = Author.objects.get(name="J.K. Rowling")
print(list(Book.objects.filter(author=rowling)))
```

Output

```
[<Book: Harry Potter and the Philosopher's Stone>,
 <Book: Harry Potter and the Chamber of Secrets>]
```

Equivalent SQL

```
SELECT * FROM book WHERE author_id = 1;
```

In Listing 3-58 this is a simple query like the other fields. First, we fetched the author with the name J.K. Rowling, then filtered the book using that author object. If we check the SQL, this also looks straightforward. We can also filter using the author, i.e., `Book.objects.filter(author_id=1)`. This is also valid. But in this case, we are using **author_id** instead of **author.**

Let us check how we can do the same filtering using reverse querying.

Listing 3-59. Reverse querying of ForeignKey

```
rowling = Author.objects.get(name="J.K. Rowling")
print(list(rowling.book_set.all()))
```

Output

```
[<Book: Harry Potter and the Philosopher's Stone>,
 <Book: Harry Potter and the Chamber of Secrets>]
```

SQL (reverse concept)

```
SELECT * FROM book WHERE author_id = 1;
```

In Listing 3-59 we are filtering using the reverse querying method. Here we first fetched the author object. Then we accessed **book_set.all**(). Did you wonder where **book_set** comes from? The name **book_set** is automatically generated by Django and represents a collection of all book objects related to the given author. The _set suffix indicates that the relationship can return multiple objects, i.e., the syntax for the reverse attribute is like **<model_name>_set**. If you see the output and SQL, it looks the same as that of the forward querying method.

The default **book_set** name works, but it may feel verbose or unclear in larger projects. Django allows you to customize the reverse relationship name using the `related_name` option on the `ForeignKey` which we have already learned in Chapter 2.

Consider the case if author value of the Book model was like.

Listing 3-60. Book model with related_name

```
class Book(models.Model):
    title = models.CharField(max_length=200)
    author = models.ForeignKey(Author, on_delete=models.CASCADE, related_
    name="books")
    genres = models.ManyToManyField(Genre, blank=True)
    price = models.DecimalField(max_digits=6, decimal_places=2, null=True,
    blank=True)
    number_of_pages = models.IntegerField(null=True, blank=True)
    published_date = models.DateField(null=True, blank=True)
    created_at = models.DateTimeField(auto_now_add=True)
```

```
    def __str__(self):
        return self.title
```

If our Book model was like Listing 3-60, it has a related_name for ForeignKey which is **books**. Then Listing 3-59 will become like Listing 3-61.

Listing 3-61. Reverse querying of ForeignKey with related_name

```
rowling = Author.objects.get(name="J.K. Rowling")
print(list(rowling.books.all()))
```

Output

```
[<Book: Harry Potter and the Philosopher's Stone>,
 <Book: Harry Potter and the Chamber of Secrets>]
```

Equivalent SQL

```
SELECT * FROM book WHERE author_id = 1;
```

If we check the example in Listing 3-61, we can see that the only difference is that instead of a default reverse attribute which is **book_set**, it changes to **books** which is the related_name specified on the ForeignKey.

Now we have learned both techniques for filtering. Let us move to ManyToManyField.

Working with ManyToManyField

In Django, querying a ManyToManyField works in two directions. They are **forward querying** and **reverse querying**. Forward querying is filtering from the model which has the ManyToManyField fields. In our case, the book has the ManyToManyField field, so filtering book is called forward querying. Reverse querying is filtering from the referenced model. In our case, the Genre model.

Let us consider the case to filter all books in the fantasy genre using forward querying.

Listing 3-62. Forward querying of ManyToManyField

```
fantasy = Genre.objects.get(name="Fantasy")
books = Book.objects.filter(genres=fantasy)
print(books)
```

Output

```
[<Book: Harry Potter and the Philosopher's Stone>,
 <Book: Harry Potter and the Chamber of Secrets>]
```

Equivalent SQL

```
SELECT * FROM book INNER JOIN book_generes on (book.id = book_generes.book_
id) WHERE book_generes.genere_id = 1
```

In Listing 3-62, we first filter the genre object with the name Fantasy. Then using that object, we can filter the books. This looks like other fields. But if we check the SQL, we can see that it is a bit different because of the intermediate table created for the `ManyToManyField`. The book table is joined with the intermediate table which stores both ids of book and genre. And the filtering is done. If we use the `through` attribute, the working is the same as the above; only the table name for the join changes.

Now we can learn how to filter the same using the reverse querying technique.

Listing 3-63. Reverse querying of ManyToManyField

```
fantasy = Genre.objects.get(name="Fantasy")
books = fastasy.book_set.all()
print(books)
```

Output

```
[<Book: Harry Potter and the Philosopher's Stone>,
 <Book: Harry Potter and the Chamber of Secrets>]
```

Equivalent SQL

```
SELECT * FROM book INNER JOIN book_generes on (book.id = book_generes.book_
id) WHERE book_generes.genere_id = 1
```

In Listing 3-63 we can see that it works exactly like the `ForeignKey` reverse filtering. Django automatically creates an attribute named **book_set**; using that we can filter the books.

If we use `related_name` while defining the model, then that attribute changes accordingly.

Now we can learn some specific methods for `ManyToManyField` which are used for adding, deleting, and updating the values in these fields.

Let us learn how to add many-to-many relations.

Listing 3-64. Adding to manytomanyfield

```
book = Book.objects.get(id=1)

fantasy = Genre.objects.get(name="Fantasy")
scifi = Genre.objects.get(name="Sci-Fi")
magic = Genre.objects.get(name= "Magic")

book.genres.add(fanstasy) # Adding single object
book.genres.add(scifi, magic) # Adding multiple
```

Equivalent SQL

```
INSERT INTO book_genres ("book_id", "genre_id") VALUES (1, 1) ON CONFLICT
DO NOTHING; # single

INSERT INTO book_genres ("book_id", "genre_id") VALUES (1, 2), (1, 3) ON
CONFLICT DO NOTHING; # multiple
```

In Listing 3-64 we filter the book and add multiple genres like fantasy, sci-fi, and magic to that book. Django provides an add method for the same; it can accept single or multiple objects. Even ids of the objects are also accepted, i.e., `book.genres.add(2, 3)`. If we check the equivalent SQL, we can see that it goes to the intermediate table.

Let us check how we can remove an item from `ManyToManyField`.

Listing 3-65. Removing from ManyToManyField

```
book = Book.objects.get(id=1)

fantasy = Genre.objects.get(name="Fantasy")
scifi = Genre.objects.get(name="Sci-Fi")
magic = Genre.objects.get(name= "Magic")

book.genres.remove(fanstasy) # Remove single object
book.genres.remove(scifi, magic) # Remove multiple
```

Equivalent SQL

```
DELETE FROM book_genres WHERE (book_id = 1 AND genre_id IN (1));
# single

DELETE FROM book_genres WHERE (book_id = 1 AND genre_id IN (2, 3));
# multiple
```

In Listing 3-65 we are removing the genres from the book. Like the example we can remove a single item or multiple items using the `remove` method. It also accepts the ids of the objects. If we check the SQL, we can see the removing record from the intermediate table.

Django ORM provides a `clear` method for clearing all relationships.

Listing 3-66. clear ManyToManyField

```
book = Book.objects.get(id=1)
book.genres.clear()
```

Equivalent SQL

```
DELETE FROM book_genres WHERE (book_id = 1);
```

In Listing 3-66 we are removing all the genres from the book objects. If we check the SQL, we can see that we are clearing all the intermediate records of the selected book objects.

The Django ORM provides a `set` method for replacing the relations with a newly given list. The set is equivalent to applying `clear` and `add` methods back-to-back.

Listing 3-67. set method example

```
book = Book.objects.get(id=1)

fantasy = Genre.objects.get(name="Fantasy")
scifi = Genre.objects.get(name="Sci-Fi")
book.genres.set([fanstasy, scifi])
```

In Listing 3-67 we are setting genres as fantasy and sci-fi. If any records exist, then they will be deleted automatically, and new records matching the given input will be generated automatically.

So we learned the querying of relationships, how we add, remove, clear, and set relationships in ManyToManyField.

Now we will move to the next one which is OneToOneField.

Querying OneToOneField

In Django, querying a OneToOneField also works in two directions, just like a ForeignKey. These are forward querying and reverse querying. The difference is that a one-to-one relationship always gives a single object instead of a collection. Before we dive into the working, let us define a model.

Listing 3-68. Sample model for OneToOneField

```
class AuthorProfile(models.Model):
    author = models.OneToOneField(Author, on_delete=models.CASCADE)
    bio = models.TextField()
    website = models.URLField()
```

Using this model let's check how we do forward querying.

In forward querying, we filter from the model that defines the OneToOneField. In this case (Refer Listing 3-68), the **AuthorProfile** model contains the AuthorProfile, so querying AuthorProfile is considered forward querying.

Listing 3-69. Forward querying of OneToOneField

```
rowling = Author.objects.get(name="J.K. Rowling")
profile = AuthorProfile.objects.get(author=rowling)
print(profile)
```

Equivalent SQL

```
SELECT * FROM author_profile WHERE (author_id = 1);
```

In Listing 3-69, we first retrieved the **Author** object and then filtered the **AuthorProfile** using that author. This works similarly to filtering a ForeignKey, but since the relationship is one to one, Django expects exactly one matching row.

Now we can check the same using the reverse querying technique.

Listing 3-70. Reverse querying of OneToOneField

```
rowling = Author.objects.get(name="J.K. Rowling")
profile = rowling.authorprofile
print(profile)
```

Equivalent SQL

```
SELECT * FROM author_profile WHERE (author_id = 1);
```

In Listing 3-70, the reverse attribute name **authorprofile** is automatically generated by Django. It is derived from the related model name (AuthorProfile) converted to lowercase. Unlike `ForeignKey`, there is no **_set** suffix, because a `OneToOneField` can return only a single object. The `OneToOneField` has a provision for giving the `related_name`; if we give a related name, then instead of an autogenerated attribute, we will use the `related_name`.

Now we will summarize this chapter.

Summary

In this chapter, we explored Django's `QuerySet`, a way of interacting with the database using the OOP concept. We began with an overview of `QuerySets`, understanding their lazy nature, their chainability, and how they translate high-level Python expressions into efficient SQL queries.

We then covered CRUD operations, learning how to `Create`, `Read/Retrieve`, `Update`, and `Delete` records using `QuerySet` and how bulk operations differ from instance-level operations. The chapter introduced set operations and logical combinations, demonstrating how `QuerySet` can be combined, intersected, or excluded.

Next, we examined advanced lookups, including field transformations, range queries, date and time lookups, and pattern matching, enabling precise and flexible data retrieval. We also discussed how to handle relationship fields, covering forward and reverse querying for `ForeignKey`, `OneToOneField`, and `ManyToManyField`, along with best practices for using `related_name` and managing many-to-many write operations.

The chapter introduced `aggregate` and `annotate` methods for showing how to compute summaries such as counts, averages, and totals and how to enrich `QuerySet` with calculated fields for reporting and analysis.

By the end of this chapter, you should be able to model real-world data access patterns using Django ORM confidently, write readable and efficient queries, and reason about the SQL generated behind the scenes.

In the upcoming chapter we will learn advanced querying techniques, methods for optimizing the queries, and database functions that Django ORM provides.

Appendix

Exercise 1: QuerySet Basics

1. Explain why Django `QuerySet` is described as lazy.
2. Write a `QuerySet` that retrieves all books ordered by published_date in descending order.
3. What happens when the same `QuerySet` is evaluated multiple times?

Exercise 2: CRUD Operations

1. Create a new book record with a title, price, and publication date.
2. Update the price of all books written by a specific author using a bulk update.
3. Delete all books that were published before the year 2000.

Exercise 3: Set Operations

1. Retrieve books that are either in the fantasy genre or have more than 500 pages.
2. Retrieve books that are in the fantasy genre and not published in the last five years.

Exercise 4: Advanced Lookups

1. Retrieve books whose title starts with the letter "H."
2. Retrieve books published between two given dates.
3. Retrieve books created on a specific weekday.

Exercise 5: Handling Relationship Fields

1. Write a forward query to retrieve all books written by a given author.
2. Write a reverse query to retrieve all books belonging to a given genre.
3. Modify a model to use related_name and update the reverse query accordingly.

Exercise 6: Many-to-Many Write Operations

1. Add multiple genres to an existing book.
2. Replace all genres of a book using a single operation.

Exercise 7: Aggregation and Annotation

1. Count the number of books written by each author.
2. Annotate each book with the total number of genres it belongs to.
3. Retrieve authors who have written more than three books.

CHAPTER 4

Advanced Queries

Efficient database management is crucial for applications that need to be scaled. Django ORM provides powerful tools to optimize queries and improve performance. This chapter covers essential optimization techniques, including index creation, raw SQL, subqueries, and aggregation, with an emphasis on why each technique is important. We will also compare SQL queries with and without these optimizations to see their impact.

Optimizing queries minimizes resource usage, reduces latency, and ensures scalability. Proper query optimization in Django ORM is key to building responsive applications that perform well under load. Without optimization, applications risk slow performance, high memory usage, and increased server costs, which impact the user experience. Let's dive into some of the techniques.

In the last chapter, we have learned some of the QuerySet methods. In this section, we will dive deeper into methods.

Before getting started, we will define the models for this chapter. We can use the same models used in the last chapter.

Listing 4-1. Model for explaining all the concepts in this chapter

```
from django.db import models

class Author(models.Model):
    name = models.CharField(max_length=100, unique=True)

    def __str__(self):
        return self.name

class Genre(models.Model):
    name = models.CharField(max_length=50)

    def __str__(self):
        return self.name
```


Afsal MS, *Mastering Django ORM*, https://doi.org/10.1007/979-8-8688-2589-7_4

```
class Book(models.Model):
    title = models.CharField(max_length=200)
    author = models.ForeignKey(Author, on_delete=models.CASCADE)
    genres = models.ManyToManyField(Genre, blank=True)
    price = models.DecimalField(max_digits=6, decimal_places=2, null=True,
    blank=True)
    number_of_pages = models.IntegerField(null=True, blank=True)
    published_date = models.DateField(null=True, blank=True)
    created_at = models.DateTimeField(auto_now_add=True)

    def __str__(self):
        return self.title
```

Deep Dive into the QuerySet Methods

We have defined the models for the chapter (Refer Listing 4-1) and let's check the methods one by one. The first one is `alias`.

alias

`alias` is used to create a temporary name for an expression inside a query. It helps us to simplify complex queries by giving a name to a calculated value. `alias` does not create a new column in the database table. It is only used internally by the ORM while constructing the SQL query. The main difference from `annotate` is that `alias` does not include the calculated value in the result set, whereas annotate adds the calculated field to each returned object. Let us check this with an example.

Listing 4-2. Using alias with Count function

```
from django.db.models import Count

books = Book.objects.alias(
    total_genres=Count("genres")
).filter(total_genres__gt=1)
```

Equivalent SQL

```
SELECT book.id, book.title, book.author_id, book.price,
book.number_of_pages, book.published_date,
book.created_at
FROM book
LEFT OUTER JOIN book_genres
ON book.id = book_genres.book_id
GROUP BY book.id
HAVING COUNT(book_genres.genre_id) > 1;
```

In Listing 4-2, we are using the alias method with the `Count` function. Here we are counting how many genres are associated with each book. Since the field genres is a `ManyToManyField`, Django automatically joins the intermediate table named **book_genres**.

We are creating a temporary name called total_genres for Count("genres"). Then we are filtering the books where total_genres is greater than 1.

If we check the equivalent SQL, we can see that Django performs a `LEFT OUTER JOIN` with the intermediate table. Because we are using an aggregate function Count, Django adds a `GROUP BY` clause on book.id. The filtering condition is placed inside the `HAVING` clause instead of the `WHERE` clause. This is because aggregate conditions are applied after grouping.

Do you observe something important here? The column total_genres is not present in the `SELECT` statement unlike `annotate`. This clearly shows that alias is only used for query construction.

If we want to access the number of genres while iterating over the QuerySet, we should use annotate instead of alias. Now let us move to `annotate` with Count which will return the aggregated value along with each book record.

Let us move to the next one which is `reverse`.

reverse

The `reverse` method of a QuerySet is used to reverse the ordering of the results. It only changes the order in which the records are returned. Let us check this with an example.

Listing 4-3. Using reverse method on QuerySet

```
books = Book.objects.all().order_by("published_date")

reversed_books = books.reverse()
```

Equivalent SQL

first QuerySet

```
SELECT book.id, book.title, book.author_id, book.price,
book.number_of_pages, book.published_date,
book.created_at
FROM book
ORDER BY book.published_date ASC;
```

reversed QuerySet

```
SELECT book.id, book.title, book.author_id, book.price,
book.number_of_pages, book.published_date,
book.created_at
FROM book
ORDER BY book.published_date DESC;
```

In Listing 4-3 we are first ordering the books by published_date in ascending order using `order_by("published_date")`. Then we are calling `reverse` on the QuerySet. If we check the equivalent SQL, we can see that Django changes the ORDER BY clause to DESC. This means the results are now returned in descending order of published_date.

The `reverse` applied on QuerySet without `order_by` gives you unpredictable results.

Listing 4-4. reverse without specifying order_by

```
books = Book.objects.all()

reversed_books = books.reverse()
```

Equivalent SQL

first QuerySet

```
SELECT book.id, book.title, book.author_id, book.price,
book.number_of_pages, book.published_date,
book.created_at
FROM book
```

reversed QuerySet

```
SELECT book.id, book.title, book.author_id, book.price,
book.number_of_pages, book.published_date,
book.created_at
FROM book
```

Do you notice something important in Listing 4-4? The `reverse` method only works properly if the QuerySet already has an ordering defined. If there is no `order_by` clause, reversing may not give predictable results because the database does not guarantee any default ordering unless specified.

The reverse method is useful when we want to dynamically flip the ordering of a query without rewriting the `order_by` clause. It is commonly used in pagination or when we want to toggle between ascending and descending order.

Let us move to the next one which is distinct.

distinct

The distinct method is used to remove duplicate records from a QuerySet. When a query involves joins, especially with `ManyToManyField` relationships, the same record can appear multiple times in the result. The distinct method ensures that each record appears only once. Let us check this with an example.

Listing 4-5. Using distinct with ManyToMany relationship

```
books = Book.objects.filter(genres__name__in=["Fantasy", "Drama"])
```

Equivalent SQL

```
SELECT book.id, book.title, book.author_id, book.price,
book.number_of_pages, book.published_date,
book.created_at
FROM book
INNER JOIN book_genres
ON book.id = book_genres.book_id
INNER JOIN genre
ON book_genres.genre_id = genre.id
WHERE genre.name IN ('Fantasy', 'Drama');
```

In Listing 4-5 we are filtering books that belong to either fantasy or drama genres. Since genres is a `ManyToManyField`, Django joins with the intermediate table book_genres and the genre table. If a book belongs to both fantasy and drama, that book will appear twice in the result. This is because the join returns one row for each matching genre.

Now let us remove the duplicates using distinct.

Listing 4-6. Using distinct to remove duplicates

```
books = Book.objects.filter( genres__name__in=["Fantasy", "Drama"]
).distinct()
```

Equivalent SQL

```
SELECT DISTINCT book.id, book.title, book.author_id, book.price,
book.number_of_pages, book.published_date,
book.created_at
FROM book
INNER JOIN book_genres
ON book.id = book_genres.book_id
INNER JOIN genre
ON book_genres.genre_id = genre.id
WHERE genre.name IN ('Fantasy', 'Drama');
```

In Listing 4-6, we are using the distinct method. If we check the equivalent SQL, we can see the `DISTINCT` keyword added to the `SELECT` statement. This ensures that duplicate book rows are removed from the result set. The distinct method is very useful when working with `ManyToManyField` relationships or complex joins where duplicates may occur.

Note If you use `order_by` using a related field and use distinct, it will not work properly. Examples like Listing 4-7 will not work properly. This is because when we add `order_by`, those fields are also added in the `SELECT` which make the row unique.

Listing 4-7. distinct with order_by

```
Book.objects.filter(genres__name__in=["Scifi", "Fantasy"]).order_
by("genres__name").distinct()
```

Let us move to `values` and `values_list`.

values and values_list

The `values` and `values_list` methods are used when we do not need full model instances. Instead of returning model objects, these methods return specific field values from the database. This can improve performance because Django will not construct full model instances.

The `values` method returns dictionaries, whereas `values_list` returns tuples. Let us check this with an example.

Listing 4-8. Using values method

```
books = Book.objects.values("title", "price")
```

Output

```
[
    {'title': 'Harry Potter', 'price': 500.00}
    {'title': 'The Hobbit', 'price': 450.00}
]
```

Equivalent SQL

```
SELECT book.title, book.price FROM book;
```

In Listing 4-8 we are using the `values` method. Instead of returning book objects, Django returns a list of dictionaries. Each dictionary contains only the fields we specified. If we observe the equivalent SQL, Django selects only the title and price columns. It does not select all columns from the book table. This makes the query more efficient when we only need specific fields.

Now let us check the `values_list` method.

Listing 4-9. Using values_list method

```
books = Book.objects.values_list("title", "price")
```

Output

```
[
    ('Harry Potter', 500.00)
    ('The Hobbit', 450.00)
]
```

Equivalent SQL

```
SELECT book.title, book.price FROM book;
```

In Listing 4-9 we are using `values_list`. The difference is that it returns tuples instead of dictionaries. The SQL query is exactly the same as the `values`. The difference is only in how Django formats the result.

We can also use `flat=True` when selecting a single field.

Listing 4-10. Using values_list with flat=True

```
titles = Book.objects.values_list("title", flat=True)
```

Output

```
[ 'Harry Potter', 'The Hobbit']
```

Equivalent SQL

```
SELECT book.title FROM book;
```

In Listing 4-10 we are selecting only one field and using `flat=True`. Instead of returning list tuples like `[('Harry Potter',),('The Hobbit',)]`, Django directly returns a flat list.

When we use `values` or `values_list`, we do not get full book objects. So, we cannot call model methods or access related objects in the same way. The `values` method is useful when we want dictionary-style data, especially for JSON responses. The `values_list` method is useful when we only need simple tuples or a single list of values.

New in 5.2+: The order in `SELECT` is not the same as the order specified in `values` and `values_list` arguments.

Let's move to `dates` and `datetimes`.

dates and datetimes

The dates and datetimes methods are used to extract unique date or datetime values from a DateField or DateTimeField. These methods are helpful when we want to group records by year, month, day, or even hour without writing raw SQL. Let us check this with an example.

Listing 4-11. Using dates method

```
dates = Book.objects.dates("published_date", "year")
```

Equivalent SQL

```
SELECT DISTINCT DATE_TRUNC('year', book.published_date) AS date
FROM book
WHERE book.published_date IS NOT NULL
ORDER BY date ASC;
```

In Listing 4-11, we are using the dates method in the published_date field. The second argument "**year**" tells Django to truncate the date to the year level. Django returns unique year values in ascending order.

If we observe the equivalent SQL, Django uses the DATE_TRUNC function to truncate the date to the year and applies DISTINCT to remove duplicates. It also excludes NULL values automatically.

Now let us see the datetimes method.

Listing 4-12. Using datetimes method

```
datetimes = Book.objects.datetimes("created_at", "month")
```

Equivalent SQL

```
SELECT DISTINCT DATE_TRUNC('month', book.created_at) AS datetime
FROM book
ORDER BY datetime ASC;
```

In Listing 4-12, we are using the datetimes method on the created_at field which is a DateTimeField. The second argument "**month**" tells Django to truncate the datetime to month level. Django returns unique month values.

The dates method works with DateField and DateTimeField, while datetimes works only with DateTimeField. Both methods return Python date or datetime objects, not full Book instances. These methods are very useful when building archive pages such as yearly archive, monthly archive, or daily archive.

Let us move to the next one which is none.

none

The none method is used to return an empty QuerySet. It does not hit the database, and it always returns no records. This method is useful when we want to return an empty result conditionally without writing complex logic. Let us check this with an example.

Listing 4-13. Using none method

```
books = Book.objects.none()
```

Output

```
<QuerySet []>
```

The none method returns a QuerySet, not a list. This means we can still call methods like filter, exclude, or order_by on it, and it will remain empty. The none method is mainly used when we want to maintain QuerySet consistency in our code while intentionally returning no results (Refer Listing 4-13).

Let us move to the next one which is very critical in performance optimization which is select_related.

select_related

The select_related method is used to retrieve related objects in a single database query using SQL JOIN. It is mainly used for ForeignKey and OneToOneField relationships. Let us check this with an example.

Listing 4-14. Accessing related object without select_related

```
books = Book.objects.all()

for book in books:
    print(book.title, book.author.name)
```

Equivalent SQL

First Query for fetch the book

```
SELECT book.id, book.title, book.author_id, book.price,
book.number_of_pages, book.published_date,
book.created_at
FROM book;
```

Second Query (executed for each book)

```
SELECT author.id, author.name
FROM author
WHERE author.id = <author_id>;
```

In Listing 4-14 we are fetching all books and then accessing `book.author.name`. Since the author is a `ForeignKey`, Django performs an additional query for each book when we access the author. This is called the **N+1 query problem**. This is one of the most common mistakes seen in the Django application. Django ORM has a solution for this which is `select_related`.

Now let us solve this using `select_related`.

Listing 4-15. Using select_related

```
books = Book.objects.select_related("author")

for book in books:
    print(book.title, book.author.name)
```

Equivalent SQL

```
SELECT book.id, book.title, book.author_id, book.price,
book.number_of_pages, book.published_date,
book.created_at,
author.id, author.name
FROM book
INNER JOIN author
ON book.author_id = author.id;
```

In Listing 4-15 we are using `select_related` on the author field. Now Django performs a single query using `INNER JOIN` between the book and author tables. The author data is fetched along with the book data in the same query.

If we observe the equivalent SQL, we can see that Django joins the author table and selects its columns. Because of this, when we access `book.author.name` inside the loop, Django does not make additional queries.

The `select_related` method works only for single-valued relationships like `ForeignKey` and `OneToOneField`. It does not work for `ManyToManyField`. For many-to-many relationships, we should use `prefetch_related` which we will learn in the next section.

The `select_related` method improves performance by reducing the number of database queries. It is especially useful when we know that we will access related objects for each record in the QuerySet.

Let us move to the next one which is `prefetch_related`.

prefetch_related

The `prefetch_related` method is used to retrieve related objects in separate queries and combine them in Python. It is mainly used for `ManyToManyField` and `reverse ForeignKey` relationships. Let us check this with an example.

Listing 4-16. Accessing ManyToMany without prefetch_related

```
books = Book.objects.all()

for book in books:
    for genre in book.genres.all():
        print(book.title, genre.name)
```

Equivalent SQL

First Query

```
SELECT book.id, book.title, book.author_id, book.price,
book.number_of_pages, book.published_date,
book.created_at
FROM book;
```

Second Query (executed for each book)

```
SELECT genre.id, genre.name
FROM genre
INNER JOIN book_genres
ON genre.id = book_genres.genre_id
WHERE book_genres.book_id = <book_id>;
```

In Listing 4-16, we are fetching all books and then accessing `book.genres.all()`. Since genres is a `ManyToManyField`, Django performs an additional query for each book. This leads to the **N+1 query** problem.

Now let us solve this using `prefetch_related`.

Listing 4-17. Using prefetch_related

```
books = Book.objects.prefetch_related("genres")

for book in books:
    for genre in book.genres.all():
        print(book.title, genre.name)
```

Equivalent SQL

First Query

```
SELECT book.id, book.title, book.author_id, book.price,
book.number_of_pages, book.published_date,
book.created_at
FROM book;
```

Second Query

```
SELECT genre.id, genre.name, book_genres.book_id
FROM genre
INNER JOIN book_genres
ON genre.id = book_genres.genre_id
WHERE book_genres.book_id IN (1, 2, 3, ...);
```

In Listing 4-17, we are using `prefetch_related` on the genres field. Django executes two queries. The first query fetches all Book records. The second query fetches all related Genre records using a `WHERE  IN` clause. Django then maps the Genre objects to their respective Book objects in Python.

Now let us see how to use the `Prefetch` object for more control.

Listing 4-18. Using Prefetch object

```
from django.db.models import Prefetch

prefetch_genres = Prefetch(
    "genres",
    queryset=Genre.objects.filter(name__icontains="F"),
)

books = Book.objects.prefetch_related(prefetch_genres)

for book in books:
    for genre in book.genres.all():
        print(book.title, genre.name)
```

Equivalent SQL

First Query

```
SELECT book.id, book.title, book.author_id, book.price,
book.number_of_pages, book.published_date,
book.created_at
FROM book;
```

Second Query

```
SELECT genre.id, genre.name, book_genres.book_id
FROM genre
INNER JOIN book_genres
ON genre.id = book_genres.genre_id
WHERE genre.name ILIKE '%F%'
AND book_genres.book_id IN (1, 2, 3, ...);
```

In Listing 4-18, we are using the `Prefetch` object. This allows us to customize the QuerySet used for prefetching. Here we are prefetching only those genres whose name contains the letter F. The Prefetch object gives more flexibility. We can filter, order, or even assign the prefetched result to a different attribute using `to_attr`.

Listing 4-19. Prefetch with to_attr example

```
from django.db.models import Prefetch

prefetch_genres = Prefetch(
    "genres",
    queryset=Genre.objects.filter(name__icontains="F"),
    to_attr="genre_starting_with_f"
)

books = Book.objects.prefetch_related(prefetch_genres)

for book in books:
    for genre in book.genre_starting_with_f:
        print(book.title, genre.name)
```

In Listing 4-19, we are using the `Prefetch` object with a `to_attr` attribute. If we check the code carefully, we can see that `book.genres.all()` is changed to `book.genre_starting_with_f`, which is the to_attr name. Also the type of the return item is a list instead of QuerySet.

The `prefetch_related` method reduces the number of queries from **N+1 to two queries**. The `Prefetch` object provides advanced control over how related objects are fetched.

Let's move to the next one which is `extra`.

extra

The `extra` method is used to add custom SQL fragments to a QuerySet. It allows us to manually specify `SELECT`, `WHERE`, or `ORDER BY` clauses when the ORM does not directly support a particular query. Let us check this with an example.

Listing 4-20. Using extra with select

```
books = Book.objects.extra(
    select={"title_length": "LENGTH(title)"}
)
for book in books:
    print(book.title, book.title_length)
```

Equivalent SQL

```
SELECT book.id, book.title, book.author_id, book.price,
book.number_of_pages, book.published_date,
book.created_at,
LENGTH(title) AS title_length
FROM book;
```

In Listing 4-20, we are using the extra method with the select parameter. We are manually adding a SQL expression `LENGTH(title)` and assigning it an alias **title_length**. Django includes this expression in the `SELECT` statement.

If we check the equivalent SQL, we can see that `LENGTH(title) AS title_length` is added to the query. Unlike `alias`, the extra method actually adds the calculated column to the result set, so we can access `book.title_length` directly.

Now let us see an example using `extra` with where condition.

Listing 4-21. Using extra with where clause

```
books = Book.objects.extra(
    where=["price > %s"],
    params=[500]
)

for book in books:
    print(book.title, book.price)
```

Equivalent SQL

```
SELECT book.id, book.title, book.author_id, book.price,
book.number_of_pages, book.published_date,
book.created_at
FROM book
WHERE price > 500;
```

In Listing 4-21, we are adding a custom `WHERE` clause. The where argument accepts a list of SQL conditions and params is used to safely pass parameters. The `extra` method gives us direct control over SQL, but it reduces database portability and makes the code harder to maintain. It should be used only when the ORM cannot express a query in a clean way.

Warning

The extra method is considered legacy and may be removed in future versions of Django. In most cases, we should prefer to use `annotate`, `filter`, or database functions instead of `extra`.

Let us move to `only` and `defer`.

only and defer

The `only` and `defer` methods are used to control which fields are loaded from the database. By default, Django selects all columns of the model. But sometimes we do not need all the fields. In such cases, we can optimize the query using only or defer. Let us check this with an example.

Listing 4-22. Using only method

```
books = Book.objects.only("title", "price")
for book in books:
    print(book.title, book.price)
```

Equivalent SQL

```
SELECT book.id, book.title, book.price FROM book;
```

In Listing 4-22, we are using the only method to load only the title and price fields. If we observe the equivalent SQL, Django selects only these columns along with the primary key. Other fields like number_of_pages, published_date, and created_at are not loaded initially. If we try to access a field that was not included only, Django will execute an additional query to fetch that specific field. This is called **deferred loading**.

Now let us see the `defer` method.

Listing 4-23. Using defer method

```
books = Book.objects.defer("price", "number_of_pages")
for book in books:
    print(book.title)
```

Equivalent SQL

```
SELECT book.id, book.title, book.author_id,
book.published_date, book.created_at
FROM book;
```

In Listing 4-23, we are using the `defer` method. Here we are telling Django not to load the price and number_of_pages fields initially. All other fields are selected. If we check the equivalent SQL, we can see that the deferred fields are not included in the `SELECT` statement.

The difference between `only` and `defer` is simple. The `only` method loads only the specified fields and defers the rest. The `defer` method loads all fields except the specified ones. Both methods are useful when working with large tables or fields that contain heavy data. They help reduce the amount of data fetched from the database and improve performance.

Let's move to the next one which is `raw`.

raw

The `raw` method is used to execute a raw SQL query and return model instances. It gives us full control over the SQL while still mapping the result to Django model objects. Let us check this with an example.

Listing 4-24. Using raw method

```
query = "SELECT * FROM book WHERE price > %s"
books = Book.objects.raw(query, [500])
for book in books:
    print(book.title, book.price)
```

Equivalent SQL

```
SELECT * FROM book WHERE price > 500;
```

In Listing 4-24, we are using the `raw` method to execute a custom SQL query. We are passing the SQL string and parameters separately. Django safely substitutes the parameter value and executes the query. If we observe carefully, the raw method returns model instances of book. That means we can access fields like book.title and book.price just like normal ORM objects.

When using raw, the SELECT statement must include the primary key column. Django needs the primary key to correctly map each row to a model instance. If the primary key is not included, Django will raise an error.

The raw method is powerful because it allows us to write complex queries that may not be easily expressed using the ORM. However, it reduces database portability and bypasses many ORM features like automatic query construction and chaining.

It is always recommended to use ORM methods whenever possible and use raw only when necessary.

Let's move to the next one which is get_or_create.

get_or_create

The get_or_create method is used to fetch an object if it exists or create it if it does not exist. It helps us avoid writing the get and create logic separately. The method returns a tuple containing the object and a Boolean value. Let us check this with an example.

Listing 4-25. Using get_or_create method

```
author, created = Author.objects.get_or_create(name="J.K. Rowling")
print(author)
print(created)
```

Output

```
J.K. Rowling
True
```

Equivalent SQL (when record does not exist)

First Query

```
SELECT author.id, author.name
FROM author
WHERE author.name = 'J.K. Rowling'
LIMIT 1;
```

Second Query

```
BEGIN
INSERT INTO author (name) VALUES ('J.K. Rowling');
COMMIT
```

In Listing 4-25, we are using `get_or_create` on the Author model. Django first performs a `SELECT` query to check whether an author with the name "J.K. Rowling" exists. If it does not exist, Django performs an INSERT query to create a new record.

The variable created will be True if a new record is created, otherwise False if the record already exists.

Now let us see another example using defaults.

Listing 4-26. Using get_or_create with defaults

```
author = Author.objects.get(name="J.K. Rowling")
book, created = Book.objects.get_or_create(
    title="Harry Potter",
    defaults={
        "author": author,
        "price": 500.00
    }
)
print(book)
print(created)
```

Equivalent SQL (when record does not exist)

First Query

```
SELECT book.id, book.title, book.author_id, book.price,
book.number_of_pages, book.published_date,
book.created_at
FROM book
WHERE book.title = 'Harry Potter'
LIMIT 1;
```

Second Query

```
INSERT INTO book (title, author_id, price) VALUES ('Harry Potter', 1,
500.00);
```

In Listing 4-26, we are searching for a book with the title "**Harry Potter**". If it does not exist, Django creates a new book using the values provided inside defaults. The lookup fields are used only for searching, and the defaults are used only when creating a new record.

The fields passed directly as arguments are used for lookup. The fields inside defaults are used only if a new object is created.

The `get_or_create` method is very useful when we want to avoid duplicate records and ensure that only one record exists for a given condition.

Important note:

For true safety, a database-level unique constraint must exist on the lookup field (e.g., title). Without a unique constraint, duplicates can still occur.

Now let us move to understanding the `update_or_create` method.

update_or_create

The `update_or_create` method is used to fetch an object if it exists and update it or create a new object if it does not exist. It helps us combine updates and create logic into a single operation. The method returns a tuple containing the object and a Boolean value. Let us check this with an example.

Listing 4-27. Using update_or_create method

```
author, created = Author.objects.update_or_create(
    name="J.K. Rowling",
    defaults={}
)

print(author)
print(created)
```

Equivalent SQL (when record does not exist)
First Query

```
SELECT author.id, author.name
FROM author
WHERE author.name = 'J.K. Rowling'
LIMIT 1;
```

Second Query

```
INSERT INTO author (name) VALUES ('J.K. Rowling');
```

In Listing 4-27, Django first performs a SELECT query to check whether the author exists. If the record is not found, Django performs an INSERT query. The variable created will be True if a new record is inserted, otherwise False.

Now let us see a more practical example with the Book model.

Listing 4-28. Using update_or_create with defaults

```
author = Author.objects.get(name="J.K. Rowling")
book, created = Book.objects.update_or_create(
    title="Harry Potter",
    defaults={
        "author": author,
        "price": 600.00,
        "number_of_pages": 500
    }
)
print(book)
print(created)
```

Equivalent SQL (when record exists)
First Query

```
SELECT book.id, book.title, book.author_id, book.price,
book.number_of_pages, book.published_date,
book.created_at
```

```
FROM book
WHERE book.title = 'Harry Potter'
LIMIT 1;
```

Second Query

```
UPDATE book
SET author_id = 1,
price = 600.00,
number_of_pages = 500
WHERE id = 1;
```

In Listing 4-28, Django first searches for a book with the title "**Harry Potter**". If it exists, Django performs an `UPDATE` query using the fields provided inside defaults. If it does not exist, Django performs an `INSERT` query with both lookup and default values.

The fields passed directly as arguments are used only for lookup. The fields inside defaults are used for updating if the object exists and also for creating if it does not exist.

The main difference between `get_or_create` and `update_or_create` is simple. The `get_or_create` method does not update an existing record; it only retrieves it. The `update_or_create` method updates the existing record if found. This method is very useful when we want to ensure a record exists and also keep it updated in a single atomic operation.

Let's move to the next one which is `in_bulk`.

in_bulk

The `in_bulk` method is used to retrieve multiple objects and return them as a dictionary instead of a QuerySet. The dictionary keys are the primary key values, and the values are the model instances. Let us check this with an example.

Listing 4-29. Using in_bulk method

```
authors = Author.objects.in_bulk([1, 2, 3])
print(authors)
```

Output

```
{
    1: <Author: J.K. Rowling>,
    2: <Author: Tolkien>,
    3: <Author: George R.R. Martin>
}
```

Equivalent SQL

```
SELECT author.id, author.name
FROM author
WHERE author.id IN (1, 2, 3);
```

In Listing 4-29, we are using the `in_bulk` method on the Author model. We are passing a list of primary key values. Django performs a single query using the `WHERE IN` clause and returns a dictionary. Unlike `filter(id__in=[...])`, the in_bulk method does not return a QuerySet. It returns a dictionary where the key is the primary key and the value is the corresponding Author instance.

This is very useful when we want a quick lookup by id without iterating over a QuerySet. Since the result is already in a dictionary format, accessing a specific object is very fast.

Now let us see how to use `in_bulk` with a different field.

Listing 4-30. Using in_bulk with field_name

```
authors = Author.objects.in_bulk(
    ["J.K. Rowling", "Tolkien"],
    field_name="name"
)
print(authors)
```

Equivalent SQL

```
SELECT author.id, author.name
FROM author
WHERE author.name IN ('J.K. Rowling', 'Tolkien');
```

In Listing 4-30, we are using the `field_name` argument. Instead of using the primary key as the dictionary key, we are using the name field. The dictionary keys will now be the author names. The `field_name` must be a unique field to get the result.

The `in_bulk` method is useful when we need multiple objects at once and want to access them directly with a key. It performs a single efficient query and avoids multiple database hits.

Let's move to the next one which is `iterator`.

iterator

The `iterator` method is used to iterate over a QuerySet without caching the results in memory. Normally when we iterate over a QuerySet, Django fetches all rows and stores them in memory. The iterator method helps us process large datasets efficiently by fetching rows directly from the database without caching them. Let us check this with an example.

Listing 4-31. Using iterator method

```
books = Book.objects.all().iterator()
for book in books:
    print(book.title)
```

Equivalent SQL

```
SELECT book.id, book.title, book.author_id, book.price,
book.number_of_pages, book.published_date,
book.created_at
FROM book;
```

In Listing 4-31, we are using the iterator method on the book QuerySet. The SQL query is the same as a normal QuerySet. The difference is not in the SQL, but in how Django handles the result. By default, when we iterate over a QuerySet, Django caches all objects after fetching them. This means that if we loop again over the same QuerySet, Django will not hit the database again. However, this also means that all records are stored in memory.

When we use `iterator`, Django does not cache the results. It fetches rows directly from the database cursor and yields them one by one. This reduces memory usage when working with large tables.

Now let us see how chunk_size works.

Listing 4-32. Using iterator with chunk_size

```
books = Book.objects.all().iterator(chunk_size=100)
for book in books:
    print(book.title)
```

Equivalent SQL

```
SELECT book.id, book.title, book.author_id, book.price,
book.number_of_pages, book.published_date,
book.created_at
FROM book;
```

In Listing 4-32, we are passing `chunk_size=100`. This means Django will fetch rows from the database in batches of 100 at a time. If there are 250 records, Django will fetch them in three batches. The SQL query remains the same. The difference is in how rows are fetched from the database cursor.

The `iterator` method is mainly useful when processing very large datasets such as exporting data or running background jobs. It helps reduce memory consumption and improves efficiency.

Let's move to `first` and `last` methods.

first and last

The `first` and `last` methods are used to retrieve a single object from a QuerySet based on its ordering. These methods return the first or last record from the result set. Let us check this with an example.

Listing 4-33. Using first method

```
first_book = Book.objects.order_by("published_date").first()
print(first_book.title, first_book.published_date)
```

Equivalent SQL

```
SELECT book.id, book.title, book.author_id, book.price,
book.number_of_pages, book.published_date,
book.created_at
```

```
FROM book
ORDER BY book.published_date ASC
LIMIT 1;
```

In Listing 4-33, we are ordering the books by published_date in ascending order and then calling `first`. Django adds LIMIT 1 and returns the first record from the ordered result.

Now let us see the last method.

Listing 4-34. Using last method

```
last_book = Book.objects.order_by("published_date").last()
print(last_book.title, last_book.published_date)
```

Equivalent SQL

```
SELECT book.id, book.title, book.author_id, book.price,
book.number_of_pages, book.published_date,
book.created_at
FROM book
ORDER BY book.published_date DESC
LIMIT 1;
```

In Listing 4-34, we are using the last method. Internally, Django reverses the ordering and applies `LIMIT 1` to fetch the last record efficiently.

Another important point is that first and last return None if no records exist. The first and last methods are very useful when we want safe access to boundary records without handling exceptions.

Let's move to `latest` and `earliest` methods.

latest and earliest

The `earliest` and `latest` methods are used to retrieve a single object based on the ordering of a field. These methods are commonly used with `DateField` or `DateTimeField`, but they can work with any field that supports ordering. Let us check this with an example.

Listing 4-35. Using earliest method

```
earliest_book = Book.objects.earliest("published_date")
print(earliest_book.title, earliest_book.published_date)
```

Equivalent SQL

```
SELECT book.id, book.title, book.author_id, book.price,
book.number_of_pages, book.published_date,
book.created_at
FROM book
ORDER BY book.published_date ASC
LIMIT 1;
```

In Listing 4-35, we are using the earliest method in the published_date field. Django orders the records in ascending order based on published_date and returns the first record.

Now let us see the latest method.

Listing 4-36. Using latest method

```
latest_book = Book.objects.latest("published_date")
print(latest_book.title, latest_book.published_date)
```

Equivalent SQL

```
SELECT book.id, book.title, book.author_id, book.price,
book.number_of_pages, book.published_date,
book.created_at
FROM book
ORDER BY book.published_date DESC
LIMIT 1;
```

In Listing 4-36, we are using the latest method. Django orders the records in descending order and returns the most recent published book. Both `earliest` and `latest` return a single model instance, not a QuerySet. If no matching record exists, Django raises a `DoesNotExist` exception.

Internally these methods are equivalent to using `order_by("field_name").first()` for `earliest` and `order_by("-field_name").first()` for `latest`. However, `earliest` and `latest` clearly express the intention of fetching the oldest or newest record.

These methods are very useful when building features such as archive pages, dashboards, or reports where we need the first or most recent entry based on a specific field.

Let's move to the next one which is `contains`.

contains

The `contains` method is used to check whether a QuerySet contains a specific model instance. It returns a Boolean value, either True or False. This method is useful when you already have a model instance and want to verify whether it is part of a QuerySet result.

Let us understand this with an example.

Listing 4-37. Using contains method

```
book = Book.objects.get(id=10)
recent_books = Book.objects.filter(published_date__year=2026)
is_present = recent_books.contains(book)
print(is_present)
```

Equivalent SQL

```
SELECT 1
FROM book
WHERE published_date BETWEEN '2026-01-01' AND '2026-12-31'
AND id = 10
LIMIT 1;
```

In Listing 4-37, we first fetch a Book instance. Then we create a QuerySet of books published in the year 2026. Using `contains`, Django checks whether the given book exists inside that QuerySet. Django optimizes this internally and performs an efficient existence check. It does not load all records into memory. The object passed to `contains` must be a saved model instance (it must have a primary key). If the instance does not have a primary key, Django raises a ValueError.

You could write: `Book.objects.filter(published_date__year=2026, id=book.id).exists()`. This achieves the same result. However, `contains` is more readable when you already have the model instance and simply want to check membership inside a QuerySet.

Let's move to the next one which is `explain`.

explain

The `explain` method exposes the database execution plan for a QuerySet, making it possible to evaluate how queries are processed internally.

Let us check with an example.

Listing 4-38. explain book query

```
qs = Book.objects.filter(price__gt=500)
print(qs.explain(analyze=True, format="TEXT"))
```

Output

```
Seq Scan on public.myapp_book  (cost=0.00..5770.02 rows=232 width=22)
(actual time=0.006..14.124 rows=231 loops=1)\n  Output: id, title,
author_id, price, number_of_pages \n  Filter: (myapp_book.price >
'500'::numberic)\n  Rows Removed by Filter: 130\nPlanning Time: 0.055 ms\
nExecution Time: 14.145 ms
```

With `analyze=True`, the database executes the query and reports actual execution statistics rather than estimates (Refer Listing 4-38). The format is used to get the preferred output format. Its value depends on the database back end. For PostgreSQL the values are TEXT, JSON, YAML, and XML. For MySQL the values are TEXT and JSON only.

This output indicates a sequential scan over the table, suggesting that the query is not using an index. On large datasets, this often points to the need for indexing or query restructuring.

So that is the end of the QuerySet methods; let us move to slicing a QuerySet.

Slicing QuerySet

Slicing in Django allows you to limit the number of records returned from a QuerySet using Python's slice syntax. It is translated into SQL `LIMIT` and `OFFSET` at the database level. The basic syntax is `QuerySet[start:end]`.

Let us understand this with examples.

Listing 4-39. Basic slicing

```
books = Book.objects.all()[0:5]
```

Equivalent SQL

```
SELECT book.id, book.title, book.author_id, book.price,
book.number_of_pages, book.published_date,
book.created_at
FROM book
LIMIT 5;
```

In Listing 4-39, we are retrieving the first five records. Django translates this into `LIMIT` 5.

Now let us see slicing with an offset.

Listing 4-40. Slicing with offset

```
books = Book.objects.all()[5:10]
```

Equivalent SQL

```
SELECT book.id, book.title, book.author_id, book.price,
book.number_of_pages, book.published_date,
book.created_at
FROM book
LIMIT 5 OFFSET 5;
```

Here (Refer Listing 4-40), Django skips the first five rows and returns the next five rows.

Important rules about slicing:

- Slicing does not immediately evaluate the QuerySet unless you iterate over it.
- Negative indexing is not supported. For example, `Book.objects.all()[-1]` will raise an error.
- You cannot use step values. For example, [0:10:2] is not allowed.
- After slicing, you cannot apply further filtering.

Example of invalid usage

```
Book.objects.all()[0:5].filter(price__gt=500)
```

This raises an error because Django does not allow filtering after slicing. However, you can filter first and then slice.

Correct usage

```
Book.objects.filter(price__gt=500)[0:5]
```

Single object using index

You can also retrieve a single object using an index syntax.

Listing 4-41. Using index

```
first_book = Book.objects.all()[0]
```

Equivalent SQL

```
SELECT ...
FROM book
LIMIT 1;
```

But be careful. If no records exist, this raises an IndexError (Refer Listing 4-41).

Difference between slicing and first()

`Book.objects.all()[0]` raises IndexError if empty.

`Book.objects.first()` returns None if empty.

So `first` is safer when you are unsure whether records exist.

Slicing is very useful for implementing pagination, limiting dashboard results, and handling large datasets efficiently at the database level.

Let's move to the next one which is using `Meta` attributes.

Using Meta Attributes

The `Meta` class is used to configure model-level behavior in Django. It controls how the table is created, how records are ordered, how constraints are applied, and how inheritance works. The `Meta` class is defined inside the model. Let us understand the important `Meta` attributes one by one using our existing models.

The first one is `ordering`.

ordering

The `ordering` attribute defines the default ordering of records.

Listing 4-42. Using ordering in Meta

```
class Book(models.Model):
    title = models.CharField(max_length=200)
    published_date = models.DateField(null=True, blank=True)
    class Meta:
        ordering = ["-published_date"]
```

If we call

```
books = Book.objects.all()
```

Equivalent SQL

```
SELECT book.id, book.title, book.published_date FROM book ORDER BY book.
published_date DESC;
```

In Listing 4-42, we define ordering as `-published_date`. The minus sign means descending order. Every time we query book without `order_by`, Django automatically applies this ordering.

Let us move to the next one which is `db_table`.

db_table

The `db_table` attribute allows us to define a custom table name.

Listing 4-43. Using db_table

```
class Book(models.Model):
    title = models.CharField(max_length=200)

    class Meta:
        db_table = "library_book"
```

By default, Django creates a table name using `app_label_modelname`. If we define `db_table`, Django uses the given name instead (Refer Listing 4-43). This is useful when working with existing databases or we are following naming conventions.

Let us move to the next one which is `indexes`.

indexes

Indexes improve query performance.

Listing 4-44. Using indexes

```
class Book(models.Model):
    published_date = models.DateField(null=True, blank=True)
    price = models.DecimalField(
        max_digits=6, decimal_places=2,  null=True, blank=True)

    class Meta:
        indexes = [
            models.Index(fields=["published_date"]),
            models.Index(fields=["published_date", "price"]),]
```

If we run

```
books = Book.objects.filter(published_date__year=2025, price__gt=500)
```

The database can use the composite index for faster lookup (Refer Listing 4-44). Indexes improve `SELECT` performance but slightly slow down `INSERT` and `UPDATE` operations because the index must also be updated.

Let's move to the next one which is `constraints`.

constraints

Constraints enforce rules at the database level. This ensures that data is matching our requirements.

Listing 4-45. Using constraints

```
class Book(models.Model):
    title = models.CharField(max_length=200)
    published_date = models.DateField(null=True, blank=True)
    price = models.DecimalField(
        max_digits=6, decimal_places=2, null=True, blank=True)

    class Meta:
        constraints = [
```

```
            models.UniqueConstraint(
                fields=["title", "published_date"],
                name="unique_title_per_date"
            ),
            models.CheckConstraint(
                check=models.Q(price__gt=0),
                name="price_must_be_positive"
            ),
        ]
```

`UniqueConstraint` prevents duplicate title and published_date combinations. `CheckConstraint` ensures price is always greater than zero. These rules are enforced by the database itself (Refer Listing 4-45).

Let us move to the next one which is `abstract`.

abstract

The `abstract` attribute is used to create abstract base models. It is used for sharing fields.

Listing 4-46. Using abstract model

```
class TimeStampedModel(models.Model):
    created_at = models.DateTimeField(auto_now_add=True)
    class Meta:
        abstract = True
class Book(TimeStampedModel):
    title = models.CharField(max_length=200)
```

In Listing 4-46, no table is created for **TimeStampedModel**. The book table will contain the created_at field. Abstract models are used for sharing common fields.

Let's move to the next one which is `proxy`.

proxy

The `proxy` attribute is used to change model behavior without creating a new table.

Listing 4-47. Using proxy model

```
class RecentBook(Book):
    pass

    class Meta:
        proxy = True
        ordering = ["-published_date"]
```

In Listing 4-47, no new table is created. **RecentBook** uses the same table as book. It only changes behavior such as default ordering.

Let's move to the next one which is `managed`.

managed

The `managed` attribute controls whether Django manages the table.

Listing 4-48. Using managed

```
class BookReport(models.Model):
    title = models.CharField(max_length=200)

    class Meta:
        managed = False
        db_table = "book_report_view"
```

If `managed` is False, Django will not create or modify this table during migrations. This is useful when working with database views or legacy tables (Refer Listing 4-48).

Let's move to `verbose_name` and `verbose_name_plural`.

verbose_name and verbose_name_plural

These attributes are used mainly in Django admin.

Listing 4-49. Using verbose names

```
class Book(models.Model):
    title = models.CharField(max_length=200)
```

```
    class Meta:
        verbose_name = "Book Item"
        verbose_name_plural = "Book Items"
```

These names are used for display purposes and do not affect the database structure (Refer Listing 4-49).

In this section we understood how Meta attributes control ordering, table naming, indexing, constraints, inheritance behavior, migration management, and display configuration. Proper use of Meta helps us design clean and optimized database schemas.

Let's move to `Subquery`.

Subquery

A `Subquery` in Django ORM allows us to use one QuerySet inside another QuerySet. In simple words, it is a query inside another query. Django provides `Subquery` and `OuterRef` to build such queries in a clean and readable way.

Subqueries are mainly used when

- We need the latest related record
- We need aggregated values per row
- We need row-wise comparison
- A simple join cannot solve the problem

The basic syntax is `Subquery(QuerySet)`.

Let us understand this step by step using our models.

Subquery with annotation

Suppose we want to annotate each author with the id of their latest book based on published_date.

Listing 4-50. Using Subquery with annotate

```
from django.db.models import Subquery, OuterRef

latest_book = Book.objects.filter(
    author=OuterRef("pk")
).order_by("-published_date").values("id")[:1]
```

```
authors = Author.objects.annotate(
    latest_book_id=Subquery(latest_book)
)

for author in authors:
    print(author.name, author.latest_book_id)
```

Equivalent SQL

```
SELECT author.id, author.name,
(SELECT book.id
FROM book
WHERE book.author_id = author.id
ORDER BY book.published_date DESC
LIMIT 1) AS latest_book_id
FROM author;
```

In Listing 4-50, we first create an inner QuerySet named latest_book.

```
Book.objects.filter(author=OuterRef("pk"))
```

Here `OuterRef("pk")` refers to the id of the current author row from the outer query. We then order the books in descending order of published_date and take only one record using [:1].

Why [:1]?

A Subquery must return only one column and one row when used inside annotate. That is why we use values("id") to select one column and [:1] to limit it to one row. Finally, we `annotate` author using `Subquery(latest_book)`. For every author row, the database runs the inner query and returns the id of the most recent book.

Understanding OuterRef

`OuterRef` is used to reference a field from the outer query inside the subquery.

In this line

```
author=OuterRef("pk")
```

It means match the book's author_id with the id of the current author row. Without `OuterRef`, the subquery cannot dynamically connect to each row of the outer query.

Subquery with filter

Now let us see another example. Suppose we want to fetch books whose price is greater than the average price of books written by the same author.

Listing 4-51. Subquery inside filter

```
from django.db.models import Avg

avg_price = Book.objects.filter(
    author=OuterRef("author")
).values("author").annotate(
    avg_price=Avg("price")
).values("avg_price")

books = Book.objects.filter(
    price__gt=Subquery(avg_price)
)
```

Equivalent SQL

```
SELECT b1.*
FROM book b1
WHERE b1.price > (
SELECT AVG(b2.price)
FROM book b2
WHERE b2.author_id = b1.author_id
);
```

In Listing 4-51, the subquery calculates the average price per `author`. `OuterRef("author")` refers to the author field of the outer book query. The outer query compares each book's price with the average price of books written by the same author. This is a row-by-row comparison. That is why a subquery is needed.

Important rules for Subquery:

- `Subquery` must return only one column.
- `OuterRef` is required when referencing fields from the outer query.
- Subquery works at the database level. Django only builds the SQL.

Subquery vs. Join

Join

- Combines tables using relationships
- Works well for simple related lookups

Subquery

- Executes a nested query inside `SELECT` or `WHERE`
- Useful for row-wise dynamic calculations
- More flexible for complex logic

If we only need related data like author names for a book, we use `select_related`.

If we need "latest book per author" or "books above author average price," we use `Subquery`.

Performance consideration

Subqueries can be powerful but must be used carefully. On large datasets, correlated subqueries may be slower. Always check the execution plan using `explain`. In some cases, rewriting using annotations or joins may be faster.

`Subquery` is an advanced but very important feature in Django ORM. It allows us to write complex SQL logic while still staying inside the ORM. Understanding `Subquery` and `OuterRef` properly helps you move from intermediate to advanced Django ORM usage.

Let us move to the next one: using a `Paginator` object.

Using a Paginator object

The `Paginator` class in Django is used to split a QuerySet into multiple pages. This is very useful when dealing with large datasets, such as displaying books in a list view. Instead of loading all records at once, we divide them into smaller chunks. The `Paginator` class is available in `django.core.paginator`. The basic syntax is `Paginator(QuerySet, per_page)`.

Let us understand this with an example using our Book model.

Basic usage of Paginator

Listing 4-52. Using Paginator

```
from django.core.paginator import Paginator

books = Book.objects.all().order_by("id")

paginator = Paginator(books, 5)

page_number = 1

page_obj = paginator.get_page(page_number)

for book in page_obj:
    print(book.title)
```

In Listing 4-52, we are fetching all books and ordering them by id. Then we create a Paginator object and specify that each page should contain five records.

```
paginator = Paginator(books, 5)
```

This means each page will have five book objects. When we call

```
page_obj = paginator.get_page(1)
```

Django returns the first page containing five records.

Equivalent SQL (conceptual for page 1)

```
SELECT book.id, book.title, book.author_id, book.price,
book.number_of_pages, book.published_date,
book.created_at
FROM book
ORDER BY book.id ASC
LIMIT 5 OFFSET 0;
```

If we request page 2

```
page_obj = paginator.get_page(2)
```

Equivalent SQL

```
SELECT ...
FROM book
ORDER BY book.id ASC
```

```
LIMIT 5 OFFSET 5;
```

Django automatically calculates the correct OFFSET value.

Accessing Paginator and page attributes

The Paginator object provides useful properties. They are

- paginator.count: To get the total number of records
- paginator.num_pages: To get the total number of pages
- paginator.per_page: To get the number of records per page

The page object also provides helpful attributes. They are

- page_obj.number: To get the current page number
- page_obj.has_next(): Returns True if the next page exists
- page_obj.has_previous(): Returns True if the previous page exists
- page_obj.next_page_number(): Returns the next page number
- page_obj.previous_page_number(): Returns the previous page number

Using page() vs. get_page()

There are two ways to get a page.

```
page_obj = paginator.page(1)
```

or

```
page_obj = paginator.get_page(1)
```

Difference

page raises an exception if the page number is invalid.

get_page handles invalid page numbers gracefully and returns a valid page instead.

For example, if the user enters a non-existing page number, get_page returns the last available page instead of raising an error.

Why use Paginator?

- Improves performance by limiting the number of records per request
- Reduces memory usage

- Essential for large datasets in list views
- Works efficiently because it uses `LIMIT` and `OFFSET` at the database level

`Paginator` works with any QuerySet. It does not load all records into memory. It applies slicing at the database level using `LIMIT` and `OFFSET`. Using the `Paginator` object is the correct and efficient way to implement pagination in Django applications.

Let us move to the next topic which is using `Q` objects for complex queries.

Using Q Objects for Complex Queries

`Q` objects allow you to build complex queries with **AND**, **OR**, and **NOT** conditions, which can't always be expressed with simple keyword arguments. They are especially useful when combining multiple conditions dynamically. The normal `filter` method combines the fields in AND logic. But in our application, we need more than that. The `Q` object solves this problem; this can be used for complex logic conditions.

Let's check how we can do **OR** conditions.

OR condition

We can do an **OR** condition using a `Q` object and | symbol.

Let's check with an example.

Listing 4-53. OR condition example

```
from django.db.models import Q

books = Book.objects.filter(
    Q(title__contains="python") | Q(title__contains="django"))
```

Equivalent SQL

```
SELECT * FROM book
WHERE title LIKE '%python%' OR title LIKE '%django%';
```

In Listing 4-53, we are filtering the books with a title that contains **python** or **Django.** For that we have created two `Q` objects with conditions `title__contains="python"` and `title__contains="django"`; then we combine them using a | symbol which says that they are combined in **OR** logic. If we see the equivalent SQL, they are combined in OR logic.

Let's check the AND condition of a Q object.

AND condition

By default, filter works in AND logic. Q object with **&** symbol we can do this explicitly. Let us check with an example.

Listing 4-54. AND logic example

```
books = Book.objects.filter(
    Q(price__gt=100) & Q(number_of_pages__gt=100)
)
```

Equivalent using filter

```
books = Book.objects.filter(price__gt=100, number_of_pages__gt=100)
```

Equivalent SQL

```
SELECT * FROM book
WHERE price > 100 AND number_of_pages > 100;
```

In Listing 4-54, we are filtering the book which has a price greater than 100 and number_of_pages also greater than 100. For that we create two Q objects and combine them using **&(AND)** logic. This is equivalent to `filter(price__gt=100, number_of_pages__gt=100`. If we check the SQL, we can see that there is AND logic applied.

Let's see how we can do the **NOT** logic using a Q object.

NOT condition

We can do the NOT logic using Q object and ~ symbol.

Let's check with an example

Listing 4-55. NOT logic using Q

```
books = Book.objects.filter(
    ~Q(title__contains="python")
)
```

SQL Equivalent:

```
SELECT * FROM book
WHERE NOT (title LIKE '%python%');
```

In Listing 4-55, we filter the book whose title does not have **python** in it. For that we are using a Q object with a ~ symbol. If we check the SQL, we can see that NOT is used.

With Q objects, you can flexibly combine conditions using AND, OR, and NOT. This helps us create complex queries with ease.

Let's check this with an example.

Combining multiple conditions

Q objects can be combined for more complex logic.

Listing 4-56. Complex query using Q

```
books = Book.objects.filter(
    (
        Q(price__gt=500) &
        Q(number_of_pages__gt=300)
    ) |
    Q(
        published_date__year=2025
    )
)
```

Equivalent SQL

```
SELECT ... FROM book WHERE (book.price > 500 AND book.number_of_pages >
300) OR EXTRACT(YEAR FROM book.published_date) = 2025;
```

In Listing 4-56 we are retrieving books where **price > 500 AND number_of_pages > 300** or **published in the year 2025**. We can see that we can achieve this by simply using the Q object and logic operator. Parentheses are important to control logical grouping.

Why use Q objects?

- To implement OR conditions
- To use NOT logic
- To build dynamically generated filters
- To write readable complex conditions

Important notes

- | means OR
- & means AND
- ~ means NOT
- Parentheses are important for correct logical grouping

Q objects are evaluated at the database level. Using Q objects allows us to express complex SQL logic cleanly inside Django ORM while keeping the code readable and maintainable.

Let's learn how to use the F expressions.

Using F Expressions

F expressions let you reference model fields directly in queries, enabling operations without fetching values into Python memory. They are efficient because calculations happen in the database.

Let us understand this with examples.

Comparing two fields

Let's see how we can compare two fields on the same table using an F expression.

Listing 4-57. Using F for field comparison

```
from django.db.models import F
books = Book.objects.filter(
    number_of_pages__gt=F("price")
)
```

Equivalent SQL

```
SELECT book.id, book.title, book.author_id, book.price,
book.number_of_pages, book.published_date,
book.created_at
FROM book
WHERE book.number_of_pages > book.price;
```

In Listing 4-57, we are comparing two columns of the same table. We are fetching all the books with a number of pages that are greater than their price. The comparison happens entirely in the database. Django does not fetch the values into Python.

Let's see how we can update using an `F` expression.

Updating a field using an F expression

One of the most powerful uses of F expressions is updating fields.

Listing 4-58. Updating using F

```
Book.objects.filter(price__isnull=False).update(
    price=F("price") + 100
)
```

Equivalent SQL

```
UPDATE book
SET price = price + 100
WHERE price IS NOT NULL;
```

In Listing 4-58, we are increasing the price of all books by 100. The calculation happens in the database itself. If we fetch each record, modify it in Python, and save it, it will result in multiple queries. Using an F expression performs the update in a single SQL query.

Let's learn `F` with `annotate`.

Using F with annotate

F expressions can also be used in annotate.

Listing 4-59. Using F inside annotate

```
from django.db.models import ExpressionWrapper, DecimalField
books = Book.objects.annotate(
    increased_price=F("price") + 50
)
for book in books:
    print(book.title, book.increased_price)
```

Equivalent SQL

```
SELECT book.id, book.title, book.price,
(book.price + 50) AS increased_price
FROM book;
```

Here in Listing 4-59 we are not modifying the database. We are just creating a calculated field as a result.

Why use F expressions?

- Avoid race conditions.
- Perform calculations in a single query.
- Compare fields directly.
- Improve performance.

Race condition example

Problem Scenario (Race Condition):

Initial price = 10

Request A reads price → 10

Request B reads price → 10

Request A decrease by one → 9

Request B decrease by one → 9

The final value becomes 9 instead of 8. One decrement is lost.

With the F expression, `price=F("price") - 1`. The database safely increments the value.

F expressions operate at the database level. They are evaluated when the query is executed. They do not pull values into Python memory. Often used with `update`, `annotate`, and `filter`, `F` expressions are essential when writing efficient and safe database operations in Django ORM.

Let's move to the next one which is using `Value` expressions.

Using Value Expressions

`Value` expressions are used to wrap constant values, so they can be used inside annotations and expressions. In simple words, `Value` allows us to treat a Python value as a database expression. The `Value` class is available in `django.db.models`. The basic syntax is `Value(constant_value)`.

Let us understand this with examples.

Using Value inside annotate

Let's see how we can use `Value` with `annotate`.

Listing 4-60. Using Value with annotate

```
from django.db.models import Value, CharField

books = Book.objects.annotate(
    category=Value("General", output_field=CharField())
)

for book in books:
    print(book.title, book.category)
```

Equivalent SQL

```
SELECT book.id, book.title,
'General' AS category
FROM book;
```

In Listing 4-60, we are adding a constant column named category to every row. The value "**General**" is added for all records. `Value("General")` tells Django to treat the string as a database expression instead of a Python value. `output_field` specifies the type of the field.

Using Value with an F expression

Value expressions are often combined with F expressions.

Listing 4-61. Combining Value and F

```
from django.db.models import F, Value, ExpressionWrapper, DecimalField

books = Book.objects.annotate(
    increased_price=ExpressionWrapper(
        F("price") + Value(50),
        output_field=DecimalField(max_digits=6, decimal_places=2)
    )
)
```

```
for book in books:
    print(book.title, book.increased_price)
```

Equivalent SQL

```
SELECT book.id, book.title,
(book.price + 50) AS increased_price
FROM book;
```

Here `Value(50)` represents the constant 50. `F("price")` refers to the price column. The addition happens at the database level. `ExpressionWrapper` is used to define the output field type explicitly (Refer Listing 4-61).

Using Value in filter

We can use `Value` in a `filter` also.

Listing 4-62. Using Value in filter

```
from django.db.models import F, Value

books = Book.objects.filter(
    price__gt=F("number_of_pages") + Value(100)
)
```

Equivalent SQL

```
SELECT ...
FROM book
WHERE book.price > (book.number_of_pages + 100);
```

In Listing 4-62 we compare price with number_of_pages plus a constant value. The calculation is performed in the database.

Why use Value expressions?

- To include constant values inside annotations
- To combine constants with F expressions
- To ensure Django treats literals as database expressions
- To define output field types when required

Value wraps Python constants for database usage. Often used with F expressions. It requires output_field when Django cannot infer the type. This is evaluated at the database level.

Value expressions are small but important building blocks when constructing advanced database expressions in Django ORM.

Now let's move to the database functions.

Using Database Functions

Django provides wrappers around many SQL functions, enabling developers to perform **string manipulation, numeric computation, date/time operations, and type conversion** directly in the database. This avoids raw SQL, keeps queries efficient, and ensures portability across supported databases.

Let's learn them one by one. The first one is Cast.

Cast

The Cast function is used to convert one field type into another type at the database level. It performs type conversion inside the SQL query without changing the actual database column. Cast is available in django.db.models.functions. The syntax is Cast(expression, output_field=FieldType()).

Let us see a simple example.

Listing 4-63. Using Cast

```
from django.db.models.functions import Cast
from django.db.models import CharField

books = Book.objects.annotate(
    price_text=Cast("price", output_field=CharField())
)
```

Equivalent SQL

```
SELECT book.id, book.title,
CAST(book.price AS VARCHAR) AS price_text
FROM book;
```

In Listing 4-63, we are converting the price field, which is a `DecimalField`, into a string type. The conversion happens only in the query result. The actual database column remains unchanged.

`Cast` is mainly used when

- Converting field types for comparison
- Preparing values for calculations
- Handling database-specific type requirements

`Cast` affects only the query output. It does not modify the stored data in the database. Also make sure the field type and `output_field` type are compatible.

Let's move to the next one which is `Coalesce`.

Coalesce

The `Coalesce` function is used to return the first non-null value from a list of expressions. It is very useful when dealing with nullable fields. It is available in `django.db.models.functions`. The syntax is `Coalesce(expression1, expression2, ..., output_field=FieldType())`.

Handling null values

Suppose some books have price as null. We want to return 0 instead of null.

Listing 4-64. Using Coalesce

```
from django.db.models.functions import Coalesce
from django.db.models import Value, DecimalField

books = Book.objects.annotate(
    final_price=Coalesce(
        "price", Value(0),
        output_field=DecimalField(max_digits=6, decimal_places=2)
    )
)
```

Equivalent SQL

```
SELECT book.id, book.title,
COALESCE(book.price, 0) AS final_price
FROM book;
```

In Listing 4-64, we are checking the price field. If the price is not null, it returns the price. If the price is null, it returns 0. The database evaluates COALESCE and returns the first non-null value.

Using multiple expressions

We can pass multiple expressions.

```
Coalesce("price", "number_of_pages", Value(0))
```

This means

- Return price if not null
- Else return number_of_pages if not null
- Else return 0

Why use Coalesce?

- To replace null values with defaults
- To avoid null-related calculation errors
- To ensure clean output in annotations

`Coalesce` works at the database level and does not modify the stored data. It only affects the query result.

Let us move to `Greatest` and `Least`.

Greatest and Least

The `Greatest` and `Least` functions are used to compare multiple expressions and return either the largest value or the smallest value. These comparisons happen at the database level. Both functions are available in `django.db.models.functions`. The syntax is `Greatest(expression1, expression2, ...)` and `Least(expression1, expression2, ...)`.

Let us understand this using our Book model.

Using Greatest

Let's check the Greatest function.

Listing 4-65. Using Greatest

```
from django.db.models.functions import Greatest

books = Book.objects.annotate(
    max_value=Greatest(
        "price", "number_of_pages", output_field=IntegerField())
)
```

Equivalent SQL

```
SELECT book.id, book.title,
GREATEST(book.price, book.number_of_pages) AS max_value
FROM book;
```

In Listing 4-65, we compare price and number_of_pages for each book. The database returns the larger value between the two fields. Since both field types are not equal, we explicitly specify the output field.

Using Least

Now let's see how Least works.

Listing 4-66. Using Least

```
from django.db.models.functions import Least

books = Book.objects.annotate(
    min_value=Least(
        "price", "number_of_pages", output_field=IntegerField())
)
```

Equivalent SQL

```
SELECT book.id, book.title,
LEAST(book.price, book.number_of_pages) AS min_value
FROM book;
```

In Listing 4-66, the database returns the smaller value between the price and number_of_pages.

Warning

If any compared field is null, the result may be null depending on the database back end. In such cases, it is common to combine `Greatest` or `Least` with `Coalesce` to handle null values properly.

Why use Greatest and Least?

- To compare multiple columns in a single query
- To compute dynamic max or min values
- To avoid performing comparisons in Python

`Greatest` and `Least` operate only at the query level. They do not modify the stored data in the database.

Let's move to the next one which is `NullIf`.

NullIf

The `NullIf` function compares two expressions and returns null if they are equal. If they are not equal, it returns the first expression. The syntax is `NullIf(expression1, expression2)`.

Let us understand this using our Book model.

Listing 4-67. Using NullIf

```
from django.db.models.functions import NullIf

books = Book.objects.annotate(
    adjusted_price=NullIf("price", Decimal(0.0))
)
```

Equivalent SQL

```
SELECT book.id, book.title,
NULLIF(book.price, 0) AS adjusted_price
FROM book;
```

In Listing 4-67 we are comparing the price with 0. If the price is 0, the result will be null. If the price is not 0, the result will be the actual price. This is useful when 0 represents an invalid or placeholder value, and we want to treat it as null at the query level.

Why use NullIf?

- To treat specific values as null in queries
- To simplify conditional logic
- To avoid writing Case expressions for simple comparisons

`NullIf` does not modify the actual data stored in the database. It only affects the value returned by the query.

Let's move to the next one which is `Chr`.

Chr

The `Chr` function returns the character corresponding to an ASCII code.

Listing 4-68. Using Chr

```
from django.db.models.functions import Chr
from django.db.models import Value

books = Book.objects.annotate(
    sample_char=Chr(Value(65))
)

for book in books:
    print(book.title, book.sample_char)
```

Equivalent SQL

```
SELECT book.id, book.title,
CHR(65) AS sample_char
FROM book;
```

CHR(65) returns "A." Chr converts a numeric ASCII value into its character representation (Refer Listing 4-68).

Let's move to the next one which is the `Concat` function.

Concat

The Concat function is used to join multiple strings into a single value. The syntax is Concat(expression1, expression2, ...).

Listing 4-69. Using Concat

```
from django.db.models.functions import Concat
from django.db.models import Value, CharField

books = Book.objects.annotate(
    full_title=Concat(
        "title",
        Value(" - "),
        "author__name",
        output_field=CharField()
    )
)

for book in books:
    print(book.full_title)
```

Equivalent SQL

```
SELECT book.id,
(COALESCE(book.title, ) || COALESCE((COALESCE( - , ) || COALESCE(author.name,
)), )) AS full_title
FROM book
INNER JOIN author ON book.author_id = author.id;
```

In Listing 4-69 we are joining the book title and author name into a single string. Concat combines multiple fields or values into one string at the database level.

Let's move to Left and Right.

Left and Right

Left and Right are used to extract characters from the beginning or end of a string.

Syntax

```
Left(expression, length)
Right(expression, length)
```

Listing 4-70. Using Left

```
from django.db.models.functions import Left

authors = Author.objects.annotate(
    first_three=Left("name", 3)
)
```

Equivalent SQL

```
SELECT author.id, author.name,
LEFT(author.name, 3) AS first_three
FROM author;
```

`Left` returns the first three characters of the author's name (Refer Listing 4-70).

Listing 4-71. Using Right

```
from django.db.models.functions import Right

authors = Author.objects.annotate(
    last_two=Right("name", 2)
)
```

Equivalent SQL

```
SELECT author.id, author.name,
RIGHT(author.name, 2) AS last_two
FROM author;
```

`Right` returns the last two characters of the author's name (Refer Listing 4-71). Both functions extract a fixed number of characters directly at the database level. Let's move to the next one which is `Length`.

Length

The `Length` function returns the number of characters in a string. The syntax is `Length(expression)`.

Listing 4-72. Using Length

```
from django.db.models.functions import Length

authors = Author.objects.annotate(
    name_length=Length("name")
)
```

Equivalent SQL

```
SELECT author.id, author.name,
LENGTH(author.name) AS name_length
FROM author;
```

Length calculates the total number of characters in the author's name at the database level (Refer Listing 4-72).

Let's move to `Lower` and `Upper` functions.

Lower and Upper

`Lower` and `Upper` are used to convert text to lowercase or uppercase.

Syntax

```
Lower(expression)
Upper(expression)
```

Listing 4-73. Using Lower

```
from django.db.models.functions import Lower

authors = Author.objects.annotate(
    lower_name=Lower("name")
)
```

Equivalent SQL

```
SELECT author.id, author.name,
LOWER(author.name) AS lower_name
FROM author;
```

Lower converts the author's name to lowercase at the database level (Refer Listing 4-73).

Listing 4-74. Using Upper

```
from django.db.models.functions import Upper

authors = Author.objects.annotate(
    upper_name=Upper("name")
)
```

Equivalent SQL

```
SELECT author.id, author.name,
UPPER(author.name) AS upper_name
FROM author;
```

Upper converts the author's name to uppercase directly in the query (Refer Listing 4-74).

Let's move to LPad and RPad functions.

LPad and RPad

LPad and RPad are used to pad a string with characters to a specified length.

Syntax

```
LPad(expression, length, fill_text)
RPad(expression, length, fill_text)
```

Listing 4-75. Using LPad

```
from django.db.models.functions import LPad

authors = Author.objects.annotate(
    padded_name=LPad("name", 10, Value("*"))
)
```

Equivalent SQL

```
SELECT author.id, author.name,
LPAD(author.name, 10, '*') AS padded_name
FROM author;
```

LPad adds the character "*" to the left side of the name until it reaches length 10 (Refer Listing 4-75).

Listing 4-76. Using RPad

```
from django.db.models.functions import RPad
from django.db.models import Value

authors = Author.objects.annotate(
    padded_name=RPad("name", 10, Value("-"))
)
```

Equivalent SQL

```
SELECT author.id, author.name,
RPAD(author.name, 10, '-') AS padded_name
FROM author;
```

RPad adds "-" to the right side of the name until it reaches length 10 (Refer Listing 4-76).

Both functions pad strings directly at the database level.

Let's move to Trim, LTrim, and RTrim.

Trim, LTrim, and RTrim

Trim, LTrim, and RTrim are used to remove whitespace from strings.

Syntax

```
Trim(expression)
LTrim(expression)
RTrim(expression)
```

Listing 4-77. Using Trim

```
from django.db.models.functions import Trim

authors = Author.objects.annotate(
    clean_name=Trim("name")
)
```

Equivalent SQL

```
SELECT author.id,
TRIM(author.name) AS clean_name
FROM author;
```

`Trim` removes whitespace from both the beginning and end of the name (Refer Listing 4-77).

Listing 4-78. Using LTrim

```
from django.db.models.functions import LTrim

authors = Author.objects.annotate(
    left_clean=LTrim("name")
)
```

`LTrim` removes whitespace only from the left side of the string (Refer Listing 4-78).

Listing 4-79. Using RTrim

```
from django.db.models.functions import RTrim

authors = Author.objects.annotate(
    right_clean=RTrim("name")
)
```

`RTrim` removes whitespace only from the right side of the string (Refer Listing 4-79).

All three functions operate directly at the database level.

Let us move to the next one which is `MD5`.

MD5

The `MD5` function returns the MD5 hash of a string. The syntax is MD5(expression).

Listing 4-80. Using MD5

```
from django.db.models.functions import MD5

authors = Author.objects.annotate(
    name_hash=MD5("name")
)
```

Equivalent SQL

```
SELECT author.id, author.name,
MD5(author.name) AS name_hash
FROM author;
```

MD5 generates a hash value for the author's name at the database level (Refer Listing 4-80). It is commonly used for hashing or generating unique string representations.

Let's move to the next one which is Ord.

Ord

The Ord function returns the ASCII code of the first character in a string. The syntax is Ord(expression).

Listing 4-81. Using Ord

```
from django.db.models.functions import Ord

authors = Author.objects.annotate(
    first_char_code=Ord("name")
)
```

Equivalent SQL

```
SELECT author.id, author.name,
ASCII(author.name) AS first_char_code
FROM author;
```

Ord returns the ASCII value of the first character of the name (Refer Listing 4-81). For example, if name starts with "A," the result will be 65.

Let's move to the next one which is Repeat.

Repeat

The Repeat function repeats a string for a specified number of times. The syntax is Repeat(expression, number).

Listing 4-82. Using Repeat

```
from django.db.models.functions import Repeat

authors = Author.objects.annotate(
    repeated_name=Repeat("name", 2)
)
```

Equivalent SQL

```
SELECT author.id, author.name,
REPEAT(author.name, 2) AS repeated_name
FROM author;
```

Repeat duplicates the name value two times at the database level (Refer Listing 4-82). For example, if the name is "John," the result will be "JohnJohn."

Let's move to the next one which is Replace.

Replace

The Replace function replaces occurrences of a substring with another substring. The syntax is Replace(expression, text, replacement).

Listing 4-83. Using Replace

```
from django.db.models.functions import Replace
from django.db.models import Value

authors = Author.objects.annotate(
    updated_name=Replace("name", Value("a"), Value("@"))
)
```

Equivalent SQL

```
SELECT author.id, author.name,
REPLACE(author.name, 'a', '@') AS updated_name
FROM author;
```

Replace substitutes all occurrences of "a" with "@" in the name at the database level (Refer Listing 4-83). For example, "author" becomes "@uthor."

Let's move to the next one which is Reverse.

Reverse

The Reverse function reverses the characters in a string. The syntax is Reverse(expression).

Listing 4-84. Using Reverse

```
from django.db.models.functions import Reverse

authors = Author.objects.annotate(
    reversed_name=Reverse("name")
)
```

Equivalent SQL

```
SELECT author.id, author.name,
REVERSE(author.name) AS reversed_name
FROM author;
```

Reverse returns the name in reverse order at the database level (Refer Listing 4-84). For example, "John" becomes "nhoJ."

Let's move to using SHA hash functions.

Using SHA functions

SHA1, SHA224, SHA256, SHA384, and SHA512 generate secure hash values of a string. Let's check a SHA256 example.

Listing 4-85. Using SHA256

```
from django.db.models.functions import SHA256

authors = Author.objects.annotate(
    name_hash=SHA256("name")
)
```

Equivalent SQL

```
SELECT author.id, author.name,
SHA256(author.name) AS name_hash
FROM author;
```

SHA256 generates a secure hash of the author's name at the database level (Refer Listing 4-85). Other SHA functions (SHA1, SHA224, SHA384, SHA512) work in the same way but produce different hash lengths.

Let's move to the next one which is StrIndex.

StrIndex

The StrIndex function returns the position of a substring inside a string. The syntax is StrIndex(expression, substring).

Listing 4-86. Using StrIndex

```
from django.db.models.functions import StrIndex
from django.db.models import Value

authors = Author.objects.annotate(
    position=StrIndex("name", Value("a"))
)
```

Equivalent SQL

```
SELECT author.id, author.name,
STRPOS(author.name, 'a') AS position
FROM author;
```

StrIndex returns the position of the first occurrence of "a" in the name (Refer Listing 4-86). If the substring is not found, it returns 0 (depending on the database back end).

Let's move to the next one which is Substr.

Substr

The Substr function extracts a portion of a string starting from a given position. The syntax is Substr(expression, position, length).

Listing 4-87. Using Substr

```
from django.db.models.functions import Substr

authors = Author.objects.annotate(
    partial_name=Substr("name", 1, 3)
)
```

Equivalent SQL

```
SELECT author.id, author.name,
SUBSTR(author.name, 1, 3) AS partial_name
FROM author;
```

Substr extracts three characters starting from position 1. Position indexing starts at 1 at the database level (Refer Listing 4-87). For example, if the name is "Author," the result will be "Aut."

Let's move to the next one which is Abs.

Abs

The Abs function returns the absolute value of a numeric expression. The syntax is Abs(expression).

Listing 4-88. Using Abs

```
from django.db.models.functions import Abs

books = Book.objects.annotate(
    absolute_pages=Abs("number_of_pages")
)
```

Equivalent SQL

```
SELECT book.id, book.title,
ABS(book.number_of_pages) AS absolute_pages
FROM book;
```

Abs converts negative numbers into positive values at the database level (Refer Listing 4-88). For example, if number_of_pages is -200, the result will be 200.

Let's move to `Ceil` and `Floor`.

Ceil and Floor

`Ceil` and `Floor` are used to round numeric values to the nearest integer.

Syntax

```
Ceil(expression)
Floor(expression)
```

Listing 4-89. Using Ceil

```
from django.db.models.functions import Ceil

books = Book.objects.annotate(
    rounded_up=Ceil("price")
)
```

Equivalent SQL

```
SELECT book.id, book.title,
CEILING(book.price) AS rounded_up
FROM book;
```

`Ceil` rounds the price up to the nearest integer (Refer Listing 4-89). If the price is 4.2, it is rounded to 5.

Listing 4-90. Using Floor

```
from django.db.models.functions import Floor

books = Book.objects.annotate(
    rounded_down=Floor("price")
)
```

Equivalent SQL

```
SELECT book.id, book.title,
FLOOR(book.price) AS rounded_down
FROM book;
```

`Floor` rounds the price down to the nearest integer (Refer Listing 4-90). If the price is 4.2, it is rounded to 4.

Let's move to the next one which is `Exp`.

Exp

The `Exp` function returns e raised to the power of a given number. The syntax is `Exp(expression)`.

Listing 4-91. Using Exp

```
from django.db.models.functions import Exp

books = Book.objects.annotate(
    exp_value=Exp("number_of_pages")
)
```

Equivalent SQL

```
SELECT book.id, book.title,
EXP(book.number_of_pages) AS exp_value
FROM book;
```

`Exp` calculates **e^number_of_pages** at the database level (Refer Listing 4-91). It performs exponential calculation directly in the query.

Let's move to `Ln` and `Log`.

Ln and Log

`Ln` and `Log` are used to calculate logarithmic values.

Syntax

```
Ln(expression)
Log(base, expression)
```

Listing 4-92. Using Ln

```
from django.db.models.functions import Ln

books = Book.objects.annotate(
    natural_log=Ln("price")
)
```

Equivalent SQL

```
SELECT book.id, book.title,
LN(book.price) AS natural_log
FROM book;
```

`Ln` returns the natural logarithm (base e) of the price (Refer Listing 4-92).

Listing 4-93. Using Log

```
from django.db.models.functions import Log
from django.db.models import Value

books = Book.objects.annotate(
    log_base_10=Log(Value(10), "price")
)
```

Equivalent SQL

```
SELECT book.id, book.title,
LOG(10, book.price) AS log_base_10
FROM book;
```

Log calculates the logarithm of the price with base 10 at the database level (Refer Listing 4-93). We can use any base for this function. If we pass `Value(2)` instead of `Value(10)`, then Log is calculated in base 2.

Let's move to the next one which is `Mod`.

Mod

The `Mod` function returns the remainder of dividing one number by another. The syntax is `Mod(expression, divisor)`.

Listing 4-94. Using Mod

```
from django.db.models.functions import Mod
from django.db.models import Value

books = Book.objects.annotate(
    remainder=Mod("number_of_pages", Value(100))
)
```

Equivalent SQL

```
SELECT book.id, book.title,
MOD(book.number_of_pages, 100) AS remainder
FROM book;
```

Mod calculates number_of_pages % 100 at the database level (Refer Listing 4-94). For example, if number_of_pages is 250, the result will be 50.

Let's move to the next one which is Power.

Power

The Power function raises a number to the power of another number. The syntax is Power(base_expression, exponent_expression).

Listing 4-95. Using Power

```
from django.db.models.functions import Power
from django.db.models import Value

books = Book.objects.annotate(
    squared_pages=Power("number_of_pages", Value(2))
)
```

Equivalent SQL

```
SELECT book.id, book.title,
POWER(book.number_of_pages, 2) AS squared_pages
FROM book;
```

Power calculates number_of_pages^2 at the database level (Refer Listing 4-95). For example, if number_of_pages is 10, the result will be 100.

Let us move to the next one which is Radians.

Radians

The Radians function converts degrees to radians. The syntax is Radians(expression).

Listing 4-96. Using Radians

```
from django.db.models.functions import Radians

books = Book.objects.annotate(
    pages_in_radians=Radians("number_of_pages")
)
```

Equivalent SQL

```
SELECT book.id, book.title,
RADIANS(book.number_of_pages) AS pages_in_radians
FROM book;
```

Radians convert the numeric value of number_of_pages from degrees to radians at the database level (Refer Listing 4-96). For example, 180 becomes **Pi** radians.

Let's move to the next one which is Random.

Random

The Random function returns a random value between 0 and 1. The syntax is Random().

Listing 4-97. Using Random

```
from django.db.models.functions import Random

books = Book.objects.annotate(
    random_value=Random()
)
```

Equivalent SQL

```
SELECT book.id, book.title,
RANDOM() AS random_value
FROM book;
```

Random generates a random number for each row at the database level (Refer Listing 4-97). Each time the query runs, different random values are returned.

Let's move to the next one which is Round.

Round

The Round function rounds a numeric value to a specified number of decimal places. The syntax is Round(expression, precision).

Listing 4-98. Using Round

```
from django.db.models.functions import Round
from django.db.models import Value

books = Book.objects.annotate(
    rounded_price=Round("price", Value(0))
)
```

Equivalent SQL

```
SELECT book.id, book.title,
ROUND(book.price, 0) AS rounded_price
FROM book;
```

Round rounds the price to 0 decimal places at the database level (Refer Listing 4-98). For example, if the price is 99.75, the result will be 100.

Let's move to the next one which is Sign.

Sign

The Sign function returns the sign of a numeric value. The syntax is Sign(expression).

Listing 4-99. Using Sign

```
from django.db.models.functions import Sign

books = Book.objects.annotate(
    price_sign=Sign("price")
)
```

Equivalent SQL

```
SELECT book.id, book.title,
SIGN(book.price) AS price_sign
FROM book;
```

Sign returns

- 1 if the value is positive
- 0 if the value is zero
- -1 if the value is negative

The calculation happens at the database level (Refer Listing 4-99).

Let's move to the next one which is Sqrt.

Sqrt

The Sqrt function returns the square root of a numeric value. The syntax is Sqrt(expression).

Listing 4-100. Using Sqrt

```
from django.db.models.functions import Sqrt

books = Book.objects.annotate(
    sqrt_pages=Sqrt("number_of_pages")
)
```

Equivalent SQL

```
SELECT book.id, book.title,
SQRT(book.number_of_pages) AS sqrt_pages
FROM book;
```

Sqrt calculates the square root of number_of_pages at the database level (Refer Listing 4-100). For example, if number_of_pages is 144, the result will be 12.

Let's move to using trigonometric functions.

Using Trigonometric Functions

Django provides several trigonometric functions that allow mathematical calculations directly at the database level. These functions are useful when working with angles, scientific calculations, or geometry-related computations.

Let us see an example using the Sin function.

Syntax

```
Sin(expression)
```

Listing 4-101. Using Sin

```
from django.db.models.functions import Sin

books = Book.objects.annotate(
    sin_value=Sin("number_of_pages")
)
```

Equivalent SQL

```
SELECT book.id, book.title,
SIN(book.number_of_pages) AS sin_value
FROM book;
```

Sin calculates the sine of the numeric value. The calculation is performed at the database level (Refer Listing 4-101), and the result is returned with the QuerySet.

Django provides the following trigonometric functions:

- ACos: Returns the arccosine
- ASin: Returns the arcsine
- ATan: Returns the arctangent
- ATan2: Returns the arctangent of expression1/expression2
- Cos: Returns the cosine

Cot: Returns the cotangent

Tan: Returns the tangent

Degrees: Converts a numeric field or expression from radians to degrees

Let's move to the next one which is Now.

Now

The Now function returns the current date and time from the database server. The syntax is Now().

Listing 4-102. Using Now

```
from django.db.models.functions import Now

books = Book.objects.annotate(
    current_time=Now()
)
```

Equivalent SQL

```
SELECT book.id, book.title,
STATEMENT_TIMESTAMP() AS current_time
FROM book;
```

Now returns the current timestamp from the database server (Refer Listing 4-102). Each row in the result will contain the same current date and time value generated at the time the query is executed.

Let's move to the next one which is Extract.

Extract

The Extract function is used to extract a specific part of a date or datetime field such as year, month, or day. The syntax is Extract(expression, lookup_name).

Listing 4-103. Using Extract

```
from django.db.models.functions import Extract

books = Book.objects.annotate(
    published_year=Extract("published_date", "year")
)
```

Equivalent SQL

```
SELECT book.id, book.title,
EXTRACT(YEAR FROM book.published_date) AS published_year
FROM book;
```

`Extract` retrieves a specific part of a date field (Refer Listing 4-103). In this example, we are extracting the year from the published_date field. Common lookup values include year, month, day, week, and hour.

Let's move to the next one which is `Trunc`.

Trunc

The `Trunc` function truncates a date or datetime field to a specific precision such as year, month, or day. The syntax is `Trunc(expression, kind)`.

Listing 4-104. Using Trunc

```
from django.db.models.functions import Trunc

books = Book.objects.annotate(
    published_month=Trunc("published_date", "month")
)
```

Equivalent SQL

```
SELECT book.id, book.title,
DATE_TRUNC('month', book.published_date) AS published_month
FROM book;
```

Trunc truncates the date to the specified precision. In this example (Refer Listing 4-104), the day part is removed, and the date is truncated to the first day of the month. Variants of Trunc are TruncDate, TruncTime, TruncYear, TruncMonth, TruncWeek, TruncDay, TruncHour, TruncMinute, and TruncSecond.

Think of Trunc as rounding down a datetime to a certain unit (like year, month, day, hour).

Example in plain English:

You have 2025-08-17 14:32:10.

If you call TruncDay, it becomes 2025-08-17 00:00:00.

If you call TruncMonth, it becomes 2025-08-01 00:00:00.

If you call TruncYear, it becomes 2025-01-01 00:00:00.

And so on.

Let's move to the next one which is JSONArray.

JSONArray

The JSONArray function creates a JSON array from the given expressions. The syntax is JSONArray(expression1, expression2, ...).

Note This is new in Django 5.2.

Listing 4-105. Using JSONArray

```
from django.db.models.functions import JSONArray

books = Book.objects.annotate(
    book_info=JSONArray("title", "price")
)
```

Equivalent SQL

```
SELECT book.id, book.title,
JSON_ARRAY(book.title, book.price) AS book_info
FROM book;
```

JSONArray combines multiple values into a JSON array. In this example (Refer Listing 4-105), the title and price are returned as a JSON array for each book.

Let's move to the next one which is JSONObject.

JSONObject

The JSONObject function creates a JSON object from the given key value pairs. The syntax is JSONObject(key=value, ...).

Listing 4-106. Using JSONObject

```
from django.db.models.functions import JSONObject

books = Book.objects.annotate(
    book_info=JSONObject(
        title="title",
        price="price"
    )
)
```

Equivalent SQL

```
SELECT book.id, book.title,
JSON_OBJECT('title', book.title, 'price', book.price) AS book_info
FROM book;
```

JSONObject creates a JSON object using the specified keys and fields. In this example (Refer Listing 4-106), the result will contain a JSON object with a title and price for each book.

Now we can move to the next section which is "Operators on QuerySet."

Operators on QuerySet

Django QuerySets support operators to combine multiple QuerySets. The operators &, |, and ^ allow us to perform AND, OR, and XOR. The QuerySets must be from the same model.

Listing 4-107. Using AND (&) operator

```
qs1 = Book.objects.filter(price__gt=100)

qs2 = Book.objects.filter(number_of_pages__gt=200)

books = qs1 & qs2
```

Equivalent SQL

```
SELECT * FROM book
WHERE price > 100 AND number_of_pages > 200;
```

The & operator returns records that satisfy both conditions (Refer Listing 4-107).

Listing 4-108. Using OR (|) operator

```
qs1 = Book.objects.filter(price__lt=100)

qs2 = Book.objects.filter(number_of_pages__gt=300)

books = qs1 | qs2
```

Equivalent SQL

```
SELECT * FROM book
WHERE price < 100 OR number_of_pages > 300;
```

The | operator combines QuerySets using OR. Records that satisfy either condition will be returned (Refer Listing 4-108).

Listing 4-109. Using XOR (^) operator

```
qs1 = Book.objects.filter(price__gt=100)

qs2 = Book.objects.filter(number_of_pages__gt=200)

books = qs1 ^ qs2
```

Equivalent SQL

```
SELECT * FROM book
WHERE (
(book.price > 100 OR book.number_of_pages > 200) AND
```

```
1 = (CASE WHEN book.price > 100 THEN 1 ELSE 0 END + CASE WHEN app_book.
number_of_pages > 200 THEN 1 ELSE 0 END)
)
```

The ^ operator returns the symmetric difference (Refer Listing 4-109). It returns records that exist in either QuerySet but not in both.

Let's move to the next section which is "Conditional Expression."

Conditional Expression

Conditional expressions allow us to apply conditions inside queries. Django provides `Case` and `When` to implement conditional logic like the SQL `CASE` statement. These expressions can be used in annotations, filtering, aggregation, and updates.

Listing 4-110. Using conditional annotation

```
from django.db.models import Case, When, Value, CharField

books = Book.objects.annotate(
    price_category=Case(
        When(price__gt=500, then=Value("Expensive")),
        When(price__gt=200, then=Value("Moderate")),
        default=Value("Cheap"),
        output_field=CharField()
    )
)
```

Equivalent SQL

```
SELECT book.id, book.title,
CASE
WHEN book.price > 500 THEN 'Expensive'
WHEN book.price > 200 THEN 'Moderate'
ELSE 'Cheap'
END AS price_category
FROM book;
```

In this example (Refer Listing 4-110), we are creating a conditional annotation. Based on the price of the book, a category value is assigned.

Listing 4-111. Using conditional filtering

```
from django.db.models import Case, When, Value, IntegerField

books = Book.objects.annotate(
    expensive_flag=Case(
        When(price__gt=500, then=Value(1)),
        default=Value(0),
        output_field=IntegerField()
    )
).filter(expensive_flag=1)
```

Equivalent SQL

```
SELECT ..., CASE WHEN book.price > 500 THEN 1 ELSE 0 END AS expensive_flag
FROM book
WHERE CASE WHEN (book.price > 500) THEN 1 ELSE 0 END = 1
```

Here the conditional expression is used to mark expensive books and then filter them (Refer Listing 4-111).

Listing 4-112. Using conditional aggregation

```
from django.db.models import Sum, Case, When, Value, IntegerField

result = Book.objects.aggregate(
    expensive_books=Sum(
        Case(
            When(price__gt=500, then=Value(1)),
            default=Value(0),
            output_field=IntegerField()
        )
    )
)
```

Equivalent SQL

```
SELECT SUM(
CASE
WHEN book.price > 500 THEN 1
ELSE 0
END
) AS expensive_books
FROM book;
```

Conditional aggregation allows for applying conditions during aggregation. In this example (Refer Listing 4-112), we are counting books whose price is greater than 500.

Listing 4-113. Using conditional update

```
from django.db.models import Case, When, Value, DecimalField

Book.objects.update(
    price=Case(
        When(number_of_pages__gt=300, then=Value(600)),
        default="price",
        output_field=DecimalField(max_digits=6, decimal_places=2)
    )
)
```

Equivalent SQL

```
UPDATE book
SET price = CASE
WHEN number_of_pages > 300 THEN 600
ELSE price
END;
```

Conditional update allows modifying field values based on conditions. In this example (Refer Listing 4-113), if the number_of_pages is greater than 300, the price is updated to 600. Otherwise, the existing price value is kept unchanged.

Let's summarize this chapter.

Summary

In this chapter, we explored advanced querying techniques available in the Django ORM. These features allow developers to write complex database queries while still working within Python code.

We started by understanding different QuerySet operations and expressions that allow modifying and evaluating query results. We also explored conditional expressions using Case and When which allow us to apply conditional logic similar to SQL CASE statements. These expressions can be used in annotations, filtering, aggregation, and updates.

The chapter also introduced database functions available in Django. These functions allow performing operations directly at the database level instead of processing data in Python. We covered different categories of functions including text functions, mathematical functions, trigonometric functions, and date and time functions.

We also learned how Django supports JSON-related functions which help generate structured JSON data directly from queries.

By using these advanced ORM features, we can write powerful and efficient database queries while keeping the code clean and readable.

In the upcoming chapter we will learn some of the common mistakes and the solutions for them.

Appendix

Exercises

1. Retrieve all books and annotate a new field that categorizes them as short, medium, or long based on the number_of_pages using a conditional expression.

2. Write a query that returns the title and length of the title using the appropriate text function.

3. Annotate each book with a new field that returns the first four characters of the title.

4. Write a query that returns all books with the title converted to uppercase.

5. Generate a JSON object containing the title and price of each book.
6. Annotate each book with the square root of the number_of_pages using the appropriate mathematical function.
7. Write a query that returns a random value for each book using a database function.
8. Extract the year from the published_date of each book.
9. Write a query that groups books by author and returns the count of books written by each author.
10. Write a query that updates the price of books to 500 when number_of_pages is greater than 300 using a conditional update.
11. Write a query that annotates each book with a flag value 1 if the price is greater than 400, otherwise 0.
12. Create a query that returns books whose title contains the word "Python."
13. Write a query that retrieves the latest published book based on published_date.
14. Write a query that annotates each book with the reverse of the title using a database function.
15. Create a query that returns the absolute value of number_of_pages using the appropriate mathematical function.

CHAPTER 5

Common Issues in Django ORM and Solutions

The Django ORM provides a powerful and expressive way to interact with databases using Python instead of writing raw SQL. While it simplifies database operations and improves developer productivity, improper usage can lead to performance bottlenecks, inefficient queries, and scalability problems.

Understanding how model fields, relationships, query evaluation, indexing, and optimization techniques work internally is essential for writing efficient and reliable applications.

In this chapter, we will explore common issues developers face when working with the Django ORM, such as N+1 query problems, improper relationship usage, inefficient aggregations, and missing indexes. For each issue, we will examine practical solutions and best practices to ensure that your application remains performant, scalable, and maintainable.

Let us check them one by one. The first one is choosing the incorrect type.

Choosing Incorrect Field Types

Selecting the wrong model field type is a common mistake in Django applications. While the ORM makes it easy to define models, choosing an inappropriate field type can lead to inefficient storage, unnecessary constraints, performance issues, or even data loss. Proper field selection is essential for maintaining data integrity and scalability.

Using incorrect field types can cause limitations that do not align with the actual nature of the data. For example, developers sometimes use `CharField` for content that may grow beyond the defined maximum length, which introduces artificial constraints and potential truncation.

Let us check with examples. The first one is using `CharField` instead of `TextField`.

Afsal MS, *Mastering Django ORM*, https://doi.org/10.1007/979-8-8688-2589-7_5

Listing 5-1. CharField instead of TextField for long descriptions

```
class Book(models.Model):
    title = models.CharField(max_length=100)
    description = models.CharField(max_length=255)
```

Here in Listing 5-1, the description field is limited to 255 characters. If a longer description is required later, the schema must be changed, and existing data might already be restricted. The `CharField` enforces a maximum length at both the database and validation levels. While this is useful for controlled inputs such as titles or codes, it becomes restrictive for large or unpredictable text content. Using it incorrectly may lead to truncated data or frequent schema migrations.

`TextField`, on the other hand, is optimized for larger text storage and avoids unnecessary length constraints. Choosing the appropriate field type ensures better data modeling, prevents avoidable errors, and keeps the application flexible as requirements evolve.

For unbounded or large text data, use TextField (Refer Listing 5-2).

Listing 5-2. Using TextField for large text

```
class Book(models.Model):
    title = models.CharField(max_length=100)
    description = models.TextField()  # Correct choice for long text
```

Let us move to another example which is using `CharField` for numerical data.

Sometimes developers use `CharField` for numerical data. This creates unwanted overheads like type casting for calculations, comparisons, validation, etc. Let us check with an example.

Listing 5-3. Using CharField for numeric data

```
class Product(models.Model):
    price = models.CharField(max_length=20)
```

Storing numeric values like price in a `CharField` is problematic (Refer Listing 5-3). It prevents proper numeric comparisons, sorting, aggregations, and validation.

Listing 5-4. Using numerical field for numerical data

```
class Product(models.Model):
    price = models.DecimalField(max_digits=10, decimal_places=2)
```

DecimalField allows accurate calculations, filtering, and aggregation (Refer Listing 5-4).

Let us check another example which is using IntegerField for Boolean values.

Sometimes we can use 0 or 1 for Boolean data. But if we use IntegerField instead of BooleanField, this reduces the readability of the code. Also, it causes confusion while handling the data.

Listing 5-5. Using IntegerField instead of BooleanField

```
class User(models.Model):
    is_active = models.IntegerField()
```

Using integers (0 and 1) to represent Boolean states reduces readability and clarity (Refer Listing 5-5).

Listing 5-6. Using BooleanField for Boolean data

```
class User(models.Model):
    is_active = models.BooleanField(default=True)
```

BooleanField clearly expresses intent and improves validation (Refer Listing 5-6).

There are so many cases like this. What we can do for this is first understand the domain deeply. We must have an understanding about what is possible data might come before starting coding.

Misconfiguring null and blank Attributes

Handling null and blank correctly is essential in Django model design. Many developers misunderstand the difference between these two attributes, which can lead to validation errors, database integrity issues, and unexpected behavior in forms and queries.

Improper configuration of null and blank can create unintended constraints. For example, if a field is meant to be optional but null=True is not set, inserting a NULL value into the database will raise an error. Similarly, forgetting blank=True can cause form validation failures even when the field is logically optional.

Consider the case publish_date is optional for a book. But we define a model like this.

Listing 5-7. Book model without null and blank not set properly

```
class Book(models.Model):
    title = models.CharField(max_length=100)
    publish_date = models.DateField()  # Causes error if date is null
```

In Listing 5-7, if **publish_date** is not provided, Django will raise an error because the field does not allow NULL values at the database level and is required during validation.

Let us see how we can fix this.

Listing 5-8. Book model with proper null and blank settings

```
class Book(models.Model):
    title = models.CharField(max_length=100)
    publish_date = models.DateField(null=True, blank=True)
```

By adding `null=True`, the database allows for storing `NULL`. By adding `blank=True`, Django forms allow the field to be optional during validation (Refer Listing 5-8).

Additional common mistake: Using null=True on CharField

For string-based fields like `CharField` and `TextField`, using `null=True` is usually discouraged. This creates two possible empty states: `NULL` and an empty string (""), which complicates filtering and querying.

For text fields, it is generally better to use `blank=True` without `null=True`, allowing empty strings instead of NULL.

Listing 5-9. Proper way for setting optional CharField

```
class Author(models.Model):
    bio = models.CharField(max_length=255, blank=True)
```

`null=True` affects the database schema and allows storing `NULL` values. `blank=True` affects form validation and determines whether a field is required (Refer Listing 5-9). They serve different purposes and should not be used interchangeably.

Understanding this distinction prevents inconsistent data states, reduces validation errors, and ensures cleaner database design. Proper configuration of `null` and `blank` improves reliability and avoids subtle bugs in queries and forms.

Let us move to the next mistake which is incorrect usage of `auto_now` and `auto_now_add`.

Incorrect Usage of auto_now and auto_now_add

Timestamp fields are commonly used to track when a record is created and when it is last updated. However, misusing `auto_now` and `auto_now_add` can lead to incorrect or misleading timestamp data, which affects auditing, reporting, and debugging.

A frequent mistake is swapping the purpose of `auto_now` and `auto_now_add`. Developers sometimes use `auto_now=True` for **created_at**, which causes the field to update every time the object is saved. This overwrites the original creation time and makes it impossible to know when the record was first created.

Let us check with an example.

Listing 5-10. Incorrect auto_now and auto_now_add

```
class Book(models.Model):
    created_at = models.DateTimeField(auto_now=True)
    updated_at = models.DateTimeField(auto_now_add=True)
```

In this example (Refer Listing 5-10), **created_at** changes every time the model is saved, which is incorrect. Meanwhile, **updated_at** is set only once during creation, which defeats its purpose of tracking modifications.

Listing 5-11. Correct usage of auto_now and auto_now_add

```
class Book(models.Model):
    created_at = models.DateTimeField(auto_now_add=True)
    updated_at = models.DateTimeField(auto_now=True)
```

Here, `auto_now_add` ensures that **created_at** is set only once when the object is first created (Refer Listing 5-11). `auto_now=True` ensures that **updated_at** is automatically refreshed every time the object is saved.

`auto_now_add` records the initial creation timestamp and never changes it afterward. `auto_now` updates the field to the current date and time on every save operation. Using them correctly preserves the original creation time and accurately tracks modifications.

Proper timestamp handling is essential for maintaining reliable audit trails, debugging changes, and implementing features like sorting recent updates.

Let us move to the next issue which is not using an index for frequently queried fields.

Not Using Indexes on Frequently Queried Fields

Indexes play a crucial role in database performance. When working with large datasets, failing to index fields that are frequently used in filter conditions can significantly slow down queries. Although Django abstracts SQL details, understanding indexing is essential for writing performance applications.

If a field is repeatedly used in `filter()`, `get()`, or lookup queries but is not indexed, the database must perform a full table scan to find matching records. As the table grows, this operation becomes increasingly slow and inefficient.

Listing 5-12. Book model without index

```
class Book(models.Model):
    title = models.CharField(max_length=100)
    description = models.TextField()
```

If you frequently execute queries such as `Book.objects.filter(title="Django ORM")`, the database will scan every row in the book table to find matches when no index exists (Refer Listing 5-12).

Listing 5-13. Book model with index

```
class Book(models.Model):
    title = models.CharField(max_length=100, db_index=True)
    description = models.TextField()
```

By `db_index=True`, Django instructs the database to create an index on those fields during migration (Refer Listing 5-13). The database uses the index to quickly locate matching rows instead of scanning the entire table. Indexes significantly improve query performance by allowing the database to locate records efficiently. Instead of scanning every row, the database uses a data structure (typically a B-tree) to narrow down results quickly.

However, indexes should be added thoughtfully. While they speed up read operations, they slightly increase storage usage and can slow down write operations (`INSERT`, `UPDATE`, `DELETE`). Therefore, indexes should be applied to fields that are frequently used in filtering, ordering, or joining operations. Proper indexing ensures better scalability and consistent performance as your application grows.

The next one, which is the N+1 problem, is very common but can cause performance issues as data grows.

N+1 Query Problem

The N+1 query problem is one of the most common and serious performance issues in Django ORM. It happens when related objects are accessed without proper optimization, causing one initial query followed by additional queries for each related object. As the number of records increases, this can drastically slow down the application.

Before we dive into this, consider these models for explanation.

Listing 5-14. Sample model

```
class Author(models.Model):
    name = models.CharField(max_length=100)

class Genre(models.Model):
    name = models.CharField(max_length=50)

class Book(models.Model):
    title = models.CharField(max_length=200)
    author = models.ForeignKey(Author, on_delete=models.CASCADE)
    genres = models.ManyToManyField(Genre, blank=True)
```

In this structure, a book belongs to one author (`ForeignKey`) and can belong to multiple genres (`ManyToManyField`) (Refer Listing 5-14).

When accessing related objects inside a loop, Django may execute a separate query for each related object. This results in one query to fetch the main objects and additional queries for each related record, leading to the N+1 problem.

First let us check the N+1 in `ForeignKey`.

Listing 5-15. N+1 in ForeignKey

```
books = Book.objects.all()
for book in books:
    print(book.title, book.author.name)
```

In Listing 5-15 we are printing all the books and the author's name. If there are 100 books, Django will execute 1 query to fetch all books and 100 additional queries to fetch each related author. Total: 101 queries. As the data grows, the number of queries increases; this will cause extra load on the database.

This can be solved by using `select_related` while querying the book. This tells Django ORM to fetch the related items in a single query. This is achieved by joining the tables.

Let us check the proper way for this.

Listing 5-16. Using select_related for fetching author

```
books = Book.objects.select_related('author').all()
for book in books:
    print(book.author.name)  # Efficient single query
```

In Listing 5-16 we are using the `select_related` method and tell Django ORM to fetch authors with books. `select_related` () performs a SQL JOIN and retrieves related foreign key data in a single query. This is efficient for `ForeignKey` and `OneToOneField`.

Let us check N+1 in `ManyToManyField`.

Listing 5-17. N+1 in ManyToManyField

```
books = Book.objects.all()
for book in books:
    print(book.title, book.genres.all())
```

In Listing 5-17 we are printing the book title and its genres. If there are 100 books, Django will execute 1 query for books and 100 additional queries for genre, again resulting in 101 queries.

This can be solved by using `prefetch_related. prefetch_related` () executes a separate query for related objects but retrieves them in bulk using an IN clause and then maps them in Python. This avoids running one query per object and is ideal for many-to-many relationships.

Listing 5-18. Using prefetch_related for genres

```
books = Book.objects.prefetch_related('genres').all()
for book in books:
    print(book.title, book.genres.all())
```

Here instead of N+1 queries, ORM executed two queries for fetching the book and for fetching genres of the selected books (Refer Listing 5-18).

The N+1 query problem increases database load, slows down response time, and reduces scalability. Using `select_related` () and `prefetch_related` () ensures related objects are fetched efficiently in bulk. Preventing N+1 issues is essential for building high-performance and scalable Django applications.

Let us move to the next issue which is not using unique constraints.

Not Using Unique Constraints

Not enforcing unique constraints at the database level can result in duplicate records, leading to data integrity problems. Sometimes we attempt to handle uniqueness only at the application (code) level by checking if a record exists before creating it. However, this approach is unsafe in concurrent environments and can still allow duplicates.

Let us check with an example.

Listing 5-19. Sample Book model

```
class Book(models.Model):
    title = models.CharField(max_length=100)
    author = models.CharField(max_length=100)
```

Let us check how we can implement code-level uniqueness check.

Listing 5-20. Code-level uniqueness check (for Model Refer Listing 5-19 and code-level uniqueness check Refer Listing 5-20)

```
if not Book.objects.filter(
        title='Django ORM',
        author='Author abc').exists():
    Book.objects.create(
        title='Django ORM Guide',
        author='Author abc'
    )
```

Problem Scenario (Concurrency Issue)

Request A checks → no record found
Request B checks → no record found
Request A inserts record
Request B inserts record

Since both checks happen before either insert completes, duplicate records are created. This is called a race condition, and it commonly occurs in high-traffic systems. Both inserts succeed because the database does not enforce uniqueness.

Define unique constraints at the database level to enforce uniqueness of specific fields or combinations of fields. The database guarantees atomicity and prevents duplicates even under concurrent requests.

Listing 5-21. Model with database-level unique constraint

```
class Book(models.Model):
    title = models.CharField(max_length=100)
    author = models.CharField(max_length=100)

    class Meta:
        constraints = [
            models.UniqueConstraint(fields=['title', 'author'],
            name='unique_title_author')
        ]
```

Now, if two concurrent inserts happen, the database allows only one and rejects the other with a duplicate key violation error. Application-level checks are not safe in concurrent environments because they are not atomic. Database-level unique constraints ensure strong data integrity by preventing duplicates at the source (Refer Listing 5-21). They eliminate race conditions, enforce business rules consistently, and make the system reliable even under heavy load.

Let's move to the next issue which is not using `values` or `values_list`.

Not Using values or values_list

Fetching full model instances when only a few fields are needed results in unnecessary memory usage and slower performance. By default, Django returns complete model objects, which include all fields and model overhead. This is inefficient when the application only needs specific columns, such as titles or IDs.

Consider this example.

Listing 5-22. Listing all the book titles

```
books = Book.objects.all()
for book in books:
    print(book.title)
```

In Listing 5-22, Django retrieves all fields (id, title, author, description, etc.) even though only the title field is being used. This increases data transfer between the database and application, especially when the table contains large text fields or many columns.

This can be fixed by using `values` or `values_list` when only specific fields are required. This limits the selected columns and improves performance.

Let us check using `values` (Refer Listing 5-23).

Listing 5-23. Using values

```
books = Book.objects.values('title')

for book in books:
    print(book['title'])
```

Let us check using `values_list` (Refer Listing 5-24).

Listing 5-24. Using values_list

```
books = Book.objects.values_list('title', flat=True)

for title in books:
    print(title)
```

Difference Between values and values_list

`values` return dictionaries.

`values_list` returns tuples. When flat=True is used with a single field, it returns a simple list of values.

Using `values` and `values_list` reduces memory usage, decreases query payload size, and improves performance by selecting only required columns. This is especially important for large datasets, API responses, reporting queries, and background processing tasks.

Let us move to the next one which is not using `Meta` options effectively.

Not Using Meta Options Effectively

Failing to configure Meta options such as `db_table`, `indexes`, and `ordering` leads to suboptimal performance and reduced control over the database structure. Without explicitly defining these options, Django applies defaults that may not align with your database naming conventions, indexing strategy, or query optimization needs. This can result in slower queries and less maintainable schemas in large applications.

Consider the example.

Listing 5-25. Sample Book model

```
class Book(models.Model):
    title = models.CharField(max_length=100)
    author = models.CharField(max_length=100)
```

In this case, Django automatically creates a table name like **appname_book**, does not add custom indexes, and does not define default ordering (Refer Listing 5-25). If we frequently order by title, the database must sort results each time the query runs.

Example query: `books = Book.objects.all().order_by('title')`

If the title field is not indexed, the database performs sorting at runtime, which becomes expensive on large datasets.

Define appropriate Meta options to optimize schema design and query performance.

Listing 5-26. Book model with proper Meta settings

```
class Book(models.Model):
    title = models.CharField(max_length=100)
    author = models.CharField(max_length=100)

    class Meta:
        db_table = 'library_book'  # Custom table name
        indexes = [
            models.Index(fields=['title']),
        ]
        ordering = ['title']
```

Now, whenever we fetch records:

```
books = Book.objects.all()
```

Since the title field is indexed and used for default ordering, the database can efficiently retrieve sorted records.

`Meta` options provide fine-grained control over how Django maps models to the database (Refer Listing 5-26). Using `db_table` ensures consistent naming conventions; `indexes` improve the query performance for frequently filtered or ordered fields, and `ordering` defines predictable default sorting. Proper configuration leads to better maintainability, optimized queries, and improved scalability in production systems.

Not Using Raw SQL for Complex Queries

Relying entirely on the Django ORM for every type of query can lead to inefficient or overly complex code when dealing with advanced database operations. While the ORM is powerful and expressive, certain complex queries such as window functions, CTEs (common table expressions), heavy aggregations, or database-specific optimizations may be clearer and more efficient when written using raw SQL. Ignoring raw SQL in such scenarios can result in suboptimal performance or unreadable ORM expressions.

Using `raw()` enables you to perform more complex queries directly on the database, providing flexibility beyond Django ORM's capabilities.

Let us move to the next one which is not using `transaction` for related updates.

Not Using Transactions for Related Updates

When updating multiple related records, failing to use `transaction` can result in inconsistent data if an error occurs midway. Database operations are committed immediately by default. If one operation succeeds and a later operation fails, the database remains in a partially updated state. For example, updating a **Book** and its related **StockLog** entry separately without wrapping them in a `transaction` may leave the stock count reduced, but no corresponding log entry recorded.

Consider the example.

Listing 5-27. Not using transaction

```
book.stock_count -= 1
book.save()
stock_log.save()  # Error here causes mismatch between book and log
```

If `book.save()` succeeds but `stock_log.save()` raises an exception (e.g., validation error or database error), the stock count is already reduced. The log entry is not created. Now the system shows reduced stock without audit history. This leads to data inconsistency and accounting issues (Refer Listing 5-27).

Wrap related updates inside a `transaction` to ensure atomicity. Django provides `transaction.atomic` to group multiple operations into a single database transaction.

Listing 5-28. Using transaction

```
from django.db import transaction

with transaction.atomic():
    book.stock_count -= 1
    book.save()
    stock_log.save()
```

In this case, none of the changes are committed.

`transaction.atomic` ensures atomicity, meaning either all operations inside the block succeed or none are committed. This prevents partial updates, eliminates data mismatches, and maintains strong data integrity. Transactions are especially critical in financial operations, inventory systems, order processing, and any workflow where multiple related records must stay consistent (Refer Listing 5-28).

Let us move to the next one which is ignoring a bulk operation's limitations.

Ignoring Bulk Operation's Limitations

Using `bulk_create` or `bulk_update` improves performance by reducing the number of database queries. However, these bulk operations bypass certain Django model behaviors. Specifically:

- Signals like `pre_save` and `post_save` are not triggered.
- Custom validation inside `save` will be skipped.

If your application depends on overridden `save` logic or signals for additional processing (e.g., updating related fields, sending notifications, maintaining audit logs), using bulk operations can silently break business logic.

Consider the scenario if your model has custom logic.

Listing 5-29. Book model with custom save logic

```
from django.db import transaction
class Book(models.Model):
    title = models.CharField(max_length=100)

    def save(self, *args, **kwargs):
        self.title = self.title.upper()
        super().save(*args, **kwargs)
```

In Listing 5-29, we have customized the `save` method. We can convert the title to uppercase before saving. Using `bulk_create` will not convert titles to uppercase because `save` is skipped.

Use bulk operations only when you do not rely on custom `save` methods, signals, or additional side effects. They are ideal for large data imports, background jobs, or initial data loading where performance is critical and no per-object logic is required.

If your application depends on signals or custom logic, create a helper function that performs the required processing explicitly before calling bulk operations.

Listing 5-30. Bulk operation with helper function

```
def prepare_books(book_list):
    for book in book_list:
        book.title = book.title.upper()
    return book_list

books = prepare_books([
    Book(title="Book 1"),
    Book(title="Book 2"),
])

Book.objects.bulk_create(books)
```

In Listing 5-30 we can add a new helper function which converts the title to uppercase and then calls the bulk operation.

Bulk operations significantly improve performance by minimizing database round trips. However, they intentionally bypass model-level hooks and signals for efficiency. Understanding these limitations prevents silent business logic failures and ensures that performance optimizations do not compromise application correctness.

Let us move to another one which is forgetting QuerySet's laziness.

Forgetting QuerySet's Laziness

QuerySets in Django are lazy, meaning they do not hit the database immediately when defined. The query is only executed when the QuerySet is evaluated (e.g., during iteration, conversion to list, slicing, or calling methods like `len`, `bool`, etc.).

This behavior can cause unexpected results if the underlying data changes between the time the QuerySet is defined and when it is evaluated.

Consider the example.

Listing 5-31. QuerySet laziness example

```
books = Book.objects.filter(published=True)
# Some books are unpublished here
list(books)  # Results may differ from when books was first assigned
```

When books are first assigned, no SQL is executed (Refer Listing 5-31). If another process updates the database (e.g., sets `published=True` on some records) before `list(books)` runs, the result will reflect the updated state not the state at the time of assignment.

The SQL runs only when list(books) is called. This can lead to

- Inconsistent business logic
- Unexpected differences in counts
- Confusing debugging situations

If you need a stable snapshot of the data for the remainder of your logic, force evaluation immediately which means

```
books = list(Book.objects.filter(published=True))
```

The result is stored in memory as a Python list, and further database changes will not affect it.

Understanding QuerySet laziness helps prevent subtle bugs. Forcing evaluation when a consistent snapshot is required ensures predictable behavior in long-running operations, background tasks, and complex business workflows. Laziness is powerful for performance optimization, but it must be handled carefully to avoid unintended side effects.

Let us move to the next one which is not using F expressions for atomic updates.

Not Using F() Expressions for Atomic Updates

Updating numeric fields in Python instead of using database-level operations can cause race conditions in concurrent environments. When you read a value, modify it in Python, and then save it, another request may modify the same record in between. This leads to lost updates and inconsistent data (Refer Listing 5-32).

Consider the example.

Listing 5-32. Decrement stock count

```
book = Book.objects.get(id=1)
book.stock_count = book.stock_count - 1
book.save()
```

Problem Scenario (Race Condition):

Initial stock_count = 10

Request A reads stock_count → 10

Request B reads stock_count → 10

Request A updates → 9

Request B updates → 9

The final value becomes 9 instead of 8. One decrement is lost.

Use `F` expressions to perform updates directly at the database level. The calculation happens inside the SQL query, making it atomic.

Listing 5-33. Using atomic update

```
from django.db.models import F
Book.objects.filter(id=1).update(stock_count=F('stock_count') - 1)
```

Here in Listing 5-33, the database handles the decrement operation internally. Even if multiple requests run simultaneously, each update correctly reduces the value.

`F` expressions allow computations to happen directly in the database, preventing race conditions and lost updates. They ensure atomic operations, improve performance by avoiding unnecessary reads, and are essential in high-concurrency scenarios such as inventory management, counters, financial balances, and analytics tracking.

Let us move to the next one which is not using `only` or `defer`.

Not Using only or defer for Large Models

By default, Django fetches all fields of a model when querying the database. If your model contains large fields (such as `TextField`, `JSONField`, or large blobs) and you do not actually need them, fetching everything increases memory usage and slows down performance.

This becomes inefficient, especially in a list of views, API responses, reporting queries, or background jobs where only a few fields are required.

Listing 5-34. Sample Book model

```
class Book(models.Model):
    title = models.CharField(max_length=100)
    author = models.CharField(max_length=100)
    description = models.TextField()
    metadata = models.JSONField()
```

Listing 5-35. Printing book titles

```
books = Book.objects.all()
for book in books:
    print(book.title)
```

Even though only the title is used, the database fetches description and metadata, which may contain large data (Refer Listing 5-35 and for the model used Refer Listing 5-34).

Using `only`

Fetch only the fields you actually need (Refer Listing 5-36).

Listing 5-36. Fetching only the title

```
books = Book.objects.only('title').all()
for book in books:
    print(book.title)
```

Other fields are deferred and will be fetched only if accessed later.

Using `defer`

Exclude specific heavy fields.

Listing 5-37. defer heavy fields

```
books = Book.objects.defer('description', 'metadata')
```

Here, description and metadata are not loaded initially (Refer Listing 5-37).

Warning

If you later access a deferred field: `print(book.description)`

Django will execute an additional query for that specific row: `SELECT description FROM book WHERE id = 1;`.

So, overusing `only` or `defer` can reintroduce N+1 query problems.

Using `only` and `defer` reduces data transfer, lowers memory usage, and improves performance when dealing with large models or large datasets. They are especially useful in read-heavy systems and API endpoints.

However, they should be used carefully to avoid triggering additional queries when accessing deferred fields later.

Let us move to the next one which is not monitoring ORM.

Not Monitoring ORM Performance

Without monitoring ORM queries, inefficient database operations can go unnoticed. Problems such as N+1 queries, missing indexes, unnecessary joins, or excessive query counts may silently degrade performance. Over time, this leads to slow API responses, high database load, and scalability issues in production systems.

Often, developers assume the ORM is generating optimal SQL, but without inspection, hidden inefficiencies remain undetected.

Listing 5-38. Code with N+1 issues

```
books = Book.objects.all()
for book in books:
    print(book.title, book.genres.all())
```

This may generate multiple queries (N+1 problem), but without monitoring, you might not realize how many queries are actually executed (Refer Listing 5-38).

Use monitoring and debugging tools during development and staging environments. The first one is using django-debug-toolbar.

Use django-debug-toolbar

The **django-debug-toolbar** provides visual inspection of SQL queries, execution time, number of queries, duplicate queries, and stack traces directly in the browser.

It helps you see

- Total query count
- Execution time per query
- Repeated queries
- Missing indexes

This is extremely useful for development.

The next one is using `connection.queries` for programmatic logging.

Use connection.queries

Django allows you to inspect executed queries manually.

Listing 5-39. Listing queries

```
from django.db import connection
print(connection.queries)
```

Output

```
[
    {
        'sql': 'SELECT id, title FROM book;',
        'time': '0.002'
    }
]
```

You can use these inside views, tests, or debugging sessions to track query counts (Refer Listing 5-39).

Note `connection.queries` works only when `DEBUG=True`.

Let us move to the next one which is using a use logger for logging queries.

Use Logger

We can use Django's default logger logging the database queries. This ensures performance issues are detected before they affect users. This can be enabled by adding logger settings in settings.py like Listing 5-40.

Listing 5-40. Logging queries

```
LOGGING = {
    "version": 1,
    "disable_existing_loggers": False,
    "handlers": {
        "console": {
            "class": "logging.StreamHandler",
        },
    },
    "loggers": {
        "django.db.backends": {
            "handlers": ["console"],
            "level": "DEBUG",
        },
    },
}
```

Monitoring ORM performance helps identify and fix slow or excessive queries early in development. It prevents scalability issues, reduces database load, and ensures efficient query patterns.

Without monitoring, performance problems remain hidden until they become critical in production.

Let's move to the next problem which is not using the <fk_field>_id attribute.

Not Using the <fk_field>_id Attribute

When you only need the ID of a related object, accessing it through the related model (e.g., `book.author.id`) can cause Django to load the related object from the database. If the related object was not already fetched using `select_related`, this results in an additional query for each row creating an N+1 query problem.

Django automatically creates a **<foreignkey_field>_id** attribute that stores the raw foreign key value directly on the model. Ignoring this attribute can lead to unnecessary database hits.

Listing 5-41. Accessing author ids the wrong way

```
for book in Book.objects.all():
    print(book.author.id)
```

In Listing 5-41, Django first fetches books. Then, for each book, it queries the author's table to retrieve the related object just to access its id. Here there is no `select_related`, so it will cause an N+1 query problem. Use the autogenerated <fk_field>_id attribute, which directly accesses the foreign key column on the current model without loading the related object.

Listing 5-42. Accessing auto <fk>_id field

```
for book in Book.objects.all():
    print(book.author_id)
```

No additional queries are executed because **author_id** is already part of the book table (Refer Listing 5-42). If you need only the id of the related field, use this method because there is no join in table.

When you actually need related fields: If you need fields like author.name, then use `select_related` to fetch both models in a single query. Accessing <fk_field>_id avoids unnecessary queries by using the raw foreign key value already stored in the current table. This improves performance, reduces database load, and prevents accidental N+1 query issues.

Let's move to the next one which is not using `exists` for existence check.

Not Using exists() for Existence Checks

Using `count` or `first` when you only need to check whether a record exists wastes database resources. These methods retrieve more information than necessary. `Count` performs a full count of matching rows and `first` fetches an entire row. When the goal is simply to verify existence, this results in unnecessary computation and data transfer.

Let's see how we can check using `count`.

Listing 5-43. Check if book exists using count

```
if Book.objects.filter(title="Django").count() > 0:
    print("Book exists")
```

Generated SQL:

```
SELECT COUNT(*) FROM book WHERE title = 'Django';
```

Here, the database counts all matching rows, even though we only need to know if at least one record exists (Refer Listing 5-43).

Now we can see how we can check using `first`.

Listing 5-44. Check book exists using first

```
if Book.objects.filter(title="Django").first():
    print("Book exists")
```

Generated SQL:

```
SELECT * FROM book WHERE title = 'Django' LIMIT 1;
```

This fetches an entire row, which is unnecessary for a simple existence check (Refer Listing 5-44).

Now we check using exists.

Use `exists` to perform an optimized existence check.

Listing 5-45. Check book exists using exists

```
if Book.objects.filter(title="Django").exists():
    print("Book exists")
```

SQL Equivalent:

```
SELECT (1) AS "a" FROM book WHERE title = 'Django' LIMIT 1;
```

The database stops scanning as soon as it finds the first matching row. exists generates a `SELECT ... LIMIT 1` query, making it significantly more efficient than count or first for simple existence checks. It reduces computation, minimizes data transfer, and improves performance, especially on large tables (Refer Listing 5-45).

Let's move to the next one which is not using `get_or_create` and `update_or_create`.

Not Using get_or_create() and update_or_create()

Manually checking for a record and then creating or updating it can cause race conditions in concurrent environments (Refer Listing 5-46). When two requests execute the same logic at the same time, both may not find the record and both may attempt to create it. This results in duplicate entries or integrity errors.

Let us see the manual checking and creating method.

Listing 5-46. Manually checking and creating

```
book = Book.objects.filter(title="Django").first()
if not book:
    book = Book.objects.create(title="Django")
```

Problem Scenario (Concurrency Issue):

Request A checks → no record found

Request B checks → no record found

Request A creates record

Request B creates record

If no unique constraint exists, duplicate rows are created. If a unique constraint exists, the second insert raises an IntegrityError. Because SELECT and INSERT are separate operations, they are not safe under concurrency.

This can be solved by using `get_or_create`.

Listing 5-47. Using get_or_create

```
book, created = Book.objects.get_or_create(title="Django")
```

Django internally wraps this in a transaction and handles integrity errors properly (Refer Listing 5-47). If another transaction inserts the row at the same time, Django catches the IntegrityError and retrieves the existing record instead. `update_or_create` works the same way; this is used when we need to update the record if it exists, otherwise create a new record.

Important note:

For true safety, a database-level unique constraint must exist on the lookup field (e.g., title). Without a unique constraint, duplicates can still occur.

`get_or_create` and `update_or_create` are designed to handle concurrent inserts safely. They reduce race conditions, simplify code, and ensure atomic behavior when combined with proper database constraints. They are especially useful in high-traffic systems where multiple requests may attempt to create the same record simultaneously.

Let us check the next one which is not using `iterator` for large QuerySets.

Not Using iterator() for Large QuerySets

When iterating over very large QuerySets, Django caches all fetched objects in memory by default. This behavior is useful for reusing the QuerySet later, but it becomes a problem when processing thousands or millions of records. The entire result set stays in memory, increasing RAM usage and potentially causing performance degradation or crashes in long-running tasks.

Listing 5-48. Looping books

```
for book in Book.objects.all():
    process(book)
```

Django fetches rows in batches internally, but it stores all model instances in the QuerySet cache as iteration continues. If the dataset is very large, memory usage keeps growing (Refer Listing 5-48).

This is especially problematic in

- Background jobs
- Data migrations
- Reporting scripts
- Batch processing
- Export tasks

Use `iterator` to disable QuerySet caching and stream results directly from the database. Here it returns a generator object, so memory is used only for the single item.

Listing 5-49. Looping books using iterator

```
for book in Book.objects.iterator():
    process(book)
```

The database query remains the same, but Django does not cache the results in memory (Refer Listing 5-49). Rows are read and processed sequentially.

You can also control batch size using the chunk_size parameter.

Listing 5-50. Looping books using iterator with batch size

```
for book in Book.objects.iterator(chunk_size=1000):
    process(book)
```

This fetches rows in chunks of 1000, reducing memory pressure further.

When using `iterator` (Refer Listing 5-50)

- QuerySet caching is disabled
- You cannot rely on reusing the same QuerySet afterward
- It is ideal for one-pass processing

`iterator` reads results without caching them in the QuerySet, significantly reducing memory usage when processing large datasets. It is essential for scalable batch operations and long-running background tasks where memory efficiency is critical.

Let's move to the next one which is not using database functions.

Not Using Database Functions

Many developers perform filtering, sorting, or transformations in Python instead of using ORM database functions. This causes unnecessary memory usage and slower performance, especially when working with large QuerySets.

Consider the example; we need to sort the book based on title in lowercase.

Listing 5-51. Sorting using python method

```
books = Book.objects.all()

sorted_books = sorted(books, key=lambda b: b.title.lower())
```

In Listing 5-51, `Book.objects.all()` fetches all records from the database. The `sorted` function then runs in Python memory, and `b.title.lower` is executed for every row in Python. This means the entire dataset must be loaded into memory before sorting happens, which is inefficient for large tables.

We have Django database functions for these.

Listing 5-52. Using database function

```
from django.db.models.functions import Lower
books = Book.objects.order_by(Lower('title'))
```

Here, `Lower('title')` tells Django to apply the SQL `LOWER` function on the title column (Refer Listing 5-52). The `order_by` clause sends the sorting instruction directly to the database. As a result, sorting happens inside the database engine, and only the properly ordered results are returned to Django. This reduces memory usage, avoids unnecessary Python-side processing, improves performance, and scales much better for large datasets.

Always prefer ORM database functions such as `Lower`, `Length`, `Coalesce`, and `Extract` instead of Python-side logic whenever possible, so computation is pushed down to the database layer.

Let us move to another example which is not handling time zone-aware queries.

Not Handling Time Zone Aware Queries

Comparing datetime objects without ensuring time zone awareness can produce incorrect results. This commonly happens when developers use Python's `datetime.now` while Django is configured with `USE_TZ=True`. In such cases, Django stores time zone-aware datetimes in the database, but `datetime.now` returns a naive datetime, which can lead to errors or incorrect comparisons.

Listing 5-53. Using datetime

```
from datetime import datetime

books = Book.objects.filter(published_at__lte=datetime.now())
```

In Listing 5-53, `datetime.now` returns a naive datetime object (no time zone information). If your Django project has time zone support enabled, the **published_at** field is time zone aware. Comparing a naive datetime with a time zone-aware datetime can either raise an exception or produce incorrect filtering results.

Django provides a `timezone` module for time zone-aware datetime. Let us check this with an example.

Listing 5-54. Using timezone module

```
from django.utils import timezone

books = Book.objects.filter(published_at__lte=timezone.now())
```

`timezone.now` returns a time zone-aware datetime that matches Django's time zone configuration (Refer Listing 5-54). This ensures consistent comparisons with datetime fields stored in the database. It prevents runtime errors and guarantees correct query results. When `USE_TZ=True`, always use `django.utils.timezone.now` instead of `datetime.now` to avoid subtle bugs and incorrect time-based filtering.

Let us move to the next one which is not handling migration dependencies while working in a team.

Not Handling Migration Dependencies While Working in a Team

When multiple developers work on the same project, migration conflicts can occur either within the same app or across different apps. These issues usually happen because Django determines migration order using the dependency attribute, not just migration file numbers. If dependencies are not defined correctly, Django cannot build a proper migration graph, which leads to conflicts or migration failures.

There are two common types of problems:

- Same-app migration conflicts
- Cross-app dependency issues

Let us check same-app migration conflict.

Same-App Migration Conflict

This happens when two developers create migrations from the same base migration.

Developer A creates: **library/0005_add_published_date.py**

Developer B creates: **library/0005_remove_isbn.py**

Both migrations contain:

```
dependencies = [
    ('library', '0004_auto'),
]
```

Now Django sees two branches starting from 0004:

```
0004
├── 0005_add_published_date
└── 0005_remove_isbn
```

Django does not know which one should run first. This results in a migration conflict error.

This can be fixed by running the command:

```
python manage.py makemigrations --merge
```

Django generates a merge migration like:

0006_merge_20260220_1520.py

Inside it:

```
dependencies = [
    ('library', '0005_add_published_date'),
    ('library', '0005_remove_isbn'),
]
```

This merges both branches into a single linear path.

Now we can check cross-app dependency issues.

Cross-App Dependency Issues

This occurs when one app depends on another app model, but the dependency is not declared properly.

Let's walk through a real-world scenario step by step, so the problem is very clear.

Consider the project structure; you have two apps:

- Library (For Initial stage Refer Listing 5-55)
- Sales (For Initial stage Refer Listing 5-56)

Consider the initial stage.

Listing 5-55. Library initial stage

```
class Book(models.Model):
    title = models.CharField(max_length=100)
```

Listing 5-56. Sales initial stage

```
class Sale(models.Model):
    quantity = models.IntegerField()
```

Now Developer A changes the library app. Developer A adds a new field to book.

Listing 5-57. Added sku to book

```
class Book(models.Model):
    title = models.CharField(max_length=100)
    sku = models.CharField(max_length=50, unique=True)
```

This generates:

library/0005_add_sku.py

Inside:

```
dependencies = [
    ('library', '0004_auto'),
]
```

This migration creates a new sku column (Refer Listing 5-57).

Then Developer B changes sales. At the same time, Developer B modifies sale to reference book by SKU.

Listing 5-58. Updated the sales model

```
class Sale(models.Model):
    book = models.ForeignKey('library.Book', to_field='sku', on_
    delete=models.CASCADE)
    quantity = models.IntegerField()
```

This generates:

sales/0003_update_sale_fk.py

But the migration contains:

```
dependencies = [
    ('sales', '0002_previous'),
]
```

Notice: There is NO dependency on library.0005_add_sku.

When running:

```
python manage.py migrate
```

Django builds the migration graph. Because **sales.0003_update_sale_fk** does not depend on **library.0005_add_sku**, Django may attempt:

sales.0003_update_sale_fk

BEFORE

library.0005_add_sku

Now the problem: The sales migration tries to create a foreign key referencing **library_book.sku**. But the sku column does not exist yet (Refer Listing 5-58).

Resulting error: **django.db.utils.ProgrammingError: column library_book.sku does not exist**

Django does NOT execute migrations strictly app by app. It builds a global directed graph using dependencies.

If a migration does not explicitly declare a dependency, Django assumes it is independent.

So even though logically sales depend on library, Django doesn't know that unless you tell it.

Correct fix:

Update sales/0003_update_sale_fk.py:

```
dependencies = [
    ('sales', '0002_previous'),
    ('library', '0005_add_sku'),
]
```

Now the migration graph becomes:

```
library.0005_add_sku
        ↓
sales.0003_update_sale_fk
```

Django now guarantees a correct order: Add sku column. Then create a foreign key referencing it. No errors.

Proper dependency management prevents migration conflicts, ensuring team workflows remain smooth, and the database stays consistent.

Let us move to another migration-related issue which is not using `get_model` in data migrations.

Not Using get_model() in Data Migrations

In data migrations, developers sometimes directly import models from the app. This is incorrect and can break migrations in the future when the model changes.

A migration must use the historical version of the model at that point in time, not the current version of the model in your codebase.

Consider the example; we are converting the title to uppercase using a data migration.

Listing 5-59. Directly importing model in data migration (wrong approach)

```
from myapp.models import Book

def update_title(apps, schema_editor):
    for book in Book.objects.all():
        book.title = book.title.upper()
        book.save()
```

In Listing 5-59, we are importing the model directly into the code. The issue with this approach is when this migration runs months later

- The Book model may have changed
- Fields may have been renamed or removed
- New required fields may have been added

This can cause migration failures such as

- AttributeError
- Field does not exist
- IntegrityError

Because the imported model reflects the latest code, not the model state at the time of the migration, Django provides a `get_model` function to get the model in that point of time.

Consider the example.

Listing 5-60. Using get_model in data migration

```
def update_title (apps, schema_editor):
    Book = apps.get_model('myapp', 'Book')

    for book in Book.objects.all():
        book.title = book.title.upper()
        book.save()
```

In Listing 5-60 `get_model` retrieves the historical version of the model as defined at that specific migration point. The first argument to the function is the **app name** and the second argument is the **model's name.** Once that is properly given, we will get the model at that point of time. This ensures

- The field structure matches the migration state
- Migration remains stable even if models change later
- Future developers can run migrations safely

Migrations represent historical database states. Direct model imports reference the current model definition, which may not match the schema at migration time. Using `get_model` ensures data migrations remain consistent, future-proof, and safe across schema changes.

Let's move to the next one which is using `IntegerField` instead of `ForeignKey`.

Using IntegerField Instead of ForeignKey

Storing related object IDs in an `IntegerField` instead of using a proper `ForeignKey` breaks ORM features and removes database-level referential integrity. While it may look simpler, it causes long-term maintainability and consistency problems.

Consider the model like this.

Listing 5-61. Wrong model implementation

```
class Book(models.Model):
    title = models.CharField(max_length=100)
    author_id = models.IntegerField()
```

In Listing 5-61, **author_id** is just a number. Django does not know if this field represents a relationship to the Author model.

This leads to several problems:

- No automatic JOIN support.
- Cannot use `select_related`.
- Cannot use reverse relationships.
- No database-level foreign key constraint.
- Invalid author IDs can be stored.
- Manual queries are required to fetch related data.

Listing 5-62. Manual lookup

```
author = Author.objects.get(id=book.author_id)
```

This can easily create N+1 query problems and makes the code harder to maintain (Refer Listing 5-62).

The correct approach is use `ForeignKey`.

Listing 5-63. Correct model definition

```
class Book(models.Model):
    title = models.CharField(max_length=100)
    author = models.ForeignKey(Author, on_delete=models.CASCADE)
```

In Listing 5-63, Django understands that **Book** is related to **Author**.

Behind the scenes

- A foreign key column author_id is still created in the database
- A proper foreign key constraint is added
- ORM relationship features become available

You can now do `Book.objects.select_related('author')` and access `book.author.name`.

Django automatically performs optimized JOIN queries.

Using `ForeignKey` enables ORM-level joins like `select_related` and `prefetch_related`, maintains referential integrity at the database level, prevents accidental invalid IDs, and significantly improves readability and maintainability of the codebase. Storing relationships as plain integers removes all these benefits and shifts responsibility from the database and ORM to manual application logic, which increases the risk of bugs.

Let's move to the next one which is not using pagination for large QuerySets.

Not Using Pagination for Large QuerySets

Passing unfiltered or very large QuerySets directly to templates can cause slow page rendering and high memory usage. When you load all records at once, the database returns the entire dataset, and Django must build model instances for every row. This becomes a serious performance issue as the table grows.

Consider this example.

Listing 5-64. Loading entire books

```
def book_list(request):
    books = Book.objects.all()
    return render(request, "books.html", {"books": books})
```

In Listing 5-64 `Book.objects.all()` fetches all rows from the database. If there are thousands (or millions) of records

- Large amount of data is transferred from the database
- High memory usage on the application server
- Slow template rendering
- Slow page load time for users
- This approach does not scale

Django provides paginator for solving this issue. Consider the example below.

Listing 5-65. Using paginator

```
from django.core.paginator import Paginator
def book_list(request):
    book_list = Book.objects.all()
    paginator = Paginator(book_list, 10)
```

```
    page = request.GET.get('page')
    books = paginator.get_page(page)
    return render(request, "books.html", {"books": books})
```

Paginator splits the QuerySet into smaller chunks (Refer Listing 5-65). Instead of loading all records, Django fetches only the records required for the current page using SQL `LIMIT` and `OFFSET`. The arguments for the paginator are the **QuerySet** for pagination and the **number of objects in a page**.

For example, page 1 generates something like:

```
SELECT * FROM book LIMIT 10 OFFSET 0;
```

Page 2:

```
SELECT * FROM book LIMIT 10 OFFSET 0;
```

Only 10 records are loaded at a time, reducing memory usage and improving response time.

Pagination limits the amount of data loaded per request. This reduces memory consumption, improves rendering performance, and makes the application scalable as data grows. Never send very large QuerySets directly to templates. Always paginate or limit results to ensure predictable performance and better user experience.

Let us move to the next one which is wrong usage of `on_delete`.

Wrong Usage of on_delete

Using the wrong `on_delete` behavior in our code can cause unintended data loss or broken references. Many developers use `models.CASCADE` by default without thinking about business impact. The `on_delete` option controls what happens to related records when the parent object is deleted, and choosing the wrong strategy can corrupt data relationships.

Consider the example.

Listing 5-66. Risky on_delete

```
class Order(models.Model):
    customer = models.ForeignKey(Customer, on_delete=models.CASCADE)
```

In Listing 5-66 we used `CASCADE`; if a customer is deleted, all related order records are automatically deleted by the database.

This may be dangerous in systems like

- Accounting systems
- Inventory systems
- Audit logs
- Financial records

Deleting one parent's record could unintentionally remove critical historical data.

Another common mistake is using `models.SET_NULL` without allowing null values.

Listing 5-67. Set null without nullable fields

```
class Order(models.Model):
    customer = models.ForeignKey(Customer, on_delete=models.SET_NULL)
```

In Listing 5-67, we are using `models.SET_NULL` so Django will try to set a null value when we delete the customer. But `null=True` is not added; this will raise an error because Django cannot set the field to `NULL`.

Listing 5-68. Corrected version

```
class Order(models.Model):
    customer = models.ForeignKey(Customer, on_delete=models.SET_NULL,
    null=True)
```

Here in Listing 5-68 we have added `null=True`. If we delete the customer, the null value is set in the order.

Let us see common `on_delete` options and when to use them:

- `CASCADE` → Deletes child records automatically. Use only when child data has no meaning without parent.
- `PROTECT` → Prevents deletion if related objects exist. Good for financial or important relational data.
- `SET_NULL` → Keeps child records but removes relation. Requires null=True.

- SET_DEFAULT → Sets a default value.
- DO_NOTHING → Does nothing at DB level (can cause integrity errors).

Choosing the correct on_delete behavior ensures data integrity and protects business-critical records. Blindly using CASCADE can result in accidental mass deletions, while incorrect configurations can cause runtime errors or broken references. on_delete is not just a technical option, it represents business logic. Always choose it based on how your data should behave when the parent record is removed, not just for convenience.

Let us move to another example which is overusing signals instead of overriding the save method.

Overusing Signals Instead of Overriding the Save Method

A common mistake in Django projects is using signals for simple, model-specific logic. While signals are powerful, they execute behind the scenes and can make code harder to trace, debug, and maintain. When logic strictly belongs to a single model, overriding the model's save method is often clearer and more predictable.

Consider the example.

Listing 5-69. Using a signal for a simple model logic

```
from django.db.models.signals import pre_save
from django.dispatch import receiver
from django.utils.text import slugify
from .models import Book

@receiver(pre_save, sender=Book)
def update_slug(sender, instance, **kwargs):
    instance.slug = slugify(instance.title)
```

In Listing 5-69, the slug is generated using a pre_save signal. Although this works, the logic is separated from the model. When someone reads the **Book** model, they won't immediately see that the slug is autogenerated. They must search the project to find the connected signal. In large codebases, this creates hidden behavior and increases cognitive load.

A better approach for model-specific logic is to override the save method.

Listing 5-70. Better approach for model-specific logic

```
from django.utils.text import slugify

class Book(models.Model):
    title = models.CharField(max_length=100)
    slug = models.SlugField()

    def save(self, *args, **kwargs):
        self.slug = slugify(self.title)
        super().save(*args, **kwargs)
```

In Listing 5-70, by overriding save, the slug generation is clearly defined inside the model. Anyone reading the model immediately understands the behavior. The logic is encapsulated, predictable, and easier to maintain.

Signals are useful when you need to react to events across models or apps, such as sending notifications, updating related models, logging changes, or triggering background tasks. In these cases, decoupling logic from the model makes sense.

Overriding save keeps logic explicit and easier to trace. Overusing signals can introduce hidden side effects and make debugging difficult. Choosing the right approach improves the readability, maintainability, and long-term stability of the codebase.

Let's move to the next one which is not handling database connection for long-running tasks.

Not Handling Database Connection for Long-Running Tasks

A common mistake in Django projects is not managing database connections properly in long-running processes such as Celery workers, background jobs, management commands, or scheduled scripts. These processes may keep database connections open for a long time. If the database server closes an idle connection, the task may later fail with errors like

- Server closed the connection unexpectedly
- Connection already closed
- MySQL server has gone away

This typically happens because the connection becomes stale while the process is still running.

Imagine a long-running background task.

Listing 5-71. Example task

```
def long_running_task():
    # Some heavy processing
    for item in large_dataset:
        process(item)
```

If this task runs for a long time or stays idle between operations, the database connection may expire. When the task tries to execute a query again, it may crash due to a closed connection (Refer Listing 5-71).

The solution for this kind of situation is explicitly closing old or unusable connections before starting the task.

Listing 5-72. Closing the connection manually

```
from django.db import close_old_connections
def long_running_task():
    close_old_connections()
    # Task logic here
```

In Listing 5-72, `close_old_connections` checks for unusable or expired database connections and closes them safely. Django will automatically open a fresh connection when the next query runs. This prevents errors caused by stale connections.

In Celery tasks, this is especially important when

- Workers stay alive for a long time
- Tasks are CPU-heavy
- There are long idle gaps between database queries

Long-running processes do not follow the typical request-response lifecycle where Django automatically manages connections. Manually handling old connections ensures they remain valid and prevents unexpected connection drop errors. For background jobs, Celery tasks, or long-running scripts, always ensure stale database connections are properly handled. Use `close_old_connections` to avoid connection-related crashes in production environments.

Let's move to the next one which is not using `select_for_update` in concurrent environments.

Not Using select_for_update in Concurrency

In concurrent environments, updating the same database row from multiple requests without proper locking can cause race conditions. This usually happens when two transactions read the same value, modify it independently, and then save it. Because both transactions started with the same original value, the final result becomes incorrect.

Consider a simple stock deduction example.

Listing 5-73. Simple stock deduction

```
book = Book.objects.get(id=1)
book.stock_count -= 1
book.save()
```

If stock_count is 1 and two users try to purchase at the same time, both requests may read the value as 1 before either of them saves. Each request subtracts 1 and saves 0. The system has now allowed two purchases even though only one item was available. This is a classic race condition caused by the absence of row-level locking (Refer Listing 5-73).

This can be fixed by using `select_for_update` inside a transaction. Let us check with an example.

Listing 5-74. Using select_for_update

```
from django.db import transaction
with transaction.atomic():
    book = Book.objects.select_for_update().get(id=1)
    book.stock_count -= 1
    book.save()
```

In Listing 5-74, `transaction.atomic` starts a database transaction. The `select_for_update` call tells the database to lock the selected row until the transaction finishes. When the first request selects the row, the database places a row-level lock on it. If a second request tries to select the same row with `select_for_update`, it must wait until the first transaction commits or rolls back.

This ensures that the second request reads the updated stock value instead of the stale one. The operations become sequential instead of overlapping, which prevents incorrect updates.

It is important to understand that `select_for_update` works only inside a transaction. Without `transaction.atomic`, the lock will not behave as expected. Also, this feature relies on database-level row locking support, such as PostgreSQL or MySQL with InnoDB.

`select_for_update` enforces row-level locking during a transaction, preventing concurrent transactions from modifying the same row simultaneously. This guarantees data consistency in situations involving counters, balances, stock management, or any shared mutable data.

When working in high-concurrency systems, proper locking is essential. Without it, even simple updates can lead to subtle and dangerous data corruption.

Let us move to the next one which is not handling `get`.

Not Handling get() Properly

A common mistake is using `get` without handling the possible exceptions it raises. The `get` method expects exactly one record. If no record exists, Django raises `DoesNotExist`. If more than one record matches the query, it raises `MultipleObjectsReturned`. If these exceptions are not handled, your application can crash at runtime.

Consider the example.

Listing 5-75. Problematic get

```
book = Book.objects.get(title="Django")
```

In Listing 5-75, we assume exactly one book with the title "**Django**" exists. If no such book exists, Django raises `Book.DoesNotExist`. If multiple books share that title, Django raises `Book.MultipleObjectsReturned`. In both cases, an unhandled exception will break the request.

Let us see what the safer approach is for using get.

Listing 5-76. Wrapping get in a try/except block

```
try:
    book = Book.objects.get(title="Django")
except Book.DoesNotExist:
    book = None
except Book.MultipleObjectsReturned:
    book = Book.objects.filter(title="Django").first()
```

In Listing 5-76, missing or duplicate records are handled gracefully. If the record does not exist, the book becomes None. If multiple records exist, the code safely retrieves the first one instead of crashing.

There is an alternative way for the same code using filter and first.

Listing 5-77. Using filter and first

```
book = Book.objects.filter(title="Django").first()
```

In Listing 5-77, if no matching record exists, the book will be None. If multiple records exist, only the first one is returned. No exceptions are raised. However, this approach should be used only when it is acceptable to receive the first matching record and when uniqueness is not strictly required.

Using `get` without handling exceptions can cause unexpected crashes. Proper handling ensures your application behaves predictably when records are missing or duplicated. Use `get` only when you are certain that exactly one record must exist, typically when querying a unique field. If uniqueness is not guaranteed, `filter` and `first` is often a safer choice.

Let us move to another one which is misusing cast for incompatible fields.

Misusing Cast for Incompatible Fields

A common mistake is forcefully casting a field to an incompatible type using `Cast` without ensuring the underlying data supports that conversion. This can cause runtime database errors and break queries in production.

`Cast` is powerful, but it does not magically fix bad data. If the database cannot convert the value safely, the query will fail.

Consider the below model where price is stored as a `CharField`, and some rows contain non-numeric values (Refer Listing 5-78).

Listing 5-78. Wrong table implementation

```
class Product(models.Model):
    price = models.CharField(max_length=20)
```

Now a developer writes cast like this.

Listing 5-79. Casting price to integer

```
from django.db.models import IntegerField
from django.db.models.functions import Cast

Product.objects.annotate(
    price_int=Cast('price', IntegerField())
).filter(price_int__gt=100)
```

In Listing 5-79, we can convert the price from `CharField` to `IntegerField`. It will work if all the values are stringified numbers. If any row contains values like "**N/A,**" "**unknown,**" or "" (**empty string**), the database will raise an error such as invalid input syntax for type integer. The entire query fails because the cast is not valid for all rows.

Let us see another one casting a `DateTimeField` to `IntegerField`.

Listing 5-80. Casting a DateTimeField to IntegerField

```
Cast('created_at', IntegerField())
```

This will fail because a datetime cannot be directly converted to an integer without proper transformation (Refer Listing 5-80).

Before casting, ensure

- The data is clean and compatible
- You filter out invalid rows
- The target type logically matches the source type

For the product example we can do cleaning like this.

Listing 5-81. Cleaning product data before casting

```
from django.db.models import IntegerField
Product.objects.exclude(price__regex=r'[^0-9]').annotate(
    price_int=Cast('price', IntegerField())
).filter(price_int__gt=100)
```

In Listing 5-81, we exclude all the products with non-number as price. But a better approach is to fix the schema and store numeric data in numeric fields like `IntegerField` or `DecimalField` instead of `CharField`.

Casting incompatible types can cause database-level errors, break API responses, and crash background tasks. Unlike Python, database engines enforce strict type rules. Improper casting results in immediate query failure. `Cast` should be used carefully and only when the data is guaranteed to be compatible. Do not use casting as a shortcut to fix poor schema design. Store data in the correct field type from the beginning to avoid unsafe conversions.

Let's move to the next one which is hardcoding database credentials in code.

Hardcoding Database Credentials Directly in settings.py

A common mistake in Django projects is defining database credentials directly inside **settings.py**. This includes hardcoding values such as database name, username, password, host, and port. While this may work in development, it creates serious security and deployment risks in real-world environments.

Listing 5-82. Hardcoding database settings in code

```
DATABASES = {
    'default': {
        'ENGINE': 'django.db.backends.postgresql',
        'NAME': 'djangoorm',
        'USER': 'postgres',
        'PASSWORD': 'supersecretpassword',
```

```
        'HOST': 'localhost',
        'PORT': '5432'
    }
}
```

In Listing 5-82, we have written the database settings directly in the code. Problems with this approach are

- Credentials are exposed in version control
- Rotating passwords requires code changes
- Different environments (development, staging, production) need different credentials
- Risk of leaking production secrets if the repository becomes public
- Hardcoding sensitive values violates security best practices

The recommended approach is to use environment variables. Instead of storing secrets in settings.py, load them from environment variables (Refer Listing 5-83).

Now our settings look like this.

Listing 5-83. Loading database settings from ENV

```
import os

DATABASES = {
    "default": {
        "ENGINE": "django.db.backends.postgresql",
        "NAME": os.environ.get("DB_NAME"),
        "USER": os.environ.get("DB_USER"),
        "PASSWORD": os.environ.get("DB_PASSWORD"),
        "HOST": os.environ.get("DB_HOST", "localhost"),
        "PORT": os.environ.get("DB_PORT", "5432"),
    }
}
```

Now the credentials are configured outside the codebase like this.

Listing 5-84. Exporting environment variables

```
export DB_NAME=djangoorm
export DB_USER=postgres
export DB_PASSWORD=supersecretpassword
```

You can also use tools like

- .env files (with python-dotenv)
- Docker environment variables
- CI/CD secret managers
- Cloud secret managers (AWS, GCP, etc.)

Separating configuration from code improves security, flexibility, and maintainability (Refer Listing 5-84).

Environment-based configuration allows

- Safe secret management
- Easy credential rotation
- Different configurations per environment
- Secure deployments

Never hardcode database credentials directly in code. Always use environment variables or a secure configuration management system to protect sensitive data and support multiple deployment environments.

Let's move to the next one which is not being aware of the order of `filter` and `annotate`.

Not Being Aware of the Order of filter() and annotate()

A common mistake in Django ORM is assuming that the order of `filter` and `annotate` does not matter. In reality, the order directly affects the generated SQL and therefore the result of the query. Since `annotate` introduces grouping and aggregation, applying `filter` before or after it can produce completely different outcomes.

Django builds queries step by step. Each QuerySet operation modifies the query state at that moment.

Let us see an example with a filter before annotating.

Listing 5-85. Filter before annotate

```
import os
from django.db.models import Count

authors = Author.objects.filter(book__rating__gte=4).annotate(
    book_count=Count('book')
)
```

In Listing 5-85, Django first filters books with rating ≥ 4, then counts them. So **book_count** includes only high-rated books.

Now let's see what happens if we change the order.

Listing 5-86. Annotate before filter

```
from django.db.models import Count


authors = Author.objects.annotate(book_count=Count('book')).filter(
    book__rating__gte=4
)
```

In Listing 5-86, Django first counts all books per author. Then it filters authors who have at least one book with rating ≥ 4.The **book_count** now includes all books, not just high-rated ones.

Even though the two queries look similar, they answer different questions.

Another common confusion is filtering on aggregates. If you want authors with more than two books.

Listing 5-87. Filter author with more than two books

```
Author.objects.annotate(book_count=Count('book')).filter(book_count__gt=2)
```

In Listing 5-87, the filter works on the annotated field because it is applied after annotating. If you tried filtering before annotating. This would fail because **book_count** does not exist yet.

`annotate` changes the query by introducing grouping (`GROUP BY`). The filter applied before aggregation affects which rows are included in the grouping. The filter applied after aggregation filters the grouped results.

The order determines whether filtering happens before aggregation (affects what gets counted) or after aggregation (affects the final grouped result).

Understanding this is crucial when working with reports, dashboards, counts, sums, or averages. The order of `filter` and `annotate` is not interchangeable. Always think about whether you want to filter the raw rows before aggregation or filter the aggregated results after grouping.

Let's move to the next one which is not specifying the `batch_size` in bulk operations.

Not Specifying batch_size in Bulk Operations

When using bulk operations such as `bulk_create` or `bulk_update` without specifying a `batch_size`, Django may attempt to send a very large number of records to the database in a single query. This can cause memory spikes, slow execution, or even database errors due to query size limits.

Bulk operations are designed for efficiency, but without batching, they can overwhelm the database when handling large datasets.

Consider the example.

Listing 5-88. Creating 100,000 books without batch_size

```
books = [Book(title=f"Book {i}") for i in range(100000)]
Book.objects.bulk_create(books)
```

In Listing 5-88, Django may try to insert all 100,000 records in one query (depending on database back-end behavior). This can lead to

- Very large SQL statements
- Database packet size limit errors
- Increased memory usage
- Slower execution
- Transaction timeouts

The same issue applies to `bulk_update` without batching; this may generate extremely large SQL queries. The correct approach is specifying `batch_size`.

Listing 5-89. bulk_create with batch_size

```
Book.objects.bulk_create(books, batch_size=1000)
```

In Listing 5-89, we have `batch_size`; by setting `batch_size=1000` Django splits the operation into smaller chunks. Instead of one massive query, it executes multiple smaller queries, each handling 1,000 records.

This reduces

- Memory pressure
- Risk of exceeding database query size limits
- Lock duration
- Risk of timeouts
- It also makes large data imports more stable and predictable.

Databases have practical limits on query size and parameter counts. Sending extremely large bulk operations in a single query can degrade performance or fail entirely. Batching ensures scalability and reliability when processing large datasets. When performing bulk operations on large datasets, always specify a reasonable `batch_size`. Bulk operations are powerful, but without batching, they can become a performance and stability risk in production systems.

Let's move to the next one which is using `len(QuerySet)` instead of the `count` method.

Using len(QuerySet) Instead of count()

A common mistake in Django ORM is using Python's `len` function to count records in a QuerySet instead of using count. Although both may return the same number, they behave very differently in terms of performance.

`len(QuerySet)` forces Django to evaluate the entire QuerySet and load all records into memory. This can be extremely inefficient for large datasets.

Consider the example.

Listing 5-90. Find the len of published books

```
books = Book.objects.filter(is_published=True)
total = len(books)
```

In Listing 5-90, Django executes a full SELECT query and fetches all matching rows. It creates model instances for each row and stores them in memory just to calculate the length. If there are 100,000 records, all 100,000 rows are loaded into memory. The correct approach is to use count.

Listing 5-91. Using count

```
 books = Book.objects.filter(is_published=True)
total = books.count()
```

In Listing 5-91, `count` is used for getting the number of books. The database calculates the count directly without returning all rows. Only a single number is returned to Django. This is much faster and memory efficient.

When len() Is Acceptable

If the QuerySet has already been evaluated and loaded into memory for other reasons, using `len` will not trigger another query.

Consider the example.

Listing 5-92. len is acceptable

```
books = list(Book.objects.filter(is_published=True))
total = len(books)
```

In Listing 5-92, the data is already in memory, so `len` does not cause additional database queries. However, this should not be done solely for counting.

count performs the counting operation at the database level using optimized SQL. `len(QuerySet)` loads full objects into memory before counting them. Using `len(QuerySet)` on large QuerySets can significantly increase memory usage and slow down your application. If you only need the number of records, always use count. Use `len` only when the QuerySet is already evaluated and stored in memory for another purpose.

Let's move to the next one which is confusing between `values`, `values_list`, `only`, and `defer`.

Confusing Between values(), values_list(), only(), and defer()

A common mistake in Django ORM is misunderstanding the difference between `values`, `values_list`, only, and defer. Although all of them deal with selecting specific fields, they behave very differently and return different types of results. Using the wrong one can lead to unexpected behavior, extra queries, or incorrect assumptions about performance.

values() and values_list()

These methods do not return model instances. They return dictionaries or tuples directly from the database.

Let us see how values works.

Listing 5-93. Using values

```
books = Book.objects.values("id", "title")
```

Output

```
[
    {"id": 1, "title": "Django Basics"},
    {"id": 2, "title": "Advanced Django"},
]
```

In Listing 5-93, we are using values; this will return the list of dictionaries. The key in that dictionary is the same as the input passed in that method. Here we are fetching ids and the title only.

Let us see `values_list` working.

Listing 5-94. Using values_list

```
books = Book.objects.values_list("id", "title")
```

Output

```
[
    (1, "Django Basics"),
    (2, "Advanced Django"),
]
```

In Listing 5-94, we are using `values_list`; here the difference is the list of tuples. The position of the item in the tuple is the same as the position in the argument list. If you use flat=True with a single field, then it will return a list.

Listing 5-95. flat=True example

```
ids = Book.objects.values_list("id", flat=True)
```

Output

```
[1, 2]
```

In Listing 5-95, we are using flat=True with a single field so we will get a list of ids. These methods are efficient when

- You only need raw data
- You are building APIs
- You are doing aggregation
- You don't need model methods or relationships

only() and defer()

These methods return full model instances, but limit which fields are initially loaded. Let us check `only` with an example.

Listing 5-96. Using only

```
books = Book.objects.only("title")
```

In Listing 5-96, Django loads only the title column initially. However, it still returns book objects. If you later access any other field like Listing 5-97, Django will execute an additional query to fetch the missing field. This can silently cause N+1 query problems.

Listing 5-97. Accessing other fields

```
book = books.first()
print(book.description)
```

`defer` works opposite of only; it fetches all the fields except what we have given in the list.

Listing 5-98. Defer example

```
books = Book.objects.defer("description")
```

This loads all fields except description (Refer Listing 5-98).

Common Confusion

Developers sometimes expect `only` to behave like `values`.

But

- `values` → returns dictionaries
- `Values_list` → returns tuples
- `only/defer` → return model instances

`only/defer` does not reduce queries if you later access deferred fields. It may even increase the number of queries.

`values` and `values_list` are optimized for raw data retrieval. `only` and `defer` are meant for optimizing model instance loading but require careful usage to avoid hidden queries.

Choosing the wrong method can cause

- Unexpected data structures
- Extra database hits
- Hard-to-debug performance issues

Use `values` or `values_list` when you only need specific fields and do not need model instances. Use `only` or `defer` when you still need model objects but want to limit initially loaded columns, and be careful not to access deferred fields unintentionally.

Let us move to the next one which is not using parameters in raw SQL queries.

Not Using Parameters in Raw SQL Queries

A serious mistake when writing raw SQL in Django is directly interpolating variables into the query string instead of using parameterized queries. This exposes your application to SQL injection attacks and can break queries when special characters are present.

Raw SQL is powerful, but it must be written safely.

Consider the example.

Listing 5-99. Raw SQL without parameters

```
query = f"SELECT * FROM library_book WHERE title = '{title}'"
books = Book.objects.raw(query)
```

In Listing 5-99, we are using the f string. If the title comes from a user input and contains malicious content like **Django' OR 1=1 --**

The final query becomes: `SELECT * FROM library_book WHERE title = 'Django' OR 1=1 --'`

This returns all rows and completely bypasses your intended filtering. This is a classic SQL injection vulnerability. Even without malicious intent, quotes or special characters in user input can break the query.

This can be solved by using parameterized queries.

Consider the example.

Listing 5-100. Using parameterized queries

```
query = "SELECT * FROM library_book WHERE title = %s"
books = Book.objects.raw(query, [title])
```

In Listing 5-100, Django safely passes the parameter to the database driver. The database treats the value strictly as data, not as executable SQL.

The %s is replaced by the item in the list in the correct order. This ensures proper escaping and protection.

Parameterized queries separate SQL structure from data. This prevents

- SQL injection attacks.
- Broken queries due to special characters.
- Security vulnerabilities in production.
- Databases and drivers are optimized to handle parameters safely and efficiently.

Never build raw SQL queries using string formatting, f-strings, or concatenation. Always use parameter placeholders (%s) and pass values separately to ensure security and correctness.

Let us move to another one which is not using `super().save()` while overriding save method.

Overriding save() Without Calling super().save()

A common mistake when customizing model behavior is overriding the save method but forgetting to call `super().save()`. When this happens, Django's built-in save logic is never executed, and the object is not properly saved to the database.

This can silently break

- Database persistence
- Autogenerated fields (like auto_now, auto_now_add)
- Primary key assignment
- Signals (pre_save, post_save)
- Many internal Django mechanisms

Consider the example.

Listing 5-101. Override save without super save

```
class Book(models.Model):
    title = models.CharField(max_length=100)
    slug = models.SlugField()

    def save(self, *args, **kwargs):
        self.slug = self.title.lower().replace(" ", "-")
        # missing the super().save()
```

In Listing 5-101, the slug is generated, but the object is never actually saved to the database because `super().save()` is not called.

The code like in Listing 5-102 will not persist the record.

Listing 5-102. Sample code

```
book = Book(title="Django Guide")
book.save()
```

Let's see the correct implementation for the same.

Listing 5-103. Correct implementation of save

```
class Book(models.Model):
    title = models.CharField(max_length=100)
    slug = models.SlugField()

    def save(self, *args, **kwargs):
        self.slug = self.title.lower().replace(" ", "-")
        super().save(*args, **kwargs)
```

In Listing 5-103, we have called the `super().save()` so Django executes its internal save logic after your custom modifications.

`super().save()` performs essential operations such as

- Executing the actual INSERT or UPDATE query
- Managing transactions
- Updating auto fields
- Triggering signals
- Maintaining ORM consistency

Without it, your override completely bypasses Django's persistence layer.

Important note:

If you need to modify behavior before saving, place your logic before `super().save()` If you need behavior after the object is saved (e.g., using the generated primary key), place your logic after calling `super().save()`.

Let us check with an example.

Listing 5-104. Logic after saving

```
def save(self, *args, **kwargs):
   is_new = self.pk is None
   super().save(*args, **kwargs)
   if is_new:
       create_related_object(self)
```

In Listing 5-104, we called `super().save()` and then called **create_related_object** only when the object is new.

Whenever you override save, always call super().save() unless you have a very specific and advanced reason not to. Forgetting this can silently prevent your model from being saved and break important Django functionality.

Let's move to the next one which is using select_for_update outside a transaction block.

Using select_for_update() Outside a Transaction

A common mistake is calling select_for_update without wrapping it inside a database transaction. select_for_update only works properly inside an active transaction. If used outside one, it either **raises an error (in most databases like PostgreSQL)** or **does not behave as expected**.

Row-level locking requires a transaction context. Without it, the lock cannot be maintained.

Consider the example.

Listing 5-105. select_for_update without transaction

```
order = Order.objects.select_for_update().get(id=1)
order.status = "completed"
order.save()
```

In databases like PostgreSQL, this fails immediately (Refer Listing 5-105). If this runs outside transaction.atomic, Django will raise:

TransactionManagementError: select_for_update cannot be used outside of a transaction.

The correct usage for this is always wrap it in transaction.atomic.

Listing 5-106. Proper use of select_for_update

```
from django.db import transaction

with transaction.atomic():
    order = Order.objects.select_for_update().get(id=1)
    order.status = "completed"
    order.save()
```

In Listing 5-106, `select_for_update` is wrapped inside `transaction.atomic`. Then the row is locked, and other transactions attempting to lock the same row will wait. The lock is released only when the transaction commits or rolls back.

Why This Matters

`select_for_update` acquires a row-level lock. But locks only exist inside transactions.

If you do not use a transaction

- There is no locking guarantee
- Race conditions can occur
- Two requests may modify the same row simultaneously
- This defeats the entire purpose of using `select_for_update`

Important Note About Django Settings

If `ATOMIC_REQUESTS=True` is enabled in database settings, each request runs inside a transaction automatically. In that case, `select_for_update` works inside views.

`select_for_update` must always be used inside `transaction.atomic`). Without a transaction, row-level locking does not work, and your concurrency protection fails.

Let us move to the summary of this chapter.

Summary

This chapter explores the most common mistakes developers make when working with Django ORM, mistakes that often don't raise errors but quietly affect correctness, performance, scalability, and data integrity. We examined how poor data modeling decisions, such as choosing incorrect field types, misconfiguring `null` and `blank`, misusing `auto_now`, ignoring unique constraints or indexes, and using an `IntegerField` instead of a proper `ForeignKey`, can weaken the foundation of an application. We saw how query-related issues, including the **N+1 problem**, misunderstanding QuerySet **laziness**, confusing `values` with `only` and `defer`, relying on `len` instead of `count`, skipping pagination, or failing to monitor ORM performance, stem from not thinking in terms of SQL execution and row-level behavior. The chapter also highlighted the importance of transactions, atomic updates with F() expressions, proper use of `select_for_update`, and handling concurrency safely to prevent race conditions and data corruption. We discussed migration discipline in team environments, the importance of using `get_model` in data migrations, avoiding hardcoded database credentials, understanding bulk operation limitations, specifying batch sizes, and managing long-running database connections. Across all these topics, the deeper message remains consistent: the Django ORM is a powerful abstraction, but it does not replace understanding how databases work. When developers think in terms of SQL, transactions, constraints, and query planning rather than just QuerySets, most of these mistakes naturally disappear, and the ORM becomes a precise, reliable tool instead of a hidden source of problems.

In the next chapter, we will learn about a cheat sheet for converting form to model.

CHAPTER 6

Forms to Models: A Django Cheat Sheet

When building web applications with Django, connecting user-facing forms to back-end models is one of the most common development tasks. Although Django provides powerful abstractions for both forms and models, correctly mapping HTML input types to Django model fields is critical for maintaining data integrity, application performance, and long-term maintainability.

Improper field mapping can lead to improper validation, inefficient database structures, and unnecessary complexity in business logic. A clear understanding of how form inputs translate into model fields allows developers to design systems that are both robust and scalable.

This chapter serves as a practical reference guide. It presents a structured mapping between common HTML form input types and their corresponding Django model fields. Real-world examples are provided to demonstrate how these mappings work in production scenarios. In addition, the chapter highlights common pitfalls, performance considerations, and best practices that help avoid architectural mistakes early in development.

Important Disclaimer

The mappings and patterns discussed in this chapter are not rigid rules. They are recommended conventions designed to reduce development effort, improve clarity, and prevent common mistakes.

Different projects may require alternative approaches depending on domain requirements, performance constraints, or architectural goals. The objective of this chapter is not to impose a strict structure, but to provide practical guidance that accelerates development while maintaining sound design principles.

Let us learn mapping one by one. The first is **Text Input** to `CharField`.

Afsal MS, *Mastering Django ORM*, https://doi.org/10.1007/979-8-8688-2589-7_6

Text Input to CharField

Text inputs are the most common form of elements in web applications. They are typically used to collect short textual data such as usernames, titles, labels, or codes.

In Django, these inputs usually map to `CharField` in the model layer. Choosing the correct field type ensures proper validation, efficient storage, and predictable behavior.

Let us check with a simple example.

Listing 6-1. Text field to CharField example

```
HTML Form Element
<input type="text" name="username"/>
Django Model
class User(models.Model):
    username = models.CharField(max_length=150)
```

In Listing 6-1, the <input type="text"> element collects short string data from the user interface. When the form is submitted, the value entered by the user is sent to the back end and mapped to the username field of the model. `CharField` is designed to store short-to-medium-length strings in the database. Internally, this is typically represented as a `VARCHAR` column with a defined maximum length.

The `max_length` parameter is mandatory for `CharField`. It serves two important purposes. First, it defines the maximum size of the column at the database level. This prevents uncontrolled growth of string data. Second, it enforces validation at the Django level. If a user attempts to submit a value of longer than 150 characters, Django will raise a validation error before attempting to save the data.

It is important that the `max_length` defined in the Django model matches the front-end validation rules. If the front end allows 200 characters, but the back end allows only 150, users may experience unexpected validation errors after submission. Consistency between front-end constraints and back-end field definitions ensures predictable behavior and better user experience.

Let us move to the next one which is Textarea to `TextField`.

Textarea to TextField

While single-line text inputs are used for short strings, many applications require storing larger blocks of text such as descriptions, comments, bios, or article content.

For these use cases, HTML provides the `textarea` element, which allows for multi-line input. In Django, this typically maps to `TextField`.

Let us check with a simple example.

Listing 6-2. Textarea to TextField example

```
HTML Form Element
<textarea name="bio"></textarea>
Django Model
class Profile(models.Model):
    bio = models.TextField()
```

In Listing 6-2 the <textarea> element allows users to enter multi-line text. Unlike <input type="text">, it does not enforce a natural length restriction unless explicitly defined using attributes like maxlength. When the form is submitted, the value is sent under the key bio. `TextField` is designed to store large or unbounded text data. Internally, most databases represent this as a `TEXT` column type, which does not require a predefined maximum length.

TextField should be used when storing

- User biographies
- Article bodies
- Product descriptions
- Comments or notes
- Long-form content

It provides flexibility for storing variable-length data without unnecessary size restrictions.

Let us check how we can map number fields.

Number Input to IntegerField/FloatField/DecimalField

Numeric inputs are commonly used in forms to collect structured numerical data such as age, quantity, price, weight, ratings, or measurements.

Choosing the correct numeric field type in Django is critical because different numeric fields behave differently in terms of precision, storage, and validation.

Let us check with a simple example.

Listing 6-3. Whole number to IntegerField

```
HTML Form Element (Whole Numbers)
<input type="number" name="age" />
Django Model
class Person(models.Model):
    age = models.IntegerField()
```

`IntegerField` stores whole numbers in the database. Internally, this maps to an integer column type such as `INTEGER`. When the user submits a value through <input type="number">, Django validates and converts the input into an integer before saving it to the database.

`IntegerField` is ideal when

- Fractions are not allowed
- Values represent counts or discrete quantities
- Mathematical precision is not a concern

Examples (Refer Listing 6-3) include age, stock count, quantity, or number of items.

Now let's move on to numbers with decimal values.

Listing 6-4. Examples of numbers with floating points

```
HTML Form Element (Decimal Values)
<input type="number" step="0.01" name="price" />
Django Model
class Product(models.Model):
    price = models.DecimalField(max_digits=10, decimal_places=2)
```

In Listing 6-4 the step="0.01" attribute allows decimal input up to two decimal places. This is commonly used for currency or measurement inputs. `DecimalField` is designed for precise decimal values. It requires two parameters: internally, databases store this as a fixed-precision numeric type such as `NUMERIC` or `DECIMAL`.

`DecimalField` should always be used for financial values, measurements requiring accuracy, and any scenario where rounding errors are unacceptable.

What About FloatField?

`FloatField` stores floating-point numbers using binary representation. It is suitable for approximate values such as percentages or statistical data where minor rounding differences are acceptable.

However, floating-point arithmetic can introduce precision errors.

Example issue:

0.1 + 0.2 may not exactly equal 0.3 due to binary floating-point representation. Because of this, `FloatField` should never be used for currency or precise financial calculations.

The choice between `IntegerField`, `FloatField`, and `DecimalField` directly impacts

- Data accuracy
- Database storage behavior
- Validation rules
- Financial correctness
- Long-term maintainability

Using `FloatField` for prices can cause subtle rounding bugs.

Using `IntegerField` for decimal values can cause data loss.

Using `DecimalField` for whole numbers may be unnecessarily complex.

Correct mapping ensures both correctness and clarity in your domain model.

Let us move to the next one, which is checkbox to `BooleanField`.

Checkbox to BooleanField

Checkbox inputs are used in forms to represent binary states such as enabled/disabled, active/inactive, subscribed/unsubscribed, or approved/rejected. In Django, checkbox inputs typically map to `BooleanField` in the model layer.

Let us check with an example.

Listing 6-5. Checkbox to BooleanField

```
HTML Form Element
<input type="checkbox" name="is_active" />
Django Model
class User(models.Model):
    is_active = models.BooleanField(default=True)
```

A checkbox represents a True/False state. When checked, the field is included in the form of submission. Checkboxes represent binary states. `BooleanField` is the correct semantic representation of such data at the database level (Refer Listing 6-5).

Providing a default value is important because

- It guarantees a consistent initial state
- It prevents ambiguity during object creation
- It avoids null-related inconsistencies

In modern Django versions, `NullBooleanField` is deprecated. Boolean values should not be nullable unless there is a clear business requirement for a tri-state logic (True, False, Unknown).

Let move to the next example which is radio button to `CharField` with `choices`.

Radio Buttons to CharField with Choices

Radio buttons are used when the user must select only one option from a fixed set of predefined values. In Django, this maps perfectly to a `CharField` with choices, which ensures controlled input at the application level.

Let us check with an example.

Listing 6-6. Radio button to CharField with choices

```
HTML Form Element
<input type="radio" name="gender" value="M"> Male
<input type="radio" name="gender" value="F"> Female
Django Model
class Person(models.Model):
    GENDER_CHOICES = [('M', 'Male'), ('F', 'Female')]
    gender = models.CharField(max_length=1, choices=GENDER_CHOICES)
```

In Listing 6-6 we used `CharField` with choices when the value must come from a restricted set of options. The choices ensure only valid options are saved. The database stores compact values ("M," "F"). This approach keeps your data consistent, clean, and validated both at the model and form levels.

Let us see how we can map Dropdowns.

Dropdown (Select) to CharField with Choices or ForeignKey

Dropdowns are used when the user selects one value from multiple options. In Django, the way we model it depends on whether the options are static (fixed values) or dynamic (coming from another model).

Let's check a static option example.

Listing 6-7. Dropdowns to CharField with choices

HTML Form Element

```
<select name="status">
  <option value="new">New</option>
  <option value="closed">Closed</option>
</select>
```

Django Model

```
class Ticket(models.Model):
    STATUS_CHOICES = [('new', 'New'), ('closed', 'Closed')]
    status = models.CharField(max_length=10, choices=STATUS_CHOICES)
```

In Listing 6-7 the <select> element allows the user to choose one value, and the selected value (e.g., "new") is what gets submitted to the back end. In the Django model, a `CharField` is used to store this value. The `choices` argument restricts the field to accept only the predefined values, ensuring validation at the model level.

Use `CharField` with `choices` when the dropdown values are fixed and predefined. This approach is ideal when the options rarely change and do not require a separate database table. It keeps the model simple, enforces strict validation, and maintains clean, controlled data.

Let us check for a dynamic option example. When dropdown values come from another table and can change over time, a `ForeignKey` should be used.

Listing 6-8. Dropdown to ForeignKey

HTML Form Element
```
<select name="category">
  {% for category in categories %}
      <option value="{{ category.id }}">{{ category.name }}</option>
  {% endfor %}
</select>
```
Django Model
```
class Category(models.Model):
    name = models.CharField(max_length=100)

class Product(models.Model):
    category = models.ForeignKey(Category, on_delete=models.CASCADE)
```

In this case, categories are stored in a separate table. Each category has its own database row and unique ID. The `ForeignKey` in the Product model creates a relationship between product and category. When rendering a form, Django automatically generates a dropdown listing of all available categories. Instead of storing the category name, the database stores the related category ID. This ensures referential integrity and maintains proper relational structure in the database (Refer Listing 6-8).

Use `ForeignKey` when dropdown options are dynamic, stored in another model, and may change over time. This approach supports normalization, prevents duplicate data, and allows administrators to manage options easily. It is the correct design when dealing with relational data rather than fixed configuration values.

Let us move to the next one which is data input to `DateField`/`DateTimeField`.

Date Input to DateField/DateTimeField

Date inputs are used when the user needs to select a specific date, such as date of birth, joining date, or event date. Django provides dedicated field types to handle dates properly instead of storing them as strings.

Listing 6-9. Date input to DateField

```
HTML Form Element
<input type="date" name="dob" />
Django Model
class Person(models.Model):
    dob = models.DateField()
```

In Listing 6-9 <input type="date"> allows the user to select a date using the browser's native date picker. The selected value is submitted in a standardized date format (YYYY-MM-DD). In the Django model, `DateField` is used to store only the date portion (year, month, day) without any time information. Django automatically handles validation, formatting, and database conversion. This ensures that the value is stored as a proper date type in the database rather than plain text.

If the application requires both date and time (e.g., order timestamp or event schedule), then `DateTimeField` should be used instead, as it stores both components together.

Let us learn how we can map file inputs.

File Input to FileField or ImageField

File inputs are used when the user needs to upload documents, images, or other files. In Django, specialized fields handle file storage and path management instead of manually storing file names as strings.

Listing 6-10. File input to FileField

```
HTML Form Element
<input type="file" name="resume" />
Django Model
class Applicant(models.Model):
    resume = models.FileField(upload_to='resumes/')
```

In Listing 6-10 <input type="file"> allows the user to upload a file from their system. In the Django model, `FileField` is used to store the uploaded file. The `upload_to` ='resumes/' argument tells Django to store the file inside the resumes/ directory within the configured media storage.

Django does not store the file content directly in the database. Instead, it saves the file in the file system (or configured storage back end like S3) and stores the file path in the database. This keeps the database clean and efficient.

If we upload only image files, then we can use `ImageField`. It works similarly to `FileField`, but it is specifically designed for image files. It performs additional validation to ensure the uploaded file is a valid image. This field requires the Pillow library to be installed because Django uses it to process and validate image files.

Listing 6-11. ImageField example

```
class Gallery(models.Model):
    photo = models.ImageField(upload_to='photos/')
```

Use `FileField` when uploading general files such as PDFs, documents, or resumes. Use `ImageField` when handling image uploads, as it provides built-in image validation (Refer Listing 6-11). Always configure proper `MEDIA_ROOT` and `MEDIA_URL` settings to serve uploaded files correctly.

Let us check how password input is mapped.

Password Input to CharField

Password fields are used to collect sensitive authentication data. Even though the HTML input hides the characters on the screen, security must be handled properly at the back-end level.

Listing 6-12. Password input to CharField

```
HTML Form Element
<input type="password" name="password" />
Django Model
class User(models.Model):
    password = models.CharField(max_length=128)
```

<input type="password"> only hides the characters in the browser (Listing 6-12). It does **not** encrypt or secure the value during submission. The real security must be implemented on the server side.

In Django, passwords must never be stored as plain text. Instead, they are stored as **hashed values**. CharField (max_length=128) is typically large enough to store hashed passwords generated by Django's hashing system.

However, in real-world applications, you should not manually manage password hashing inside a custom model like this. Django already provides a secure and fully tested authentication system.

Recommend Approach

In Django, passwords must never be stored as plain text. Instead, they are stored as hashed values, and this is handled automatically when using built-in user models such as AbstractUser (Listing 6-12-1). This is the recommended starting point because password hashing is done automatically, the authentication system is ready to use, and we can add extra fields if needed.

Listing 6-12-1. Using AbstractUser

```
from django.contrib.auth.models import AbstractUser
class User(AbstractUser):
    pass
```

If you need more control over the field, we can use AbstractBaseUser. This gives us more control over the field, but we must handle some feature like user management by ourselves (Refer Listing 6-12-2).

Listing 6-12-2. Using AbstractBaseUser

```
from django.contrib.auth.models import AbstractBaseUser
from django.db import models
class User(AbstractBaseUser):
    password = models.CharField(max_length=128)
```

Handling Hashing Manually

In cases where you manage passwords yourself, Django provides utilities for that. Consider the example below.

Listing 6-12-3. Handling hashing manually

```
from django.contrib.auth.hashers import make_password, check_password
hashed = make_password("mypassword")
check_password("mypassword", hashed)
```

In Listing 6-12-3, functions such as `make_password` are used to handle password storage securely. Plain-text passwords must never be stored in the database. Instead, the password should always be converted into a hashed value using `make_password` before saving it.

During authentication, the user's input should not be manually hashed for comparison. Rather, the `check_password` function should be used, as it safely compares the provided password with the stored hashed value.

Let's move to the next one which is mapping multiselect to `ManyToManyField`.

Multiselect to ManyToManyField

When a form allows selecting multiple related objects, such as products in an order or tags in a blog post, the correct relational design in Django is usually a `ManyToManyField`.

This pattern is useful when one object can be linked to multiple other objects, and those objects can also be linked back to multiple records. For example, one order can contain multiple products, and one product can appear in multiple orders.

Listing 6-13. Multiselect to ManyToManyField

```
HTML Form Element
<select name="products" multiple>
  {% for product in products %}
      <option value="{{ product.id }}">{{ product.name }}</option>
  {% endfor %}
</select>
Django Model
class Product(models.Model):
    name = models.CharField(max_length=100)
class Order(models.Model):
    customer = models.CharField(max_length=100)
    products = models.ManyToManyField(Product)
```

In Listing 6-13, multiselect shares the same name="products". When the form is submitted, multiple product IDs are sent to the back end. In the Django model, `ManyToManyField` defines a many-to-many relationship between order and product. Django automatically creates an intermediate join table in the database to manage this relationship. This table stores the mapping between order IDs and product IDs. Useful when selecting multiple related objects (e.g., products in an order, tags in a blog post).

Let us check the next one which is email input to `EmailField`.

Email Input to EmailField

Email inputs are used when collecting email addresses from users. Since emails have a specific format, Django provides a dedicated `EmailField` instead of using a simple `CharField`.

Listing 6-14. Email input to EmailField

```
HTML Form Element
<input type="email" name="email" />
Django Model
class Contact(models.Model):
    email = models.EmailField(unique=True)
```

<input type="email"> provides basic browser-level validation and ensures the user enters a properly formatted email address (Refer Listing 6-14). However, front-end validation alone is not enough. In the Django model, `EmailField` is specifically designed to store email addresses. It extends `CharField` but includes built-in validation to ensure the format matches a valid email pattern. This adds back-end-level validation in addition to front-end checks.

Let us see how we can work with URL inputs.

URL Input to URLField

URL inputs are used when collecting website links, portfolio links, or social media profiles from users. Since URLs follow a specific structure, Django provides a dedicated `URLField` for proper validation.

Listing 6-15. URL input to URLFields

```
HTML Form Element
<input type="url" name="website"/>
Django Model
class Profile(models.Model):
    website = models.URLField(blank=True)
```

<input type="url"> provides a basic browser-level validation and ensures the value entered follows a valid URL format (e.g., including http:// or https://). However, front-end validation alone is not sufficient.

In the Django model, `URLField` is used to store valid URLs. It extends `CharField` but includes built-in validation to ensure the value matches a proper URL pattern (Refer Listing 6-15). This ensures back-end-level validation and prevents storing invalid links in the database.

Let us see how we can store value from a color picker.

Color Picker to CharField(max_length=7)

Color inputs are used when allowing users to pick a color value using a browser-based color picker. The value returned from this input is a hexadecimal color code.

Listing 6-16. Color picker to CharField

```
HTML Form Element
<input type="color" name="favorite_color" />
Django Model
class ThemePreference(models.Model):
    favorite_color = models.CharField(max_length=7)
```

<input type="color"> provides a visual color picker in the browser. When a user selects a color, the submitted value is a hexadecimal code in the format #RRGGBB, for example, #FF5733. Since the value is just a string representing a hex code, a `CharField` is sufficient to store it in the database. The length of a standard hex color code is seven characters (including the # symbol), so `max_length` =7 is appropriate (Refer Listing 6-16). If stricter validation is required, a regex validator can be added to ensure the value always follows the correct hex color pattern.

Let us see how range slider can be mapped in Django.

Range Slider to IntegerField or FloatField with Validators

Range sliders are used when selecting a value within a fixed numeric range, such as ratings, percentages, volume levels, or scores. Even though the front end defines minimum and maximum values, back-end validation is still required.

Listing 6-17. Range slider example

HTML Form Element

```
<input type="range" name="rating" min="1" max="10" />
```

Django Model

```
from django.core.validators import MinValueValidator, MaxValueValidator
class Review(models.Model):
    rating = models.IntegerField(
        validators=[MinValueValidator(1), MaxValueValidator(10)]
    )
```

<input type="range"> allows the user to select a numeric value within a defined range using a slider. The `min` and `max` attributes restrict the selection in the browser, but these limits can still be bypassed if someone manipulates the request manually. In the Django model, `IntegerField` is used because the slider returns numeric values (Refer Listing 6-17). To enforce the same limits at the back-end level, `MinValueValidator` and `MaxValueValidator` are added. This ensures that only values between 1 and 10 are accepted, regardless of front-end manipulation. If the slider uses decimal steps (e.g., step="0.5"), then `FloatField` should be used instead of `IntegerField`.

Let us summarize this chapter.

Summary

In this chapter, we mapped common HTML form inputs to their appropriate Django model fields and understood why selecting the correct field type is critical for data integrity, validation, and clean database design. Rather than storing all inputs as plain text, Django provides specialized field types that enforce structure and validation at the model level.

We explored how `CharField` is suitable for short text inputs such as usernames and controlled selections, while `TextField` is designed for large or unbounded content like bios and descriptions. For numeric data, we discussed when to use `IntegerField` for whole numbers, `FloatField` for approximate decimals, and `DecimalField` for precise values such as currency.

We saw how `BooleanField` represents checkbox inputs and how `CharField` with `choices` is ideal for radio buttons and static dropdowns. For dynamic dropdowns and relational data, `ForeignKey` ensures proper normalization and referential integrity.

We also covered `DateTimeField` and `DateField` for handling dates correctly, `FileField` and `ImageField` for file uploads, and the importance of storing passwords as hashed values using Django's built-in authentication system. For multiple relational selections like line items, `ManyToManyField` provides a clean relational design. Structured inputs such as emails and URLs are best handled using `EmailField` and `URLField`, while color pickers can be stored using a `CharField` for hex values. Numeric range sliders require proper back-end validation using validators, and hidden inputs must never be blindly trusted but validated on the server side.

The core principle of this chapter is that while the front end controls user interaction, the Django model is responsible for enforcing structure, validation, and database integrity. Choosing the correct model field is not just about storing data; it is about designing a reliable, scalable, and maintainable system.

In the upcoming chapter, we will learn about some advanced Django ORM topics.

Appendix A

Cheat Sheet

HTML Element	Django Model Field	Notes
`<input type="text">`	`CharField(max_length=...)`	Basic short text
`<textarea>`	`TextField()`	Long-form text
`<input type="number">`	`IntegerField`, `DecimalField`	Use `DecimalField` for currency
`<input type="checkbox">`	`BooleanField`	Always use default

(continued)

HTML Element	Django Model Field	Notes
<input type="radio">	CharField + choices	Enum-style selection
<select> (static)	CharField + choices	Predefined options
<select> (dynamic)	ForeignKey	Link to another model
<input type="date">	DateField()	Calendar date
<input type="file">	FileField, ImageField	Requires upload_to
<input type="password">	CharField	Use AbstractUser for secure storage
Checkboxes for multiple items	ManyToManyField()	Auto-managed join table
<input type="email">	EmailField	Built-in format validation
<input type="url">	URLField	Validates URLs
<input type="color">	CharField(max_length=7)	Store hex color code
<input type="range">	IntegerField / FloatField + validators	Match min/max HTML attributes

Appendix B

Exercise 1: User Registration Form

Design a Django model for the following HTML inputs:

```
<input type="text" name="full_name" />
<input type="email" name="email" />
<input type="password" name="password" />
<input type="date" name="dob" />
<input type="checkbox" name="is_subscribed" />
```

1. Create an appropriate Django model.
2. Ensure the email cannot be duplicated.

3. Apply correct field types instead of using only CharField.
4. Mention why passwords should not be stored as plain text.

Exercise 2: Product Creation Form

Design a Django model for the following HTML inputs:

```
<input type="text" name="name" />
<input type="number" step="0.01" name="price" />
<input type="file" name="image" />
<select name="status">
  <option value="draft">Draft</option>
  <option value="published">Published</option>
</select>
```

Tasks:

1. Create the Django model.
2. Use correct field types for price and image.
3. Implement status using proper choices.

Exercise 3: Blog Post with Tags

Design Post and Tag models. Implement proper relationships between them.

Exercise 4: Field Selection Reasoning

For each scenario below, choose the correct Django field type and explain why:

1. Storing latitude and longitude coordinates
2. Storing a short four-digit OTP
3. Storing a long legal agreement text
4. Storing a percentage value between 0 and 100
5. Storing a portfolio image

CHAPTER 7

Mastering Advanced Django ORM

So far in this book, you've used Django's ORM to model data, express relationships, and write expressive queries with confidence. You've seen how Django abstracts away raw SQL while still giving you enough power to build real-world applications efficiently. But as applications grow, so do the expectations around correctness, performance, and control.

This chapter goes beneath the surface of the ORM to explore how Django manages data beyond simple queries. You'll learn how to encapsulate query logic using custom managers and QuerySets, ensuring your data access layer remains clean, reusable, and intention revealing. We'll then look at Django signals and how they interact with ORM operations, understanding both their strengths and the pitfalls that can arise when business logic is triggered implicitly.

Data integrity becomes critical when multiple operations must succeed or fail together. To address this, we'll dive into database transactions, how Django handles them, how to control them explicitly, and how to avoid subtle bugs caused by partial writes. From there, we'll move into migrations and schema evolution, examining how Django tracks, applies, and maintains changes to your database structure over time in a safe and predictable way.

Finally, no advanced ORM usage is complete without understanding what actually reaches the database. We'll conclude the chapter with techniques for profiling and debugging ORM queries, helping you identify inefficiencies, unexpected queries, and performance bottlenecks before they become production issues.

In Chapter 3, we just mentioned managers; now we are digging deeper into managers.

Afsal MS, *Mastering Django ORM*, https://doi.org/10.1007/979-8-8688-2589-7_7

Managers

A manager is the interface between Django models and the database. By default, every model has a manager named `objects`. You can define custom managers to control what data gets retrieved by default or to add reusable query logic.

Managers are accessed at the model level, not on individual instances. Their primary purposes are

- Controlling which records are returned by default
- Exposing commonly used queries as readable methods
- Acting as the entry point to custom QuerySets

By defining a custom manager, you can encapsulate filtering logic that should consistently apply whenever data is retrieved.

Consider a scenario where only published books should be visible in most parts of the application. Instead of repeatedly filtering by **is_published=True**, you can define a custom manager.

Listing 7-1. Defining custom manager

```
from django.db import models

class PublishedManager(models.Manager):
    def get_queryset(self):
        return super().get_queryset().filter(is_published=True)

class Book(models.Model):
    title = models.CharField(max_length=100)
    is_published = models.BooleanField(default=False)

    objects = models.Manager()
    published = PublishedManager()
```

Usage:

```
Book.published.all()
```

Equivalent SQL

```
SELECT "myapp_book"."id", "myapp_book"."title", "myapp_book"."is_published"
FROM "myapp_book"
WHERE "myapp_book"."is_published" = TRUE;
```

In Listing 7-1 we are defining a custom manager with the name **PublishedManager.** Then we have override the `get_queryset` method. Here we are filtering the published books only.

We have added a new attribute `published = PublishedManager()`. This says the model has one more manager other that the `objects`. Now we can filter books like normal managers.

`Book.published.all()` filters only the published books. If we need all the books, then we can use the default manager. If we check the SQL, we can see that is_published=True is automatically appended to the SQL, which means that if we use this manager, the result will only contain the published books.

Now we can move to the next section which is "Custom `QuerySet`."

Custom QuerySet

A custom `QuerySet` allows you to define reusable, chainable query logic that behaves exactly like Django's built-in `QuerySet` methods. Unlike custom managers, `QuerySet` methods can be freely combined with other filters, exclusions, annotations, and orderings.

In practice, a custom `QuerySet` is the preferred way to implement domain-specific queries while preserving flexibility and composability.

Let us consider the case if our application contains logic for filtering a book with a price greater than 500 frequently. For that we can create a new method called **expensive** and chain it whenever required.

Listing 7-2. Defining custom QuerySet

```
class BookQuerySet(models.QuerySet):
    def expensive(self):
        return self.filter(price__gt=500)
```

```
class Book(models.Model):
    title = models.CharField(max_length=100)
    price = models.DecimalField(max_digits=10, decimal_places=2)

    objects = BookQuerySet.as_manager()
```

Usage:

```
Book.objects.expensive().filter(title__contains="Django")
```

Generated SQL:

```
SELECT "myapp_book"."id", "myapp_book"."title", "myapp_book"."price"
FROM "myapp_book"
WHERE "myapp_book"."price" > 500
AND "myapp_book"."title" LIKE '%Django%';
```

In Listing 7-2 we are defining a new class named **BookQuerySet** which is a child of `models.QuerySet` and create a new method named expensive. Its logic filters books with a price greater than 500. Then we override the default manager and set the new **BookQuerySet** as the default manager. This new method can be chained with filters. Here what we are doing is filtering all the expensive books with the title containing Django. If we check the SQL, we can see that price > 500 is automatically added to the SQL query. We can create multiple methods and use their combinations according to the requirements.

Now let's move to the next section which is "Signals and ORM Interaction."

Signals and ORM Interaction

Django's ORM provides a built-in event system known as signals, which allows developers to execute custom logic in response to model lifecycle events such as saving, deleting, or modifying relationships. Signals enable behavior to be attached to ORM operations without embedding that logic directly inside model methods.

Conceptually, signals follow a **publish-subscribe** pattern. When a specific ORM event occurs, Django emits a signal, and any registered receivers are notified automatically. Common events include creating or updating a model instance, deleting an instance, or changing a many-to-many relationship.

Each signal is designed for a specific moment in the data flow. Pre-action signals such as `pre_save` and `pre_delete` are best suited for validation or modifying data before it persisted, while post-action signals such as `post_save` and `post_delete` are commonly used for side effects like logging, cache invalidation, or triggering asynchronous tasks. Relationship-specific signals like `m2m_changed` allow applications to respond to changes in many-to-many associations.

This decoupled approach can improve modularity, particularly for cross-cutting concerns such as logging, cache invalidation, or analytics. However, signals also introduce implicit behavior that is not visible at the call site. As a result, excessive or inappropriate use of signals can make application behavior harder to trace, debug, and test.

Consider the case where the book has slug fields which are generated from the title. So, we catch the `pre_save` hook and generate the value for that field.

Listing 7-3. Auto slug generator using pre_save

```
from django.db.models.signals import pre_save
from django.dispatch import receiver
from django.utils.text import slugify
@receiver(pre_save, sender=Book)
def add_slug(sender, instance, **kwargs):
    if not instance.slug:
        instance.slug = slugify(instance.title)
```

In Listing 7-3, the `pre_save` signal of the **Book** model is handled using a `receiver` function. The `receiver` is registered by specifying two key pieces of information: the signal to listen for and the sender, which identifies the model associated with that signal. In this case, the signal is `pre_save`, and the sender is the Book model.

Whenever a Book instance is saved through Django's ORM either by calling `save()` on an instance or by using `Book.objects.create()`, Django emits a `pre_save` signal. This causes the **add_slug** receiver to be executed before the object is written to the database.

Inside the receiver function, a slug is generated for the book using Django's built-in `slugify` utility, but only if the slug field has not already been set. This ensures that existing slugs are preserved while automatically populating missing values.

Note Django does not fire signals for these methods: `bulk_create, update,` and `bulk_update`. These methods bypass signals for performance reasons. So, we must consider these cases while writing code using signals. It is better not to write critical business logic here.

Let us move to transactions.

Transactions

Many real-world operations require multiple database changes to be treated as a single unit of work. If one operation succeeds while another fails, the application can be left in an inconsistent state. Django addresses this problem through database transactions, which ensure that either a group of SQL statements succeed or all fail together.

A transaction represents an `atomic` operation at the database level. All queries executed within a transaction are isolated from other concurrent transactions and are only made permanent when the transaction is successfully committed.

By default, Django operates in **autocommit** mode, meaning that each database query is immediately committed as its own transaction. While this behavior is convenient for simple operations, it is insufficient for workflows that involve multiple related updates. To explicitly group such operations, Django provides the `atomic` context manager and decorator, which allows developers to define clear transactional boundaries.

The sections that follow demonstrate how transactions work in practice, how Django uses `savepoint` and nested transactions internally, and how to avoid common pitfalls when working with concurrent database access.

Consider a simple money transfer between two accounts. Both balance updates must succeed together; otherwise, funds could be lost or duplicated.

Listing 7-4. Simple bank transfer using atomic block

```
from django.db import transaction
with transaction.atomic():
    sender.balance -= 100
    receiver.balance += 100
```

```
    sender.save()
    receiver.save()
```

Equivalent SQL

```
BEGIN;
UPDATE "accounts" SET "balance" = balance - 100 WHERE "id" = 1;
UPDATE "accounts" SET "balance" = balance + 100 WHERE "id" = 2;
COMMIT;
```

In Listing 7-4 we are writing the database operations inside an atomic block. All the database operations inside will be committed if and only if completed code is executed; nothing is saved, which means the balance of the receiving account is only incremented if the balance of the sender is decreased. If we check the SQL, we can see that it starts with `BEGIN`, which means it is a starting transaction. Then we can see two update operations the in the end `COMMIT` is called as this point all the changes are written to database. If any error occurs between all the changes, it rolls back to the previous stage.

In some cases, we don't need to roll back the entire transactions, instead we need to control the behavior where `savepoint` comes. Let us check with a sample code.

Listing 7-5. savepoint example

```
from django.db import transaction
with transaction.atomic():
    sp1 = transaction.savepoint()
    try:
        expensive_operation()
        transaction.savepoint_commit(sp1)
    except Exception:
        # Roll back only to sp1, not the whole transaction
        transaction.savepoint_rollback(sp1)
```

In Listing 7-5, we demonstrate the use of `savepoint` within an atomic transaction. A `savepoint` allows us to mark an intermediate state inside a transaction to which we can later roll back without discarding the entire transaction.

The transaction begins when the `atomic()` block is entered. Immediately after that, a save point (sp1) was created. This `savepoint` represents a rollback point within the ongoing transaction.

Inside the try block, the **expensive_operation**() is executed. If this operation completes successfully, **savepoint_commit(sp1)** is called, which confirms all changes made after the save point and merges them into the surrounding transaction.

If an exception occurs during **expensive_operation**(), execution moves to the except block, where **savepoint_rollback(sp1)** is called. This rolls back the database state to the moment the savepoint was created, while keeping the outer transaction active. Any changes made before the savepoint remain intact.

This approach is useful when a portion of a larger transactional workflow is allowed to fail independently, and the failure should not invalidate the entire transaction.

In complex database workflows, some operations are allowed to fail without requiring the entire transaction to be rolled back. Django supports this pattern through **nested transactions**, implemented using savepoint under the hood. Each nested atomic() block creates a savepoint, allowing Django to roll back only the failing portion of the transaction while preserving the outer transaction.

Listing 7-6. Nested transactions using atomic()

```
with transaction.atomic():
    step1()
    try:
        with transaction.atomic():
            step2()  # fails
    except Exception:
        # Rolled back to savepoint, step1 remains valid
        pass
    step3()
```

In Listing 7-6, the outer atomic() block starts a database transaction. The operation **step1**() executes as part of this transaction, and its changes are retained unless the outer transaction is rolled back.

When the inner atomic() block is entered, Django creates an implicit savepoint within the existing transaction. Operation **step2**() is executed inside this nested block. If **step2**() raises an exception, Django rolls back the database state to the savepoint created at the start of the inner block.

The exception is then caught by the surrounding try-except block, allowing execution to continue. Because the rollback is limited to the inner savepoint, the changes made by step1() remain intact, and the outer transaction continues.

Finally, **step3**() is executed as part of the outer transaction. If no exception escapes the outer atomic() block, the transaction is committed, and all valid changes - including those from step1() and step3() - are written to the database.

In addition to explicit transaction control using atomic(), Django also supports **request-level transactions** through the ATOMIC_REQUESTS database setting. By default, this setting is disabled. When enabled, Django automatically wraps each HTTP request in a database transaction.

With ATOMIC_REQUESTS enabled, the transaction begins at the start of request processing. If the request completes successfully, Django commits the transaction. If an unhandled exception occurs during request handling, the transaction is rolled back automatically. This behavior provides a convenient safety net for view-level database operations and helps prevent partial updates.

However, wrapping every request in a transaction can introduce performance overhead, particularly for high-traffic or read-heavy endpoints. Long-running requests may also hold database locks for an extended period, increasing contention under concurrent load.

For performance-critical endpoints, you can disable wrapping in a transaction.

Listing 7-7. Disabling transaction using non_atomic_requests

```
from django.db import transaction

@transaction.non_atomic_requests
def fast_view(request):
    # Executes outside of any transaction
    ...
```

In Listing 7-7, the non_atomic_requests decorator ensures that the view executes in **autocommit mode**, even if ATOMIC_REQUESTS is enabled for the database. Each query is committed immediately, avoiding the overhead of a long-lived transaction.

Although transactions are essential for maintaining data consistency, incorrect usage can introduce subtle and hard-to-diagnose problems. One common pitfall is relying on Django's default autocommit behavior without realizing that, in the absence of an explicit atomic() block, each database query is executed and committed independently. This can lead to partial updates when multiple related operations are expected to succeed together.

Another significant risk is the possibility of **deadlocks**. Long-running transactions or transactions that lock rows across multiple tables can block concurrent operations, especially under high load. When different transactions acquire locks in inconsistent orders, the database may detect a deadlock and forcibly terminate one of them. These issues are often difficult to reproduce and typically surface only in production environments.

Transactions should also be kept isolated from external side effects. Calling external APIs, sending emails, or writing files inside an `atomic()` block is dangerous because these actions cannot be rolled back if the database transaction fails. If an exception occurs after such an operation, the database state may be reverted, but the external system will remain unchanged, leading to inconsistent behavior.

To avoid these issues, transactions should be kept as short and narrowly scoped as possible, encompassing only the operations that truly need to be atomic. In longer or more complex workflows, `savepoint` can be used to allow partial rollbacks without discarding the entire transaction. For operations involving shared or critical resources, `select_for_update()` should be used to acquire row-level locks explicitly and prevent concurrent modifications.

Finally, transactional behavior should always be tested under concurrent load. Many transaction-related issues such as race conditions, deadlocks, and lock contention do not appear in single-user testing environments. Simulating concurrent access is essential to ensure that transactional logic behaves correctly in real-world scenarios.

Now we are moving to how we can write data migrations in Django.

Data Migration in Django

So far, we have focused on schema migrations, which modify the structure of the database by adding, removing, or altering tables and columns. **Data migrations**, on the other hand, are used to transform or populate the data stored in those tables while a migration is being applied. They are especially useful when a new field is introduced, and existing rows need to be updated accordingly.

Consider a scenario where you introduce a new **slug** field to the **Book** model. While new records can generate this value automatically, existing rows in the database will not have a slug. To ensure data consistency, we need a data migration to populate the slug field for all existing books.

After the model change, the Book model looks like that shown in Listing 7-8.

Listing 7-8. Update model with slug field

```
class Book(models.Model):
    ....
    Old fields
    ....
    slug = models.SlugField(null=True)
```

Once the new field is added, do the normal schema migrations and migrate the changes to the database. This results in a new field created in the database. The slug value of existing records is now null. Using data migration, we can populate the slug fields. Let's see how.

Step one is to create an empty migration.

Creating Empty Migration File

We can create an empty migration file by running the following command.

Listing 7-9. Update model with slug field

```
python manage.py makemigrations <app_name> --name <migration file
name> --empty
```

Listing 7-9 is a command for generating an empty migration file. `--name` is an optional argument if we don't specify it. Django automatically generates a name in the usual pattern. But it is better to give a name for data migration because it helps us to find it in the future. Once the command is executed, a file will be generated in the migration folder. If we open the file, it looks like Listing 7-10.

Listing 7-10. Empty migration file

```
from django.db import migrations

class Migration(migrations.Migration):
    dependencies = [
        ("myapp", "0002_add_slug_field"),
    ]

    operations = [

    ]
```

Let us move to step two which is populate data.

Populate Data

Next, edit the generated migration file to include a data migration that populates the slug field for existing rows.

Let us check with an example.

Listing 7-11. Populating slug field

```
from django.db import migrations
from django.utils.text import slugify

def generate_slugs(apps, schema_editor):
    Book = apps.get_model("myapp", "Book")
    for book in Book.objects.all():
        book.slug = slugify(book.title)
        book.save()

def reverse_slugs(apps, schema_editor):
   Book = apps.get_model("myapp", "Book")
   for book in Book.objects.all():
        book.slug = None
        book.save()

class Migration(migrations.Migration):
    dependencies = [
        ("myapp", "0002_add_slug_field"),
    ]

    operations = [
        migrations.RunPython(generate_slugs, reverse_slugs),
    ]
```

In this migration (Refer Listing 7-11), Django provides access to historical versions of models through the app's registry. The `get_model()` method ensures that the migration operates on the correct version of the Book model as it existed at the time the migration was created. The **generate_slugs** function iterates over all existing book records and assigns a slug derived from the book title using Django's built-in slugify utility. The reverse_slug function is used to revert the migration needed in the future. The **reverse_slugs** set the slug field back to none.

When this migration is applied, Django first ensures that the schema change has been executed and then runs the data migration, populating the new column for existing records. That is the use of dependencies; all the migrations mentioned in the dependencies will be executed before running this. Django automatically populates dependencies with the previous migration file but in some cases if there is dependency with other apps, we must manually add the value here.

We have learned how to do data migration; now we can check some pitfalls in data migrations.

Pitfalls of Data Migrations

While data migrations are powerful, they must be written with care. Running heavy data migrations on large tables can lock rows or entire tables, potentially slowing down or blocking production traffic. For large datasets, it may be necessary to batch updates or run migrations during maintenance windows.

Migrations should also be fully self-contained and deterministic. Avoid calling model methods that depend on external services, signals, or business logic that may change over time. A migration should only interact with the database and should always produce the same result when applied.

It is critical to use `apps.get_model()` instead of importing models directly from the application code. Direct imports reference the current version of the model, which may not match the historical state expected by the migration, leading to subtle and dangerous bugs.

Finally, data migrations should always be tested against a copy of production data before deployment. Issues such as duplicate slugs, unexpected null values, or performance bottlenecks often only surface when real data volumes are involved.

Now we move to query profiling and debugging.

Query Profiling and Debugging

As Django applications scale, performance problems frequently arise from inefficient database access rather than incorrect business logic. Although Django's ORM provides a high-level abstraction over SQL, it can obscure critical details such as query count, execution time, and index usage. Query profiling and debugging techniques help surface these details and provide visibility into how ORM queries interact with the underlying database.

Django supports multiple levels of query inspection, ranging from low-level execution plans to request-level profiling and structured logging. When used together, these tools form a robust workflow for diagnosing and optimizing database performance.

The first one is using `explain`.

Analyzing Queries with explain()

The `explain()` method exposes the database execution plan for a QuerySet, making it possible to evaluate how queries are processed internally.

Let us check with an example.

Listing 7-12. explain book query

```
qs = Book.objects.filter(price__gt=500)
print(qs.explain(analyze=True, format="TEXT"))
```

Output

```
Seq Scan on public.myapp_book  (cost=0.00..5770.02 rows=232 width=22)
(actual time=0.006..14.124 rows=231 loops=1)\n  Output: id, title,
author_id, price, number_of_pages \n  Filter: (myapp_book.price >
'500'::numberic)\n  Rows Removed by Filter: 130\nPlanning Time: 0.055 ms\
nExecution Time: 14.145 ms
```

With `analyze=True`, the database executes the query and reports actual execution statistics rather than estimates (Refer Listing 7-12). The `format` is used to get the preferred output format. Its value depends on the database back end. For PostgreSQL, the values are TEXT, JSON, YAML, and XML. For MySQL the values are TEXT and JSON only.

This output indicates a sequential scan over the table, suggesting that the query is not using an index. On large datasets, this often points to the need for indexing or query restructuring.

Let us move to the next one which is `connection.queries`.

Inspecting Queries via connection.queries

Django stores executed SQL statements for the current request when `DEBUG=True`. This can be useful to see all the query sessions.

Listing 7-13. Printing queries

```
from django.db import connection
print(connection.queries)
```

Output

```
[{'sql': 'SELECT "app_book"."id", "app_book"."author_id", "app_
book"."title", "app_book"."price" FROM "app_book" LIMIT 21',
  'time': '0.001'},
{'sql': 'SELECT "app_author"."id", "app_author"."name" FROM "app_author"
LIMIT 21',
  'time': '0.000'},
{'sql': 'INSERT INTO "app_author" ("name") VALUES (\'author 123\')
RETURNING "app_author"."id"',
  'time': '0.000'}]
```

In Listing 7-13, we have printed all the queries during the session. This will give all the queries executed during the session. This is very useful for finding the N+1 queries which are some of the main issues we face in Django applications.

Let us move to the next one which is `coLogging Queries` using `Logging Framework`.

ORM Query Logging Using Django's Logging Framework

In addition to ad hoc inspection, Django supports structured query logging through its built-in logging framework. This approach is particularly useful for debugging slow queries and monitoring ORM behavior without modifying application code.

To enable SQL logging, configure the `django.db.backends` logger in the project settings.

Listing 7-14. Logging Queries

```
LOGGING = {
    "version": 1,
    "disable_existing_loggers": False,
    "handlers": {
        "console": {
```

```
            "class": "logging.StreamHandler",
        },
    },
    "loggers": {
        "django.db.backends": {
            "handlers": ["console"],
            "level": "DEBUG",
        },
    },
}
```

Once enabled, Django logs every SQL query executed by the ORM, including parameter bindings and execution time (Refer Listing 7-14).

This logging method is especially useful for

- Identifying slow queries in specific code paths
- Auditing ORM behavior during background tasks or management commands
- Correlating database activity with application-level logs

SQL logging should be used selectively and is generally unsuitable for production environments due to the volume of log output and potential performance impact.

So far, we have discussed the built-in method for debugging; now we can move to populate a third-party tool which is `Django Debug Toolbar`.

Using Django Debug Toolbar

For interactive, request-level profiling during development, **the Django Debug Toolbar** provides a comprehensive visual interface.

The toolbar displays

- Total query count per request
- Individual SQL statements and timings
- Stack traces linking queries back to Python code
- Duplicate and similar queries
- Transaction and cache usage

Installation and Configuration

First install the package using pip.

Listing 7-15. Installation

```
pip install django-debug-toolbar
```

Add the toolbar to the project settings.

Listing 7-16. Adding toolbar to project

```
INSTALLED_APPS = [
    ...
    "debug_toolbar",
]
MIDDLEWARE = [
    ...
    "debug_toolbar.middleware.DebugToolbarMiddleware",
]

INTERNAL_IPS = ["127.0.0.1"]
```

Then include the toolbars urls to our project.

Listing 7-17. Include the toolbar urls to project

```
from django.urls import include, path

urlpatterns = [
    path("__debug__/", include("debug_toolbar.urls"))
]
```

We can install the Debug Toolbar by running the command in Listing 7-15. Once installation is done, then update the **settings.py** file. Update INSTALLED_APPS and MIDDLEWARE as given in Listing 7-16. Add the INTERNAL_IPS setting. This contains the list of IPs where we need the toolbar. Usually we give the IPs of local and QA environments. Also make sure that don't include product serves Ip because its show sensitive information's like database settings. We must include the toolbars URL pattern to our project (Refer Listing 7-17).

Once enabled, the toolbar appears in rendered pages and provides immediate insight into ORM performance issues. The output of the toolbar looks like this (Refer Figure 7-1).

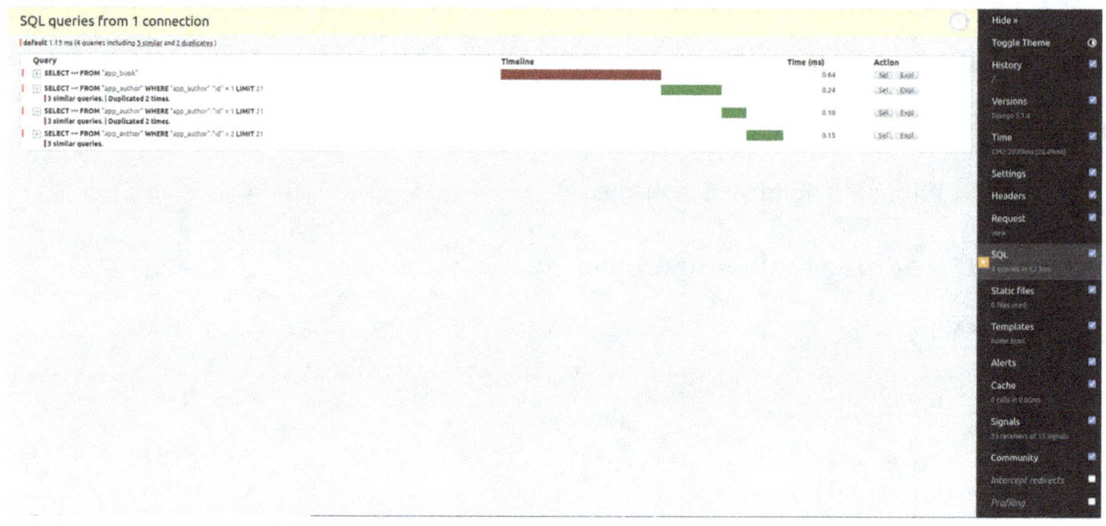

Figure 7-1. *Django Debug Toolbar screenshot*

Each profiling technique serves a different purpose. `explain()` is best suited for understanding execution plans and index usage. Query logging and `connection.queries` expose query volume and redundancy. Django Debug Toolbar ties this information together in an interactive format; that is ideal for diagnosing performance problems during development.

Used collectively, these tools enable developers to move confidently from symptom to root cause when addressing ORM-related performance issues.

Let us summarize this chapter.

Summary

In this chapter, we explored advanced Django ORM techniques that are essential for building scalable, maintainable, and high-performance applications. We began by examining custom managers and custom `QuerySet`, learning how to encapsulate reusable query logic and enforce consistent data access patterns across the application.

We then moved into signals and ORM interaction, understanding how Django provides lifecycle hooks such as `post_save`, `pre_save`, etc. While signals enable decoupled, cross-cutting behavior, we also discussed their hidden complexity and the importance of using them carefully.

Next, we studied database transactions, focusing on `atomic` operations, `savepoint`, nested transactions, and request-level transaction management using `ATOMIC_REQUESTS`. Practical examples demonstrate how transactions protect data integrity, as well as common pitfalls such as long-running transactions and external side effects.

The chapter continued with schema and data migrations, highlighting how to safely evolve both database structure and existing data. We covered empty migrations and best practices for writing production-safe migration code.

Finally, we explored query profiling and debugging, using tools such as `explain()`, query logging, Django's logging framework, and Django Debug Toolbar. These techniques make ORM behavior visible and allow developers to identify performance bottlenecks, inefficient queries, and scalability issues early in the development lifecycle.

So far, we have discussed Django ORM in a synchronous world. In the next chapter we will look into Django ORM async capabilities.

Appendix

Custom Manager Design

Create a custom manager for a Book model that returns only books published in the last 30 days. Add an additional QuerySet method that filters books by minimum price, and chain both methods together.

Signal Behavior Analysis

Implement a post_save signal that updates a related model's counter field. Then rewrite the same logic without signals using an explicit function call. Compare clarity, testability, and maintainability.

Transactional Safety

Write a transaction that transfers inventory between two warehouse models. Introduce an artificial exception and verify that the transaction rolls back correctly. Extend the example using savepoints to partially recover from errors.

Data Migration Practice

Add a new code field to an existing model and populate it using data migration. Implement both forward and reverse migration logic. Test rolling the migration backward and forward.

Query Profiling

Identify a QuerySet that triggers multiple database hits. Use connection.queries and Django Debug Toolbar to count queries, then optimize it using select_related() or prefetch_related().

Execution Plan Analysis

Use .explain() on a complex QuerySet involving joins or annotations. Add an index and compare the execution plan before and after the optimization.

CHAPTER 8

Django ORM in the Async World

Traditionally, Django handled requests synchronously: one request → one thread → one response. This is fine for most apps, but in **high-concurrency scenarios** (chat applications, streaming APIs, long-polling, WebSockets), synchronous blocking can become a bottleneck.

With **async support**, Django can

- Handle multiple requests concurrently without blocking.
- Allow parallel execution of I/O-bound tasks (API calls, file reads, DB queries). However, database queries are executed in thread pools, not truly in parallel at the driver level.
- Improve throughput under high load.

However, Django ORM is still backed by synchronous database drivers (like `psycopg2`). Async queries run in thread pools, meaning each query still occupies a thread and does not make individual queries faster.

Let us check how the async methods look.

Async QuerySet Methods

Django now provides async variants of common QuerySet methods. The naming of the methods is very intuitive.

Let us check how to fetch a single object using an id.

Afsal MS, *Mastering Django ORM*, https://doi.org/10.1007/979-8-8688-2589-7_8

Listing 8-1. Fetching a single object asynchronously

```
book = await Book.objects.aget(id=1)
```

Equivalent SQL:

```
SELECT "myapp_book"."id", "myapp_book"."title"
FROM "myapp_book"
WHERE "myapp_book"."id" = 1;
```

In Listing 8-1 we are fetching a book with id 1. Here the method for this is `aget`. Since it is an async method, we are adding `await` to get the result. If `await` is not used, the result will be a coroutine object. So always add `await` to get the result.

Let us check the other async methods provided by Django ORM:

- `acreate`: This is the async equivalent of `create` method. By passing the required model fields, we can create an object. The object is created only when awaited; otherwise, a coroutine object is returned.
- `asave`: This is the async equivalent of the `save` method. By calling this we can save the changes asynchronously. This is reflected in the database when used with `await`.
- `aget_or_create`: This is the async equivalent of the `get_or_create` method. By calling this method, we can get the object if it exists; otherwise it is created if it does not exist.
- `aupdate_or_create`: This is the async equivalent of the `update_or_create` method. By calling, we can update the object if it exists; otherwise it is created if it does not exist.
- `acount`: This is the async equivalent of the `count` method. By calling, we will get the number of records.
- `aexists`: This is the async equivalent of the `exists` method. By calling, we check if records exist or not.
- `afirst`: This is the async equivalent of the `first` method. By calling, we fetch the first record from the QuerySet.

- `alast`: This is the async equivalent of the `last` method. By calling, we fetch the last record from the QuerySet.
- `aaggregate`: This is the async equivalent of the `aggregate` method. By calling, we can get the aggregated results.
- `acontains`: This is the async equivalent of the `contains` method. Using this method, we can check if an object exists in a QuerySet.
- `aearliest`: This is the async equivalent of the `earliest` method. This is used to get the first record of a result in a specific order.
- `abulk_create`: This is the async equivalent of the `bulk_create` method. This is used to create records as bulk operations.
- `ain_bulk`: This is the async equivalent of the `in_bulk` method which can be used to fetch a list of items as a mapping.
- `alatest`: This is the async equivalent of the `latest` method which can be used to get the last record of the result in a specific order.
- `abulk_update`: This is the async equivalent of the `bulk_update` method which is used to update a list of instances as a bulk.
- `aupdate`: This is the async equivalent of the `update` method which is used to update QuerySets with the same value for all records.

Methods like `filter()`, `exclude()`, and `annotate()` remain synchronous because they are lazy and do not execute a query immediately.

Let us see how we can iterate over a QuerySet.

Async Iteration over QuerySets

QuerySets can be asynchronously iterated, which is useful when streaming results in APIs or WebSockets. As discussed earlier, Django does not provide an async equivalent for `filter()`, since it is a lazy QuerySet operation that does not trigger database execution.

Let us check with an example.

Listing 8-2. Async iteration

```
async for book in Book.objects.filter(is_published=True):
    print(book.title)
```

Equivalent SQL:

```
SELECT "myapp_book"."id", "myapp_book"."title"
FROM "myapp_book"
WHERE "myapp_book"."is_published" = TRUE;
```

In Listing 8-2 we can see that the async iteration looks similar to a normal iteration but requires `async for` and executes queries lazily. The generated SQL remains the same.

Let us check how transactions work in the async world.

Async Transactions

Transactions in Django ensure atomicity, either all database operations inside the block succeed, or none of them are committed. This guarantees data consistency, especially when multiple related operations must succeed together.

In asynchronous views, Django allows the use of `transaction.atomic()`, but it is important to understand that it is still synchronous in nature. Even though we are writing an async code, the database driver and transaction handling remain synchronous. Django executes database operations in a thread pool so that the event loop remains responsive.

However, `transaction.atomic()` does not support `async with`. It can still be used inside the async code, but it executes synchronously.

Let us consider the example.

Listing 8-3. Async transaction

```
from django.db import transaction
from asgiref.sync import sync_to_async

@sync_to_async
def create_books():
    with transaction.atomic():
```

```
        Book.objects.create(title="Async Django")
        Book.objects.create(title="Advanced Async")

async def create_book(request):
    await create_books()
```

Equivalent SQL:

```
BEGIN;
INSERT INTO "myapp_book" ("title") VALUES ('Async Django');
INSERT INTO "myapp_book" ("title") VALUES ('Advanced Async');
COMMIT;
```

In Listing 8-3 we are creating two books inside a transaction. Even though the view is async, the transaction itself runs synchronously. If any statement inside the block fails, Django issues a ROLLBACK instead of COMMIT, and none of the changes are saved.

Although the outer code uses async, the underlying transaction behavior remains identical to synchronous Django. The database still locks rows and manages isolation levels in the same way. Async does not change database transactional guarantees; it only prevents the Python event loop from blocking while waiting for database I/O.

It is important to understand that long-running transactions are dangerous in async code just as they are in synchronous code. Holding a transaction open for too long increases lock contention and reduces overall throughput.

Let us check with an example.

Listing 8-4. Transaction with blocking code

```
from django.db import transaction
from asgiref.sync import sync_to_async
import time

@sync_to_async
def bad_example():
    with transaction.atomic():
        Book.objects.create(title="Temp")
        time.sleep(5)  # Bad practice
```

In Listing 8-4, the transaction remains open during the sleep period. Other database operations may be blocked depending on isolation level and locking. Async does not eliminate locking problems. Async improves concurrency at the application level, but it does not make transactions faster, lighter, or safer by default.

Good transactional design principles are as follows:

- Keep transactions short.
- Lock only what is necessary.
- Avoid external calls inside atomic blocks.
- Avoid blocking operations inside transactions.
- Test behavior under concurrent load.

Now we can check how we can mix sync and async code.

Mixing Sync and Async

In real-world Django applications, it is common to have both synchronous and asynchronous code. Since Django originally evolved as a synchronous framework, many internal components including parts of the ORM, middleware, signals, and third-party packages are still synchronous.

Understanding how to correctly mix sync and async code is critical to avoid performance issues and runtime errors.

Async views run inside an event loop. If you call synchronous code directly inside an async view, it can block the event loop and reduce concurrency.

Listing 8-5. Incorrect usage

```
async def book_count(request):
    count = Book.objects.count()  # Synchronous ORM call
    return JsonResponse({"count": count})
```

In Listing 8-5 `Book.objects.count()` is synchronous. When executed inside an async view, it blocks the event loop until the database query completes. This defeats the purpose of using async.

The correct approach is to either use async ORM methods or explicitly wrap synchronous code using `sync_to_async`.

Listing 8-6. Using async ORM function

```
async def book_count(request):
    count = await Book.objects.acount()
    return JsonResponse({"count": count})
```

Listing 8-7. Using sync_to_async

```
from asgiref.sync import sync_to_async

async def book_count(request):
    count = await sync_to_async(Book.objects.count)()
    return JsonResponse({"count": count})
```

In Listing 8-6, we are using the async method of Django ORM. In Listing 8-7 we are using the `sync_to_async` function to wrap the synchronous code. `sync_to_async` executes the synchronous function in a thread pool, allowing the event loop to continue handling other requests.

It is important to understand that repeatedly switching between sync and async contexts adds overhead. Each boundary crossing involves context switching and thread scheduling.

The best practice is to maintain consistency within a view:

- Use fully synchronous views with synchronous ORM.
- Use fully asynchronous views with async ORM methods.

Another common issue occurs when calling async functions from synchronous views. In such cases, Django does not allow direct `await`. Instead, you must use `async_to_sync`.

Listing 8-8. Using async_to_sync

```
from asgiref.sync import async_to_sync

def sync_view(request):
    result = async_to_sync(async_function)()
    return JsonResponse({"result": result})
```

In Listing 8-8 we use the `async_to_sync` function to convert the async function to sync function. This bridges async code back into a synchronous context.

However, excessive conversion between sync and async layers should be avoided. It increases complexity and makes debugging harder.

Let us check how we can write async view in Django.

Async Views with ORM

Async views in Django allow the application to handle multiple concurrent requests efficiently, especially when the request lifecycle involves I/O-bound operations such as database queries, external API calls, file handling, or network communication.

An async view is defined using `async def` instead of `def`. When running under ASGI (such as with Uvicorn or Daphne), Django executes these views inside an event loop, enabling cooperative multitasking.

Listing 8-9. Using Async view

```
from django.http import JsonResponse

async def book_count(request):
    count = await Book.objects.acount()
    return JsonResponse({"books": count})
```

In Listing 8-9, the database query runs in a thread pool while the event loop remains free to serve other requests. This improves concurrency under high traffic. Each awaited call yields control back to the event loop while waiting for database I/O. This allows other requests to be processed simultaneously.

It is important to understand that

- Async does not reduce database execution time
- Async does not reduce query costs
- Async does not eliminate locking

Limitations of Async ORM

Although Django provides async ORM support, it is important to understand its current limitations. Async ORM improves application-level concurrency, but it does not fundamentally change how the database driver or database engine operates.

Let us check the limitations one by one.

Synchronous Database Drivers

The most important limitation is that Django still relies on synchronous database drivers by default (such as psycopg2 for PostgreSQL). When you use async ORM methods like aget() or acreate(), Django executes the database SQL inside a thread pool using sync-to-async wrappers.

This means

- Database queries are not truly non-blocking at the driver's level.
- Each query still consumes a thread.
- Async improves concurrency handling, not raw query execution speed.

Async ORM is therefore a scalability enhancement at the application layer, not a database performance upgrade.

Migrations Remain Synchronous

Database migrations are entirely synchronous. Commands such as:

```
python manage.py makemigrations
python manage.py migrate
```

run in a synchronous context. Schema alterations, table creation, and data migrations are blocking operations. Async does not apply to schema management.

This is intentional because migrations are administrative operations, not high-concurrency request-handling tasks.

Signals Are Not Async-Aware

Django signals (such as `pre_save`, `pre_delete`, `post_save`, etc.) execute synchronously. Even if triggered from an async view, the signal handlers run in synchronous context. The signal handlers cannot be effectively declared using `async def`. Attempting to make them asynchronous will make them not behave as expected.

Transaction and Locking Behavior Is Unchanged

Async does not change database transaction semantics. Row locking, isolation levels, deadlocks, and blocking behavior remain identical to synchronous Django. If you use `select_for_update()` or long-running `transaction.atomic()` blocks, database contention can still occur.

Async does not eliminate

- Deadlocks
- Lock waits
- Transaction blocking
- Isolation conflicts

It only prevents the Python event loop from blocking while waiting for database I/O.

Limited Benefit for CPU-Bound Work

Async ORM is not beneficial for CPU-heavy workloads. The CPU-bound processing still blocks execution. Async does not provide parallel CPU execution within a single worker.

For CPU-intensive tasks, use background workers or multiprocessing.

Async ORM has practical and architectural limitations. It enhances concurrency for I/O-bound workloads but does not replace proper database design, indexing strategy, or system architecture. Understanding these limitations prevents unrealistic expectations and ensures async is used where it provides genuine value.

Let us examine the best practices for the async ORM.

Best Practices for Async ORM

Using async ORM effectively requires architectural discipline. Async is not simply a syntax upgrade; it changes how request handling interacts with concurrency, database access, and system scalability.

Following these best practices ensures that async improves your system instead of introducing unnecessary complexity.

Use Async Only for I/O-Bound Workloads

Async provides real benefit when the request performs multiple I/O operations such as

- Database queries
- External API calls
- File system operation
- Network communication

If a view performs only a single quick query, async may not provide measurable improvement. In such cases, synchronous views are simpler and more effective.

Async should be chosen based on workload characteristics, not trends.

Maintain Consistency per View

Avoid mixing sync and async ORM methods within the same view. Frequent switching between sync and async contexts introduces overhead and makes code harder to reason. Consistency reduces complexity and improves maintainability.

Keep Transactions Short

Transactions should remain minimal and focused. Async does not change database locking behavior.

Good practice:

- Perform only essential database operations inside atomic blocks.
- Move external API calls outside transactions.
- Avoid long-running logic inside transactions.

Optimize Queries First

Async does not solve inefficient queries. Always ensure

- Proper indexing of frequently filtered fields
- Usage of `select_related()` and `prefetch_related()` to prevent N+1 queries
- Filtering at the database level instead of Python
- Avoiding unnecessary data retrieval

Query efficiency is more important than async usage.

Async ORM best practices revolve around intentional usage, consistency, optimized queries, and infrastructure alignment. When applied correctly, async enhances concurrency and responsiveness. When misused, it only adds complexity without measurable benefit.

Use async strategically for

- High-concurrency APIs
- Real-time applications
- Streaming endpoints
- WebSocket integrations

The Future of Async in Django

Async support in Django is still evolving. While the framework now supports async views, middleware adaptation, and async ORM methods, the ecosystem is transitioning gradually toward deeper asynchronous integration.

Understanding where Django stands today helps developers anticipate future improvements and make informed architectural decisions.

Movement Toward True Async Database Drivers

Currently, Django ORM relies primarily on synchronous database drivers such as psycopg2 for PostgreSQL. Even when using async ORM methods like `aget()`, `acreate()`, and `acount()`, queries are executed in a thread pool.

The next major step in Django's async evolution is the broader adoption of truly asynchronous database drivers, such as psycopg (psycopg3) in async mode.

When native async drivers become fully integrated

- Database I/O may become fully non-blocking.
- Threadpool overhead can be reduced.
- Event loop efficiency can improve under high concurrency.

This would represent a significant architectural shift.

Expanded Async ORM Coverage

Django continues to expand async-compatible ORM methods. Over time, more QuerySet operations and internal components may gain native async support.

Future improvements may include

- Broader async manager support
- Enhanced async transaction handling
- Better async bulk operations
- Improved async aggregation workflows

The goal is to reduce reliance on sync wrappers and increase consistency across the ORM API.

Async Middleware and Ecosystem Maturity

Although Django supports async middleware, many third-party packages are still synchronous.

As the ecosystem matures

- More libraries will provide async-compatible APIs.
- Authentication backends may improve async integration.
- Caching backends may evolve toward async-first implementations.

A mature async ecosystem is essential for real-world scalability benefits.

Improved Concurrency Patterns

As async adoption grows, architectural patterns within Django projects are likely to evolve.

We may see

- Greater use of streaming responses
- Increased WebSocket-based architecture
- Event-driven service designs
- Reduced dependency on background workers for lightweight I/O tasks

Async opens opportunities for more responsive, real-time systems.

Let us summarize this chapter.

Summary

This chapter explores Django's async ORM capabilities and their role in modern web application architecture.

Django traditionally operated in a synchronous request-response model. With the introduction of async support, Django can now handle multiple concurrent I/O-bound operations more efficiently when running under ASGI.

We learned that async improves concurrency rather than raw database speed. The ORM still relies on synchronous database drivers, and async methods execute queries inside a thread pool. This means query optimization remains just as important as in synchronous applications.

The chapter examined why async exists and when it provides real benefit. It covered async QuerySet methods such as `aget()`, `acreate()`, and `acount()`, along with async iteration over QuerySets and async bulk operations. We also explored async transactions using `transaction.atomic()` and discussed how to properly mix synchronous and asynchronous code without blocking the event loop.

Further sections explained how async views work in real-world applications and clarified the current limitations of Django's async ORM. Best practices were outlined to ensure that async is used strategically, especially in high-concurrency, I/O-heavy systems. Finally, the chapter looked ahead at the future direction of async support in Django and the gradual movement toward more native asynchronous components.

A key architectural insight from this chapter is that async should be used intentionally. It is most valuable in environments where multiple I/O operations must be handled concurrently, such as APIs, streaming endpoints, and real-time systems.

Async does not solve slow queries, remove locking issues, eliminate database contention, replace proper indexing, or improve CPU-bound performance. It enhances scalability when used correctly, but it adds unnecessary complexity when applied without clear need.

The correct mindset is to design scalability first, optimize queries thoroughly, and then apply async where concurrency genuinely provides architectural value.

Appendix

Sync vs. Async ORM Methods in Django

Operation	Sync Method	Async Method
Create object	`Book.objects.create(...)`	`await Book.objects.acreate(...)`
Get single object	`Book.objects.get(id=1)`	`await Book.objects.aget(id=1)`
Filter QuerySet	`Book.objects.filter(author="J.K. Rowling")`	`Book.objects.filter(author="J.K. Rowling")`
Get first object	`Book.objects.first()`	`await Book.objects.afirst()`
Get last object	`Book.objects.last()`	`await Book.objects.alast()`
Get the number of rows	`Book.objects.count()`	`await Book.objects.acount()`
Check if records exist	`Book.objects.exists()`	`await Book.objects.aexists()`

(continued)

Operation	Sync Method	Async Method
Delete records	Book.objects.filter(...).delete()	await Book.objects. filter(...).adelete()
Update QuerySet	Book.objects.filter(...).update(...)	await Book.objects. filter(...).aupdate(...)
Save the changes	book_obj.save()	await book_obj.asave()
Get or create record	Book.objects.get_or_ create(...)	await Book.objects. aget_or_create(...)
Update or create record	Book.objects.update_ or_create(...)	await Book.objects. aupdate_or_create(...)
Check a specific object in a QuerySet	<QuerySet>.contains (<object>)	await <QuerySet>. acontains(<object>)
Get the first record by order of a field	Book.objects. earliest(...)	await Book.objects. aearliest(...)
Get the last record by order of a field	Book.objects. latest(...)	await Book.objects. alatest(...)
Do bulk creation	Book.objects.bulk_ create([...])	await Book.objects. abulk_create([...])
Get the list of items as mapping	Book.objects. in_bulk([...])	await Book.objects. ain_bulk([...])
Bulk update	Book.objects.bulk_ update([...])	await Book.objects. abulk_update([...])

Index

A

MS. Afsal, *Mastering Django ORM*, https://doi.org/10.1007/979-8-8688-2589-7

B

C

D

E

H

I

O

P

Q

S

T

U

V

W, X, Y, Z

GPSR Compliance
The European Union's (EU) General Product Safety Regulation (GPSR) is a set of rules that requires consumer products to be safe and our obligations to ensure this.

If you have any concerns about our products, you can contact us on

ProductSafety@springernature.com

In case Publisher is established outside the EU, the EU authorized representative is:

Springer Nature Customer Service Center GmbH
Europaplatz 3
69115 Heidelberg, Germany

www.ingramcontent.com/pod-product-compliance
Lightning Source LLC
Chambersburg PA
CBHW080027210726
48503CB00023B/714

9798868825880